Charles Colcock Jones

A Roster of General Officers

Heads of departments, senators, representatives, military organizations

Charles Colcock Jones

A Roster of General Officers
Heads of departments, senators, representatives, military organizations.

ISBN/EAN: 9783337175092

Printed in Europe, USA, Canada, Australia, Japan

Cover: Foto ©Suzi / pixelio.de

More available books at **www.hansebooks.com**

A ROSTER

OF

GENERAL OFFICERS,

HEADS OF DEPARTMENTS,

SENATORS, REPRESENTATIVES,

MILITARY ORGANIZATIONS, &c., &c.,

IN

CONFEDERATE SERVICE DURING THE WAR BETWEEN THE STATES.

BY

CHARLES C. JONES, JR.

Late Lieut. Colonel of Artillery, C. S. A.

RICHMOND, VA.:
SOUTHERN HISTORICAL SOCIETY.
1876.

PREFATORY NOTE.

In consequence of the general loss and destruction of Confederate records, and a refusal on the part of the War Department to permit free access to such as have been preserved at Washington, the preparation of the following Roster was environed with no inconsiderable difficulty. The accompanying pages embody the result of much toil and inquiry. Fortunately many important war documents, original returns and official reports still exist in private hands, and from them material aid has been derived. In not a few instances the necessary information touching the commissions and commands of general officers has been obtained either from the officers themselves or from the friends of such as fell in the Confederate struggle, or have since died. While perfectness cannot be claimed for it, this Roster may nevertheless be accepted as nearly complete. No labor like the present having been as yet attempted, it is offered in the hope that it will supply an existing deficiency and prove a convenient roll of the Confederate Dramatis Personæ of the greatest of modern Revolutions—of which, in the language of Phinius Minor, it may be truthfully affirmed, *Si computes annos, exiguum tempus; si vices rerum, ævum putes.*

CHARLES C. JONES, JR.

New York City, May 1st, 1876.

CONFEDERATE ROSTER.

THE PRESIDENT AND VICE PRESIDENT.

His Excellency Jefferson Davis, Mississippi, President of the Confederate States and Commander-in-Chief of the Army and Navy.

Hon. Alexander H. Stephens, Georgia, Vice President of the Confederate States and President of the Senate.

THE PRESIDENT'S MILITARY FAMILY.

Colonel Joseph R. Davis, Mississippi, A. D. C., with rank of Colonel of Cavalry; in 1863 entered the field as Brigadier-General.

Colonel G. W. Custis Lee, Virginia, A. D. C., with rank of Colonel of Cavalry; subsequently entered the field and rose to the grade of Major-General.

Colonel Joseph C. Ives, A. D. C., with rank of Colonel of Cavalry.

Colonel Wm. Preston Johnston, Kentucky, A. D. C., with rank of Colonel of Cavalry.

Colonel Wm. M. Browne, Georgia, A. D. C., with rank of Colonel of Cavalry; subsequently entered the field and rose to the grade of Brigadier-General.

Colonel John Taylor Wood, Louisiana, A. D. C., with rank of Colonel of Cavalry.

Colonel James Chestnut, Jr., South Carolina, A. D. C., with rank of Colonel of Cavalry; subsequently entered the field and rose to the grade of Brigadier-General.

Colonel Francis R. Lubbock, Texas, A. D. C., with rank of Colonel of Cavalry; also a Confederate Governor of Texas.

Robert Josselyn, Mississippi, Private Secretary to the President during the Provisional Government.

Burton N. Harrison, Mississippi, Private Secretary to the President during the Permanent Government.

Colonel John M. Huger, A. D. C., with rank of Colonel of Cavalry.

Colonel John B. Sale, Military Secretary, with rank of Colonel of Cavalry, to General Braxton Bragg, who was assigned to duty at the Seat of Government at Richmond, and, under the direction of the President, was charged with the conduct of military operations in the armies of the Confederacy. See General Orders, No. 23, A. and I. General's office, Richmond, Virginia, February 24th, 1864. Colonel Sale was thus brought into intimate relationship with the President's military family.

DEPARTMENT OF STATE.

Hon. Robert Toombs, Georgia, First Secretary of State; subsequently entered the Confederate army with the rank of Brigadier-General; also a Delegate to Provisional Congress.

Hon. R. M. T. Hunter, Virginia, succeeded General Toombs as Secretary of State; Delegate to Provisional Congress and Confederate Senator from Virginia.

Hon. Judah P. Benjamin, Louisiana, succeeded Mr. Hunter as Secretary of State.

DEPARTMENT OF JUSTICE.

Hon. Judah P. Benjamin, Louisiana, first Attorney General.

Hon. Thomas Bragg, North Carolina, second Attorney General.

Hon. T. H. Watts, Alabama, third Attorney-General; subsequently elected Governor of Alabama.

Hon. George Davis, North Carolina, fourth Attorney-General; Delegate to Provisional Congress, Senator from North Carolina, &c.

Hon. Wade Keys, Assistant Attorney-General.

TREASURY DEPARTMENT.

Hon. Charles G. Memminger, South Carolina, first Secretary of the Treasury.

Hon. George A. Trenholm, South Carolina, second Secretary of the Treasury.

Hon. E. C. Elmore, Alabama, Treasurer.

Hon. Philip Clayton, Georgia, Assistant Secretary of the Treasury.

Lewis Cruger, South Carolina, Comptroller and Solicitor.

Bolling Baker, Georgia, First Auditor.

Robert Tyler, Virginia, Register.

WAR DEPARTMENT.

Hon. Leroy P. Walker, Alabama, first Secretary of War; afterwards entered the army with the rank of Brigadier-General.

Hon. Judah P. Benjamin, Louisiana, second Secretary of War; also Secretary of State and Attorney-General.

Hon. George W. Randolph, Virginia, third Secretary of War; at one time in the army with the rank of Brigadier-General.

Hon. James A. Seddon, Virginia, fourth Secretary of War; Delegate from Virginia to Provisional Congress.

Major-General John C. Breckinridge, Kentucky, fifth Secretary of War; summoned from the field [where he was serving with the rank and command of a Major-General] to discharge the duties of this office.

ADDENDA.

Colonel I. M. St. John, of Georgia, was First Chief of the Nitre and Mining Corps, and held the position until he was promoted and made Commissary General in the early part of 1865.

Colonel Morton was the Assistant of Colonel St. John, and was made Chief of the Bureau upon his transfer.

Albert Taylor Bledsoe, LL. D., Virginia, Assistant Secretary of War.

Hon. John A. Campbell, Louisiana, Assistant Secretary of War.

General Samuel Cooper, Virginia, Adjutant and Inspector General.

Colonel A. C. Myers, first Quartermaster-General.

Brigadier-General A. R. Lawton, Georgia, second Quartermaster-General; summoned from the field, where he was serving with the rank and command of Brigadier-General, to discharge the duties of this office.

Colonel L. B. Northrup, South Carolina, first Commissary-General.

Colonel L. M. St. John, second Commissary-General; afterwards promoted to the grade of Brigadier-General.

Colonel Josiah Gorgas, Virginia, Chief of Ordnance; afterwards promoted to the grade of Brigadier-General.

Colonel T. S. Rhett, in charge of the Ordnance Bureau.

Colonel J. F. Gilmer, North Carolina, Chief of the Engineer Bureau; afterwards promoted to the grade of Major-General.

Colonel S. P. Moore, M. D., South Carolina, Surgeon-General; afterwards promoted to the grade of Brigadier-General.

Colonel John S. Preston, South Carolina, Chief of the Bureau of Conscription; afterwards promoted to the grade of Brigadier-General.

Colonel T. P. August, Superintendent of the Bureau of Conscription.

Brigadier-General John H. Winder, Maryland, Commanding Prison Camps and Provost Marshal General.

Colonel Robert Ould, Virginia, Chief of the Bureau of Exchange.

Colonel Richard Morton, Chief of the Nitre and Mining Bureau.

Colonel R. G. H. Kean, Chief of the Bureau of War.

Lieutenant-Colonel I. H. Carrington, Virginia, Assistant Provost Marshal General, on duty at Richmond, Virginia.

Colonel Thomas L. Bayne, Louisiana, Chief of the Bureau of Foreign Supplies.

NAVY DEPARTMENT.

Hon. Stephen R. Mallory, Florida, Secretary of the Navy.

Captain French Forrest, Virginia, Chief of the Bureau of Orders and Detail.

Commander John M. Brooke, Florida, Chief of the Bureau of Ordnance and Hydrography.

POST OFFICE DEPARTMENT.

Hon. John H. Reagan, Texas, Postmaster-General; Delegate from Texas to the Provisional Congress.

H. St. George Offutt, Virginia, Chief of Contract Bureau.

B. N. Clements, Tennessee, Chief of Bureau of Appointment.

J. L. Harrell, Alabama, Chief of Finance Bureau.

Colonel Rufus R. Rhodes, Mississippi, Commissioner of Patents.

GENERALS CONFEDERATE STATES

	NAME.	STATE.	TO WHOM TO REPORT.	Date of Appointment.	Date of Rank.
1	Samuel Cooper........	Virginia ...	....	Aug. 31, 1861.	May 16, 1861.
2	Albert S. Johnston.....	Texas......	....	Aug. 31, 1861.	May 30, 1861.
3	Robert E. Lee.........	Virginia ...	....	Aug. 31, 1861.	June 14, 1861.
4	Joseph E. Johnston....	Virginia ...	....	Aug. 31, 1861.	July 4, 1861.
5	Gustav. T. Beauregard.	Louisiana..	....	Aug. 31, 1861.	July 21, 1861.
6	Braxton Bragg..	Louisiana..	....	Apl. 12, 1862.	Apl. 12, 1862.

GENERAL PROVISIONAL ARMY

1	Edmund Kirby Smith..	Florida....	Trans-Miss. Dept.....	Feb. 19, 1864.	Feb. 19, 1864.

GENERAL WITH

1	John B. Hood..........	Texas......	....	July 18, 1864.	July 18, 1864.

NOTE.—At the times of their resignations from the United States army in 1861, five of the above named officers held the following ranks respectively:
General Joseph E. Johnston was Quartermaster-General U. S. A., with the rank of Brigadier General.
General Samuel Cooper was Adjutant-General U. S. A., with the rank of Colonel.

ARMY, IN ORDER OF RANK.

Date of Confirmation.	Date of Acceptance.	REMARKS.
Aug. 31, 1861, and Apl. 23, 1863.	....	Adjutant and Inspector-General.
Aug. 31, 1861.	....	Killed at the Battle of Shiloh; assigned by Special Order No. 149, A. & .I G. O., Sept. 10, 1861, to the command of Department Number 2, embracing Tennessee and Arkansas, that part of Mississippi west of the N. O. J. & G. N. R. R. and the G. N. & C. R. R., and the military operations in Kentucky, Missouri, Kansas, and the Indian country west of Missouri and Arkansas, &c., &c.
Aug. 31, 1861, and Apl. 23, 1863.	....	Nominated and confirmed as "General-in-Chief of the Armies of the Confederate States of America" January 31, 1865; at first appointed Major-General of the military forces of Virginia; in command of the operations in the Trans-Alleghany region; in the winter of 1861 in command of the South Carolina and Georgia coast; from the spring of 1862 to the close of the war in command of the Army of Northern Virginia, &c., &c.
Aug. 31, 1861, and Apl. 23, 1863.	....	At first Major-General of Virginia State forces; assigned by President Davis to command at Harper's Ferry; at Manassas; in command, on the Peninsula, of the Department of Northern Virginia; June 9, 1863, assigned to command of forces in Mississippi; December 18, 1863, assigned to command of the Army of Tennessee; February 23, 1865, again in command of the Army of Tennessee in North Carolina and of all troops in the Department of South Carolina, Georgia and Florida, &c., &c.
Aug. 31, 1861, and Apl. 23, 1863.	....	Assigned to command at Charleston, S. C.; at Manassas; in command of the District of the Potomac; March 5, 1862, assumed command of the Army of the Mississippi; subsequently in command of the Department of South Carolina, Georgia and Florida, of North Carolina and South Virginia, &c., &c.
Apl. 12, 1862.	....	Assigned to duty at the Seat of Government, and, under the direction of the President, charged with the conduct of military operations in the armies of the Confederacy; see General Orders No. 23; A. & I. General's office, Richmond, Va., February 24, 1864; had previously commanded Department of the West, Army of Tennessee, Second Corps, Army of the Mississippi, &c., &c.

CONFEDERATE STATES.

....	....	Commanding District of Louisiana, occupied by Taylor's [afterwards Buckner's] corps, consisting of Walker's and Polignac's divisions and Green's cavalry brigade; the District of Texas, defended by Magruder's corps, consisting of Forney's, McCulloch's and Wharton's divisions; the District of Arkansas, held by Price's corps, consisting of the divisions of Price and Churchill and the brigades of Fagan, Shelby and Marmaduke, and the district of the Indian Territory—the whole constituting the Trans-Mississippi Department.

TEMPORARY RANK.

....	....	Commanding Army of Tennessee.

General Albert S. Johnston was Colonel of the Second cavalry U. S. A. with the rank of Brevet Brigadier-General.
General Robert E. Lee was Colonel of the First cavalry U. S. A.
General G. T. Beauregard was Captain and Brevet Major Corps of Engineers U. S. A.
See Official Army Register for September, 1861, page 61

LIEUTENANT-GENERALS,

	NAME.	STATE.	To WHOM TO REPORT.	Date of Appointment.	Date of Rank.
1	James Longstreet......	Alabama...	Gen. R. E. Lee........	Oct. 11, 1862.	Oct. 9, 1862.
2	E. Kirby Smith..........	Florida	Gen. B. Bragg........	Oct. 11, 1862.	Oct. 9, 1962.
3	Leonidas Polk.........	Louisiana..	Gen. B. Bragg........	Oct. 11, 1862.	Oct. 10, 1862.
4	Theophilus H. Holmes.	N. Carolina	....	Oct. 13, 1862	Oct. 10, 1862.
5	William J. Hardee.....	Georgia....	Gen. B. Bragg........	Oct. 11. 1862.	Oct. 10, 1862.
6	Thomas J. Jackson....	Virginia ...	Gen. R. E. Lee........	Oct. 11, 1862.	Oct. 10, 1862.
7	John C. Pemberton...	Virginia ...	Gen. B. Bragg........	Oct. 13, 1862.	Oct. 10, 1862.
8	Richard S. Ewell.......	Virginia ...	Gen. R. E. Lee........	May 23, 1863.	May 23, 1863.
9	Ambrose P. Hill........	Virginia ...	Gen. R. E. Lee........	May 23, 1863.	May 24, 1863.
10	Daniel H. Hill.........	N. Carolina	....	July 11, 1863.	July 11, 1863.
11	John B. Hood..	Texas......	Gen. J. E. Johnston..	Feb. 11, 1864.	Sept. 20, 1863.
12	Richard Taylor........	Louisiana..	Gen. E. K. Smith.....	May 16, 1864.	April 8, 1864.
13	Stephen D. Lee........	S. Carolina.	....	June 23, 1864.	June 23, 1864.
14	Jubal A. Early.........	Virginia....	Gen. R. E. Lee........	May 31, 1864.	May 31, 1864.

IN ORDER OF RANK.

Date of Confirmation.	Date of Acceptance.	REMARKS.
Oct. 11, 1862.	....	In command of 1st corps, Army of Northern Virginia, &c., &c. At the Battle of Fredericksburg, in November, 1862, General Longstreet's corps was composed of the divisions of Anderson, Pickett, Ransom. Hood and McLaws, and the artillery battalions of Colonels Alexander and Walton; in October, 1863, commanding corps in the Army of Tennessee, composed of the divisions of McLaws, Preston, Walker and Hood, and the artillery battalions of Alexander, Williams, Leyden and Robertson; Pickett's division belonged to this corps.
Oct. 11, 1862.	....	Promoted General P. A. C. S. February 19, 1864; commanded Department of East Tennessee and Kentucky, North Georgia and West North Carolina, with infantry divisions of Stevenson, McCown and Heth, and the cavalry brigades of Forrest, Morgan, Scott and Ashby; also in command of Trans-Mississippi Department.
Oct. 11, 1862.	....	Killed, June 14, 1864, on Pine Mountain, near Marietta, Georgia; at the time of his death in command of the Army of Mississippi, co-operating with the Army of Tennessee, both under command of General Joseph E. Johnston; commanded corps Army of Tennessee, composed of the divisions of Cheatham, Withers and McCown; commanded Army of Tennessee at Chattanooga. August, 1863; also, in 1863 and 1864, commanded Department of Alabama, Mississippi and East Louisiana; assigned to command of Trans-Mississippi Department.
Oct. 13, 1862.	....	In command, August, 1863, of the paroled prisoners of Mississippi, Arkansas, Missouri, Texas and Louisiana, recently forming part of the garrisons of Vicksburg and Port Hudson.
Oct. 11, 1862.	....	In command of the Department of South Carolina, Georgia and Florida; his corps, in the Army of Tennessee, composed of the Divisions of Cheatham, Clayburne, Stevenson and Walker; subsequently Stevenson's division was exchanged for Bates' division; in command of the Army of Tennessee at Dalton, Georgia, December 21, 1863.
Oct. 11, 1862.	....	Died May 10, 1863; commanding Second corps Army of Northern Virginia. At the Battle of Fredericksburg this corps was composed of the divisions of A. P. Hill, D. H. Hill, Early and Taliaferro. Colonel Brown's regiment of artillery and numerous light batteries.
Oct. 13, 1862.	....	Resigned May 18, 1864; assigned to the command of the Department of Mississippi and East Louisiana.
Feb. 2, 1864.	....	Commanding Second corps Army of Northern Virginia, the Department of Richmond, &c.
Jan. 15, 1864.	....	Killed in front of Petersburg, Va.; commanding Third corps Army of Northern Virginia, &c., composed of the divisions of Anderson, Heth and Pender.
....	....	In October, 1863, commanding corps, Army of Tennessee, composed of the divisions of Cleburne and Stewart; corps afterwards composed of the divisions of Cleburne and Breckinridge.
Feb. 11, 1864.	....	Promoted General with temporary rank July 18, 1864; commanding corps in the Army of Tennessee, composed of the divisions of Hindman, Stevenson and Stewart.
May 16, 1864.	....	Commanding Department of Alabama, Mississippi and West Tennessee.
....	....	Assigned to the command of the Department of Alabama, Mississippi, East Louisiana and West Tennessee; subsequently in command of Hood's old corps, Army of Tennessee, composed of the divisions of Hill, Stevenson and Clayton.
May 31, 1864.	....	Commanded Second corps Army of Northern Virginia, composed of the divisions of Rodes, Gordon and Ramseur, and three battalions of light artillery under command of Brigadier-General Long.

CONFEDERATE ROSTER.

LIEUTENANT–GENERALS, IN

	NAME.	STATE.	TO WHOM TO REPORT.	Date of Appointment.	Date of Rank.
15	Richard H. Anderson..	S. Carolina.	Gen. R. E. Lee........	June 1, 1864.	May 31, 1864.
16	Ambrose P. Stewart....	Tennessee.	Gen. J. E. Johnston..	June 23, 1864.	June 23, 1864.
17	Nathan B. Forrest.....	Tennessee.	Gen. Beauregard.....	Feb. 28, 1865.	Feb. 28, 1865.
18	Wade Hampton.......	S. Carolina.	Gen. J. E. Johnston..	....	....
19	Simon B. Buckner.....	Kentucky..	....	............1865.	....
20	Joseph Wheeler........	Georgia....	Gen. J. E. Johnston..	Feb. 28, 1865.	Feb. 28, 1865.
21	John B. Gordon........	Georgia....	Gen. R. E. Lee........	............1865.	....

ORDER OF RANK—Continued.

Date of Confirmation.	Date of Acceptance.	REMARKS.
June 1, 1864.	....	Commanded Longstreet's corps while he was disabled by wounds encountered in the Battle of the Wilderness.
....	....	Corps composed of the divisions of French, Loring and Walthall, Army of the West.
March 2, 1865.	....	Command composed of the cavalry divisions of Chalmers, Jackson and Buford, McCulloch's Second Missouri cavalry regiment as a special scouting force, and the Mississippi militia; Army of the West.
....	....	Commanding cavalry in General Joseph E. Johnston's army during General Sherman's march through the Carolinas, and Butler's division of cavalry from the Army of Northern Virginia.
....	....	Commanding District of Louisiana.
....	....	Commanding cavalry divisions of Allen, Humes and Dibbrell, composed of the brigades of Allen, Anderson, Breckinridge, Crews, Dibbrell, Ferguson, Harrison, Iverson and Lewis; again, commanding cavalry corps, Army of Tennessee, composed of the divisions of Martin, Kelley and Humes, and at another time a cavalry division in the Army of Tennessee, composed of the brigades of Hagan, Wharton and Morgan.
....	....	Commanding Second Army Corps, Army of Northern Virginia; at the time of General Lee's surrender, General Longstreet was in command of one wing of the Army of Northern Virginia and General Gordon of the other.

MAJOR-GENERALS,

	Name.	State.	To Whom to Report.	Date of Appointment.	Date of Rank.
1	David E. Twiggs......	Georgia....	...............….........	May 22, 1861.	May 22, 1861.
2	Leonidas Polk.........	Louisiana..	....	June 25, 1861.	June 25, 1861.
3	Braxton Bragg........	Louisiana..	...............…..........	Sept. 12, 1861.	Sept. 12, 1861.
4	Earl Van Dorn....... `.	Mississippi.	....	Sept. 19, 1861.	Sept. 19, 1861.
5	Gustavus W. Smith....	Kentucky...	....	Sept. 19, 1861.	Sept. 19, 1861.
6	Theophilus II. Holmes.	N. Carolina	....	Oct. 7, 1861.	Oct. 7, 1861.
7	William J. Hardee...`..	Georgia....	....	Oct. 7, 1861.	Oct. 7, 1861.
8	Benjamin Huger.......	S. Carolina.	....	Oct. 7, 1861.	Oct. 7, 1861.
9	James Longstreet......	Alabama...	....	Oct. 7, 1861.	Oct. 7, 1861.
10	J. Bankhead Magruder.	Virginia ...	....	Oct. 7, 1861.	Oct. 7, 1861.
11	Mansfield Lovell.......	Maryland..	....	Oct. 7, 1861.	Oct. 7, 1861.
12	Thomas J. Jackson....	Virginia ...	....	Oct. 7, 1861.	Oct. 7, 1861.
13	E. Kirby Smith........	Florida	....	Oct. 11, 1861.	Oct. 11, 1861.
14	George B. Crittenden..	Kentucky..	....	Nov. 9, 1861.	Nov. 9, 1861.
15	John C. Pemberton.. .	Virginia ...	Gen. R. E. Lee........	Feb. 23, 1862.	Jan. 14, 1862.
16	Richard S. Ewell.......	Virginia ...	....	Jan. 24, 1862.	Jan. 24, 1862.
17	William W. Loring....	Florida	Maj. Gen. Huger.....	Feb. 15, 1862.	Feb. 15, 1862.
18	Sterling Price.........	Missouri...	....	March 6, 1862.	March 6, 1862.

IN ORDER OF RANK.

Date of Confirmation.	Date of Acceptance.	REMARKS.
Aug. 29, 1861.		Died July 15th, 1862; in command, at New Orleans, of the Military Department of Louisiana.
Aug. 29, 1861.		Promoted Lieutenant-General October 10, 1862; commanding First corps, Army of the Mississippi, composed of the divisions of Clark and Cheatham, and Maxey's detached brigade; originally assigned to command of Department No. 2, comprising the defences of the Mississippi river; also in command of the Armies of Mississippi and Kentucky on the retreat from Kentucky.
Dec. 13, 1861.		Promoted General C. S. A. April 12, 1862; commanding Army of Tennessee, &c., &c.
Dec. 13, 1861.		Commanding Army of the District of the Mississippi.
Dec. 13, 1861.		Resigned February 17, 1863; assigned to the command of the Second corps Army of the Potomac; afterwards in command of the First division in General J. E. Johnston's Army of Virginia; subsequently relieved General Holmes of the command at Fredericksburg; at Yorktown commanded division composed of the brigades of Whiting, Hood, Hampton, Pettigrew and Hatton, &c., &c.
Dec. 13, 1861.		Promoted Lieutenant-General October 10, 1862; assigned to the command of Confederate forces in North Carolina; subsequently in command of the District of Arkansas, &c., &c.; at one time in command of Daniel's, Walker's and Wise's brigades, Army of Northern Virginia.
Dec. 13, 1861.		Promoted Lieutenant-General October 10, 1862; commanding Third corps, Army of the Mississippi, composed of Liddell's, Cleburne, Wood, Marmaduke and Hawthorne.
Dec. 13, 1861.		In command at Norfolk, Virginia; division in the field n ar Richmond, Vn., composed of the brigades of Mahone, Wright, Blanchard and Armistead.
Dec. 13, 1861.		Promoted Lieutenant-General October 9, 1862; commanding First corps Army of Northern Virginia, &c., &c.; division composed of the brigades of Kemper, Pickett, Wilcox, Anderson, Pryor and Featherston; Army of Northern Virginia.
Dec. 13, 1861.		On duty on the Peninsula; subsequently in command of the District of Texas, New Mexico and Arizona.
Dec. 13, 1861.		In command of New Orleans, &c., &c.; afterwards in command of First division, Army of the District of Mississippi, composed of the brigades of Rust, Villepique and Bowen.
Dec. 13, 1861.		Promoted Lieutenant-General October 10, 1862; assigned to the command of the Army of the Monongahela; later command consisted of the divisions of A. P. Hill, Ewell, Rodes, and Jackson's old division.
Dec. 13, 1861.		Promoted Lieutenant-General October 9, 1862; commanded reserve division, Army of the Potomac, consisting of Trimble's, Taylor's and Elzey's brigades.
....	....	Resigned October 23, 1862; commanding military operations in East Tennessee and East Kentucky.
Jan. 13, 1862.		Promoted Lieutenant-General October 10, 1862; assigned to the command of the Department of South Carolina, Georgia and Florida.
Jan. 24, 1862.		Promoted Lieutenant-General May 23, 1863; commanding Department of Richmond; division composed of the brigades of Elzey, Trimble and Taylor.
Feb. 15, 1862, and Feb. 17, 1864.	....	Commanding Department of Western Virginia; subsequently commanded division in Jackson's corps, and afterwards a division in the Department of Alabama, Mississippi and East Louisiana.
March 6, 1862.		Major-General commanding Missouri State Guard, and received with that rank into Confederate service; commanding District of Arkansas, Trans-Mississippi Department; in 1862 in command of the Army of the West; in 1864 division composed of the brigades of Drayton, Churchill, Tappan and Parsons.

MAJOR-GENERALS, IN

	NAME.	STATE.	TO WHOM TO REPORT.	Date of Appointment.	Date of Rank.
19	Benjamin F. Cheatham	Tennessee.	....	Mch. 14, 1862.	Mch. 10, 1862.
20	Samuel Jones..........	Virginia ...	....	Mch. 14, 1862.	Mch. 10, 1862.
21	John P. McCown......	Tennessee.	....	Mch. 14, 1862.	Mch. 10, 1862.
22	Daniel Harvey Hill....	N. Carolina	Gen. J. E. Johnston..	Mch. 26, 1862.	Mch. 26, 1862.
23	Jones M. Withers......	Alabama....	Gen. B. Bragg........	Aug. 16, 1862.	April 6, 1862.
24	T. C. Hindman.........	Arkansas ..	Gen. Beauregard.....	Apl. 18, 1862.	Apl. 14, 1862.
25	John C. Breckinridge..	Kentucky..	Gen. Beauregard.....	Apl. 18, 1862.	Apl. 14, 1862.
26	Lafayette McLaws.....	Georgia....	Gen. J. E. Johnston..	May 23, 1862.	May 23, 1862.
27	Ambrose P. Hill........	Virginia ...	Gen. J. E. Johnston..	May 26, 1862.	May 26, 1862.
28	Richard H. Anderson..	S. Carolina.	Gen. R. E. Lee........	July 14, 1862.	July 14, 1862.
29	J. E. B. Stuart.........	Virginia....	Gen. R. E. Lee........	July 25, 1862.	July 25, 1862.
30	Richard Taylor........	Louisiana..	Gen. R. E. Lee........	July 28, 1862.	July 28, 1862.
32	Simon B. Buckner.....	Kentucky..	Gen. B. Bragg........	Aug. 16, 1862.	Aug. 16, 1862.

ORDER OF RANK—CONTINUED.

Date of Confirmation.	Date of Acceptance.	REMARKS.
Mch. 14, 1862.		Division composed of the brigades of Maney, Smith, Wright and Strahl; in January, 1864, in command of Hardee's corps; division afterwards composed of the brigades of Maney, Wright, Strahl and Vaughan; at another time, of the brigades of Jackson, Maney, Smith, Wright and Strahl; Army of Tennessee.
Mch. 14, 1862.		In 1864 in command of the Department of South Carolina, Georgia and Florida; in 1862 commanding Second corps, Army of the Mississippi, composed of the brigades of Anderson, Richard and Walker; again in command of the Department of West Virginia and East Tennessee.
Mch. 14, 1862.		Commanding Army of the West, composed of the divisions of Little, McCown and Maury; again, in command of a division in Polk's corps, Army of Tennessee, composed of the brigades of Ector, Vance and McNair.
Mch. 26, 1862.		Division composed of the brigades of Deas, Manigault, Shoup and Brantley; also commanding division, Army of Northern Virginia, composed of the brigades of Doles, Iverson, Ramseur, Rodes and Colquitt.
Sept. 26, 1862.		Commanding reserve corps, Army of the Mississippi, composed of the brigades of Gardner, Chalmers, Jackson and Manigault; also commanded division in Polk's corps, Army of Tennessee, composed of the brigades of Deas, Chalmers, Walthall and Anderson.
Apl. 18, 1862.		Division composed of the brigades of Deas, Walthall, Manigault and Anderson, Polk's corps, Army of Tennessee; at one time in command of a corps in the Army of Tennessee, composed of the divisions of Hindman, Breckinridge and Stewart; again, division composed of the brigades of Tucker, Deas, Manigault and Walthall.
Apl. 18, 1862.		Afterwards Secretary of War; division composed of the brigades of Helm, Dan'l W. Adams and Stovall; in 1862 commanding division, Van Dorn's Army, District of Mississippi; in December, 1862, commanding cavalry division, Polk's corps, Army of Tennessee, composed of the brigades of Hanson, Palmer and Walker; in 1863 division composed of the brigades of Helm, Preston, Brown and Adams.
Sept. 26, 1862.		Division composed of the brigades of Kershaw, Wofford, Humphreys and Bryan; in 1864 in command of the District of Georgia; at the battle of Chancellorsville, division composed of the brigades of Wofford, Kershaw, Barksdale and Semmes.
Sept. 26, 1862.		Promoted Lieutenant-General May 24, 1863; commanding division in Army of Northern Virginia.
Sept. 26, 1862.		Promoted Lieutenant-General shortly after the battle of Spotsylvania; division composed of Mahone's, Wright's, Armistead's and Martin's brigades; Posey's, Wilcox's and Pryor's brigades were subsequently added; all attached to the Army of Northern Virginia; at the battle of Fredericksburg his division was composed of the brigades of Perry, Featherston, Wright, Wilcox and Mahone.
Sept. 26, 1862.		Died of wounds May 12, 1864; division composed of the brigades of Hampton, Fitzhugh Lee and W. H. F. Lee; Chief of Cavalry Army of Northern Virginia; succeeded Lieutenant-General A. P. Hill in command of the Second corps, Army of Northern Virginia, during battle of Chancellorsville.
Sept. 26, 1862.		Promoted Lieutenant-General April 8, 1864; commanding Department of Louisiana; also District of Western Louisiana.
Sept. 26, 1862.		Promoted Lieutenant-General 1865; command composed of the division of Major-General A. P. Stewart, consisting of the brigades of Johnson, Brown, Bate and Clayton, and the division of Brigadier-General Wm. Preston, consisting of the brigades of Gracie, Trigg and Kelly, and of three battalions of light artillery; Army of Tennessee.

MAJOR-GENERALS, IN

	NAME.	STATE.	TO WHOM TO REPORT.	Date of Appointment.	Date of Rank.
32	S. G. French............	Mississippi.	Maj. Gen. G. W. Smith	Oct. 22, 1862.	Aug. 31, 1862.
33	C. L. Stevenson........	Virginia ...	Lt. Gen. E. K. Smith.	Oct. 13, 1862.	Oct. 10, 1862.
34	George E. Pickett......	Virginia ...	Gen. R. E. Lee........	Oct. 11, 1862.	Oct. 10, 1862.
35	John B. Hood..........	Texas......	Gen. R. E. Lee........	Oct. 11, 1862.	Oct. 10, 1862.
36	D. R. Jones.....	Georgia....	Gen. R. E. Lee........	Oct. 11, 1862.	Oct. 11, 1862.
37	John H. Forney........	Alabama,...	....	Oct. 27. 1862.	Oct. 27, 1862.
38	Dabney H. Maury......	Virginia ...	Lt. Gen. Pemberton..	Nov. 4, 1862.	Nov. 4, 1862.
39	M. L. Smith............	Florida	Lt. Gen. Pemberton..	Nov. 4, 1862.	Nov. 4, 1862.
40	John G. Walker.......	Missouri...	Lt. Gen. T. H. Holmes	Nov. 8, 1862.	Nov. 8, 1862.
41	Arnold Elzey..........	Maryland..	Maj. Gen. G. W. Smith	Dec. 4, 1862.	Dec. 4, 1862.
42	Frank Gardner........	Louisiana..	Lt. Gen. Pemberton..	Dec. 20, 1862.	Dec. 13, 1862.
43	Patrick R. Cleburne....	Arkansas ..	Gen. J. E. Johnston..	Dec. 20, 1862.	Dec. 13, 1862.
44	Isaac R. Trimble......	Maryland..	Gen. R. E. Lee........	Apl. 23, 1863.	Jan. 17, 1863.
45	D. S. Donelson.........	Tennessee.	Gen. J. E. Johnston..	Apl. 22, 1863.	Jan. 17, 1863.
46	Jubal A. Early.........	Virginia ...	Gen. R. E. Lee........	Apl. 23, 1863.	Jan. 17, 1863.
47	Joseph Wheeler........	Georgia. ..	{ Gen. Command'g Army of Tenn. }	Feb. 4, 1864.	Jan. 20, 1863.
48	W. H. C. Whiting.... .	Mississippi.	Lt. Gen. Longstreet..	Apl. 22, 1863.	Feb. 28, 1863.
49	Edward Johnson......	Virginia ...	Gen. R. E. Lee........	Apl. 22, 1863.	Feb. 28, 1863.

ORDER OF RANK—Continued.

Date of Confirmation.	Date of Acceptance.	REMARKS.
Apl. 22, 1863.	....	Commanding Department of North Carolina and Southern Virginia, with defensive line from the mouth of the Appomattox to Cape Fear river.
Oct. 13, 1862.	....	Division composed of the brigades of Brown, Cumming, Pettus and Reynolds, and the light batteries of Anderson, Rowan, Corput and Carne; at another time, of the brigades of Pettus, Palmer and Cumming.
Oct. 11, 1862.	....	Commanding Department of North Carolina in 1864; commanded division in Longstreet's corps, Army of Northern Virginia, composed of the brigades of Garnett, Armistead, Kemper and Jenkins, to which Corse's brigade was subsequently added.
Oct. 11, 1862.	....	Promoted Lieutenant-General September 20, 1863; General with temporary rank, July 18, 1864; division composed of the brigades of Robertson, Law, Benning and Jenkins; at the Battle of Fredericksburg, division composed of the brigades of Law, Toombs, Robertson and Anderson.
Oct. 11, 1862.	....	Commanding division, Longstreet's corps, Army of Northern Virginia, composed of the brigades of Toombs, Anderson, Drayton, Kemper, Garnett and Jenkins.
Apl. 22, 1863.	....	Division consisted at first of Hebert's and Moore's brigades, and, subsequently, of the brigades of King, Waterhouse, Waul and McLain; at another time General Forney commanded a division composed of the brigades of Cockrell and Green, Army of the Mississippi.
Apl. 22, 1863.	....	Commanding Department of the Gulf; previously in command of the Third division, Army of the West.
Apl. 30, 1863.	....	In command of the Second District, Department of Mississippi and East Louisiana.
Apl. 22, 1863.	....	Division composed of Hawes', McCulloch's and Randall's brigades.
Apl. 22, 1863.	....	Commanding brigade, Army of Northern Virginia; also in command of the Department of Richmond, Virginia.
June 10, 1864.	....	In command at Mobile, Alabama, &c., &c.
Apl. 22, 1863.	....	Killed at the Battle of Franklin, Tennessee; division composed of the brigades of Polk, Wood and Deshler, and the light batteries of Calvert, Semple and Douglass; division afterwards composed of the brigades of Polk, Lowry, Govan and Granberry, and again of the brigades of Wood, Johnson, Liddell and Polk; Army of Tennessee.
Apl. 23, 1863.	....	Commanded Stonewall Jackson's old division, of the Second corps, Army of Northern Virginia; at the Battle of Chancellorsville, division composed of the brigades of Colston, Paxton, Nicholls and Jones.
Apl. 22, 1863.	....	Died April 17, 1863; in command of the First division of the right wing of the Army of the Mississippi, composed of the brigades of Savage, Stewart and Maney.
Apl. 23, 1863.	....	Promoted Lieutenant-General May 31, 1864; division composed of Early's, Hays', Lawton's and Trimble's brigades; at the Battle of Chancellorsville, division composed of the brigades of Hays, Gordon, Hoke and Smith, Army of Northern Virginia.
Feb. 4, 1864.	....	Promoted Lieutenant-General February 28, 1865; commanding cavalry in Tennessee, consisting of the divisions of Wharton, Martin and Kelly, and the brigades of Roddy and Morgan.
Apl. 22, 1863.	....	Commanding at Wilmington, North Carolina, in 1864; division composed of the brigades of Hood and Law, and the light batteries of Reilly and Balthis.
Apl. 22, 1863.	....	Commanding division in Ewell's corps, Army of Northern Virginia, composed of the brigades of Walker, Steuart and J. M. Jones.

MAJOR-GENERALS, IN

	NAME.	STATE.	TO WHOM TO REPORT.	Date of Appointment.	Date of Rank.
50	R. E. Rodes............	Alabama...	Gen. R. E. Lee........	May 7, 1863.	May 2, 1863.
51	William II. T. Walker.	Georgia....	Gen. J. E. Johnston..	May 27, 1863.	May 23, 1863.
52	Henry Heth............	Virginia ...	Gen. R. E. Lee........	May 23, 1863.	May 24, 1863.
53	John S. Bowen........	Missouri ...	Gen. J. E. Johnston..	May 29, 1863.	May 25, 1863.
54	Robert Ransom, Jr....	N. Carolina	Lt. Gen. D. H. Hill....	May 27, 1863.	May 26, 1863.
55	W. D. Pender..........	N. Carolina	Gen. R. E. Lee........	May 27, 1863.	May 27, 1863.
56	A. P. Stewart..........	Tennessee.	Gen. B. Bragg........	June 5, 1863.	June 2, 1863.
57	Stephen D. Lee........	S. Carolina.	Gen. J. E. Johnston..	Aug. 3, 1863.	Aug. 3, 1863.
58	Cadmus M. Wilcox....	Tennessee.	Gen. R. E. Lee........	Aug. 13, 1863.	Aug. 3, 1863.
59	J. F. Gilmer..........	N. Carolina	Gen. Beauregard.....	Aug. 16, 1863.	Aug. 16, 1863.
60	Wade Hampton........	S. Carolina.	Gen. R. E. Lee........	Sept. 3, 1863.	Aug. 3, 1863.
61	Fitzhugh Lee..........	Virginia....	Gen. R. E. Lee........	Sept. 3, 1863.	Aug. 3, 1863.
62	William Smith.........	Virginia....	Gen. R. E. Lee........	Aug. 13, 1863.	Aug. 12, 1863.
63	Howell Cobb..........	Georgia....	....	Sept. 19, 1863.	Sept. 9, 1863.
64	John A. Wharton......	Texas	Gen. B. Bragg........	Nov. 12, 1863.	Nov. 10, 1863.
65	William T. Martin.....	Mississippi.	Gen. B. Bragg........	Nov. 12, 1863.	Nov. 10, 1863.
66	Nathan B. Forrest.....	Tennessee.	Gen. J. E. Johnston..	Dec. 4, 1863.	Dec. 4, 1863.
67	Charles W. Field......	Kentucky..	Lt. Gen. Longstreet..	Feb. 12, 1864.	Feb. 12, 1864.
68	J. Patton Anderson....	Florida	Gen. J. E. Johnston..	Feb. 17, 1864.	Feb. 17, 1864.
69	W. B. Bate............	Tennessee.	Gen. J. E. Johnston..	March 5, 1864.	Feb. 23, 1864.
70	Robert F. Hoke........	N. Carolina	....	Apl. 23, 1864.	Apl. 20, 1864.

ORDER OF RANK—Continued.

Date of Confirmation.	Date of Acceptance.	REMARKS.
Jan. 25, 1864.	....	Killed at Winchester, Va., 19th Sept., 1864; division composed of the brigades of Doles, Battle, Daniel and Ramseur.
Jan. 25, 1864.	....	Killed in the battle around Atlanta, Georgia; division composed of the brigades of Liddell, Walthall, Ector and Wilson; division afterwards composed of the brigades of Mercer, Jackson, Gist and Stevens; in October, 1863, division composed of the brigades of Gregg, Gist and Wilson.
Feb. 17, 1864.	....	Division composed of Pettigrew's, Archer's, Davis', Cook's and Brockenborough's brigades, Army of Northern Virginia.
....	....	Died July 16, 1863, from disease contracted during the siege of Vicksburg; commanded division known as the Missouri division, composed of the brigades of Cockrell and Green.
Feb. 17, 1864.	....	Commanding Department of Richmond, in 1864; at the Battle of Fredericksburg, division composed of the brigades of Ransom and Cook.
....	....	Died July 18, 1863, from wounds received at Gettysburg; division composed of his old brigade and the brigades of McGowan, Lane and Thomas, Army of Northern Virginia.
Jan. 25, 1864.	....	Promoted Lieutenant-General June 23, 1864; division composed of the brigades of Brown, Johnson, Strahl and Clayton; afterwards, of the brigades of Brown, Bate, Clayton and Stovall; subsequently of the brigades of Stovall, Clayton, Gibson and Baker; Army of the West.
Jan. 25, 1864.	....	Promoted Lieutenant-General; assigned to the command of all the cavalry in the Department of Alabama, Mississippi, East Louisiana and West Tennessee.
Feb. 17, 1864.	....	Division composed of the brigades of Generals Lane, Scales, McGowan and Thomas.
Jan. 25, 1864.	....	Chief of the Engineer Bureau.
Jan. 25, 1864.	....	Promoted Lieutenant-General; division composed of the cavalry brigades of Young, Butler, Rosser and Gordon, Army of Northern Virginia.
Jan. 25, 1864.	....	Division composed of Wickham's and Lomax's brigades; subsequently in command of the cavalry corps, Army of Northern Virginia, composed of the divisions of W. H. F. Lee, Rosser and Munford.
Jan. 25, 1864.	....	Resigned December 31, 1863, because elected Governor of Virginia; consequently, did not assume command of a division or remain in the field.
Jan. 25, 1864.	....	In 1864 in command of the reserve forces of Georgia.
Jan. 25, 1864.	....	Commanding division in Wheeler's cavalry corps, Army of Tennessee.
Jan. 25, 1864.	....	Commanding cavalry corps in East Tennessee, under General Longstreet; subsequently a division in Wheeler's cavalry corps, composed of the brigades of Morgan and Iverson.
Jan. 25, 1864.	....	Promoted Lieutenant-General February 28, 1865; assigned to the command of all cavalry in West Tennessee and North Mississippi, consisting of those of his own brigade and those of Chalmers, McCulloch, Richardson, Bell and Jeffrey Forrest; Lyon's brigade was afterwards added; the whole was organized into two divisions, commanded respectively by Chalmers and Buford.
Feb. 12, 1864.	....	Division composed of Jenkins', Law's, Benning's, Anderson's and Gregg's brigades, Army of Northern Virginia.
Feb. 17, 1864.	....	In 1864 assigned to the command of the District of Florida.
May 11, 1864.	....	Division composed of the brigades of Tyler, Lewis and Finley, and of the light batteries of Slocum, Cobb and Mebane; Army of Tennessee.
May 11, 1864.	....	Commanding in North Carolina; division in General Beauregard's army composed, May, 1864, of the brigades of Martin, Hagood, Clingman and Colquitt; Army of Northern Virginia.

MAJOR-GENERALS, IN

	NAME.	STATE.	TO WHOM TO REPORT.	Date of Appointment.	Date of Rank.
71	W. H. F. Lee	Virginia	Gen. R. E. Lee	Apl. 23, 1864.	Apl. 23, 1864.
72	John B. Gordon	Georgia	Gen. R. E. Lee	May 14, 1864.	May 14, 1864.
73	Bushrod R. Johnson	Tennessee.	Gen. Beauregard	May 26, 1864.	May 21, 1864.
74	J. B. Kershaw	S. Carolina.	Gen. R. E. Lee	June 2, 1864.	May 19, 1864.
75	C. J. Polignac	France	Lt. Gen. E. K. Smith.	June 13, 1864.	Apl. 8, 1864.
76	J. F. Fagan	Arkansas	Lt. Gen. E. K. Smith.	June 13, 1864.	Apl. 25, 1864.
77	William Mahone	Virginia	Gen. R. E. Lee	Aug. 3, 1864.	July 30, 1864.
78	S. D. Ramseur	N. Carolina	Gen. R. E. Lee	June 1, 1864.	June 1, 1864.
79	E. C. Walthall	Mississippi.	Gen. J. E. Johnston	June 10, 1864.	June 6, 1864.
80	H. D. Clayton	Alabama	Gen. J. E. Johnston	July 8, 1864.	July 7, 1864.
81	John C. Brown	Tennessee.	Gen. J. B. Hood	Aug. 4, 1864.	Aug. 4, 1864.
82	L. L. Lomax	Virginia	Gen. R. E. Lee	Aug. 10, 1864.	Aug. 10, 1864.
83	Henry W. Allen	Louisiana		..1864.	..1864.
84	J. L. Kemper	Virginia	Gen. R. E. Lee	Mch. 1, 1864.	Mch. 1, 1864.
85	J. S. Marmaduke	Missouri	Gen. E. K. Smith	..1864.	..1864.
86	A. R. Wright	Georgia	Gen. Beauregard	Nov. 23, 1864.	Nov. 23, 1864.
87	John Pegram	Virginia	Gen. R. E. Lee	..1864.	..1864.
88	Pierce M. B. Young	Georgia	Gen. B. Bragg	Dec. 12, 1864.	Dec. 12, 1864.
89	M. Calvin Butler	S. Carolina.	Gen. J. E. Johnston	..1864.	..1864.
90	T. L. Rosser	Texas	Gen. R. E. Lee	..1864.	..1864.
91	G. W. Custis Lee	Virginia	Gen. R. E. Lee	Jan. 1, 1865.	Jan. 1, 1865.
92	William Preston	Kentucky	Gen. E. K. Smith	Jan. 1, 1865.	Jan. 1, 1865.
93	William B. Taliaferro	Virginia	Gen. Wm. J. Hardee.	Jan. 1, 1865.	Jan. 1, 1865.
94	Bryan Grimes	N. Carolina	Gen. R. E. Lee	Feb. 23, 1865.	Feb. 23, 1865.

ORDER OF RANK—Continued.

Date of Confirmation.	Date of Acceptance.	REMARKS.
June 9, 1864.	....	Division composed of the cavalry brigades of Chambliss, Barringer and Roberts, and of two batteries horse artillery, Captain McGreggor, Army of Northern Virginia.
May 14, 1864.	....	Lieutenant-General in the spring of 1865 by promotion at the hands of General R. E. Lee; division composed of the brigades of Evans, Terry and York, Army of Northern Virginia.
May 26, 1864.	Oct. 13, 1862.	Division was composed of Ransom's, Johnson's, Wise's, Elliott's and Gracie's brigades, and the Sixty-fourth Georgia regiment, Army of Northern Virginia.
June 2, 1864.	....	Division composed of the brigades of Conner, Wofford, Humphreys and Bryan, Army of Tennessee.
June 13, 1864.	....	Division composed of the Second Texas brigade and Mouton's brigade.
June 13, 1864.	....	Commanding District of Arkansas.
....	Oct. 13, 1862.	Assigned to command of Anderson's old division, composed of the brigades of Generals Wright, Weisiger, Saunders, Harris and Finnegan, Army of Northern Virginia.
June 1, 1864.	....	Assigned to the command of General Early's old division, at that time composed of the brigades of Pegram, Johnston and Godwin, Army of Northern Virginia.
June 10, 1864.	....	Division composed of the brigades of Canty, Reynolds and Quarles, Army of Tennessee; again, of the brigades of Quarles, Shelley and D. H. Reynolds, Stewart's corps, Army of Tennessee.
		Division composed of the brigades of Stovall, Baker and Henry R. Jackson; at another time, of the brigades of M. A. Stovall, R. L. Gibson, A. Baker and J. T. Holtzclaw; Army of Tennessee.
		Division composed of Govan's and Smith's brigades, Army of Tennessee.
		Division composed of the cavalry brigades of Johnson, Jackson, Imboden, Vaughn and McCausland, Army of Northern Virginia.
		Commanding division in Trans-Mississippi Department.
		In command of the reserve forces of Virginia.
		Division composed of the brigades of Clarke and Harrison.
Febr'y, 1865.	....	Commanding division during the siege of Savannah in December, 1864, composed of the brigades of Mercer and John K. Jackson.
		Killed in action at Hatcher's Run; commanding Early's old division, Army of Northern Virginia.
Dec. 22, 1864.	....	Division composed of the cavalry brigades of Lewis, Ferguson and Hannon, Wheeler's corps.
		Division composed of the cavalry brigades of Wright and Logan, Army of Northern Virginia.
		Division composed of the cavalry brigades of McCausland and Dearing, and subsequently of the brigades of Payne and Munford, Army of Northern Virginia.
		In command of local brigade and reserves for the immediate defence of Richmond, Virginia.
		Assigned to the command of the division of Major-General Polignac, after his return to France; in October, 1863, in command of a division, Longstreet's corps, Army of the Tennessee, composed of the brigades of Gracie, Twiggs and Kelly.
		Commanding division of mixed troops after the evacuation of Charleston; previously in command of James Island, South Carolina.
Feb. 23, 1865.	....	Division composed of his old brigade and the brigades of Battle, Cook and Cox, Army of Northern Virginia.

CONFEDERATE ROSTER.

MAJOR–GENERALS, IN

	NAME.	STATE.	TO WHOM TO REPORT.	Date of Appointment.	Date of Rank.
95	William W. Allen......	Alabama...	Gen. Jos. Wheeler....	March, 1865.	March, 1865.
96	W. Y. C. Humes.......	Tennessee.	Gen. Jos. Wheeler....	March, 1865.	March, 1865.
97	Harry T. Hays.........	Louisiana..	Gen. E. K. Smith.....	April, 1865.	April, 1865.
98	E. M. Law.............	Alabama...	Gen. J. E. Johnston..	April 9, 1865.	April, 1865.
99	M. W. Gary............	S. Carolina.	Gen. R. E. Lee.......	..........1865.	..........1865.

ORDER OF RANK—CONTINUED.

Date of Confirmation.	Date of Acceptance.	REMARKS.
....	....	Commanding cavalry division composed of the brigades of Crews and Hagan ; Brigadier-General Robert H. Anderson's cavalry brigade was subsequently added.
....	....	Commanding division in Lieutenant-General Wheeler's cavalry corps, composed of the brigades of Ashby, Harrison and Williams.
....	....	On special duty in Trans-Mississippi Department.
....	....	Commanding General Hampton's old cavalry division.
....	....	Division assigned, but never concentrated, consisting of his old brigade and Robert's brigade of North Carolina cavalry.

BRIGADIER–GENERALS OF THE CONFEDERATE

	NAME.	STATE.	TO WHOM TO REPORT.	Date of Appointment.	Date of Rank.
1	Adams, Charles W.....	Arkansas..	Maj. Gen. Price......	..........1862.	..........1862.
2	Adams, Daniel W.....	Louisiana..	Gen. Beauregard.....	May 23, 1862.	May 23, 1862.
3	Adams, John..........	Tennessee.	Gen. J. E. Johnston..	May 23, 1863.	Dec. 29, 1862.
4	Adams, Wirt.........	Mississippi.	Gen. Wm. J. Hardee..	Sept. 2S, 1863.	Sept. 25, 1863.
5	Alcorn, J. L...	....	....	....	....
6	Alexander, E. Porter..	Georgia....	Lt. Gen. Longstreet..	Mch. 1, 1864.	Feb. 26, 1864.
7	Allen, Henry W........	Louisiana..	Gen. E. K. Smith.....	Aug. 19, 1863.	Aug. 19, 1863.
8	Allen, William W......	Alabama...	Gen. J. E. Johnston..	Mch. 1, 1864.	Feb. 26, 1864.
9	Anderson, C. D........	Georgia....	Gen. G. W. Smith. ..	May, 1864.	May, 1864.
10	Anderson, George B...	N. Carolina	Gen. R. E. Lee........	June 9, 1862.	June 9, 1862.
11	Anderson, George T...	Georgia....	Gen. Longstreet......	Nov. 1, 1862.	Nov. 1, 1862.
12	Anderson, Joseph R...	Virginia ...	Gen. R. E. Lee........	Sept. 3, 1861.	Sept. 3, 1861.
13	Anderson, J. Patton...	Florida	Gen. B. Bragg........	Feb. 10, 1862.	Feb. 10, 1862.
14	Anderson, R. H........	S. Carolina.	Gen. R. E. Lee........	July 19, 1861.	July 19, 1861.
15	Anderson, Robert H...	Georgia....	Gen. J. B. Hood......	July 26, 1864.	July 26, 1864.
16	Anderson, Samuel R...	Tennessee.	Gen. R. E. Lee........	July 9, 1861.	July 9, 1861.
17	Archer, J. J............	Virginia ...	Gen. R. E. Lee........	June 3, 1862.	June 3, 1862.
18	Armistead, L. A........	Virginia ...	Gen. Huger..........	Apl. 1, 1862.	Apl. 1, 1862.
19	Armstrong, Frank C...	Arkansas..	Gen. J. E. Johnston..	Apl. 23, 1863.	Jan. 20, 1863.

STATES ARMY, ALPHABETICALLY ARRANGED.

Date of Confirmation.	Date of Acceptance.	REMARKS.
.........1862.	....	Commanding brigade in Major-General Price's army.
Sept. 30, 1862.	....	Commanding Mississippi brigade, General Breckinridge's division. Army of Tennessee, composed of the 13th, 20th, 16th, 25th and 19th Louisiana and 32d Alabama regiments, Austin's battalion of sharp-shooters and Slocomb's light battery.
Feb. 17, 1864.	....	Killed at Battle of Franklin; commanded brigade in Loring's division, Stewart's corps, Army of Tennessee, composed of the 6th, 14th, 15th, 20th, 23d and 43d Mississippi regiments.
Jan. 25, 1864.	....	Brigade composed of Colonel Wood's regiment, the 11th and 17th Arkansas regiments consolidated, the 14th Confederate regiment, the 9th Tennessee battalion and King's light battery.
....	....	Commanding a brigade of Mississippi State troops at Columbus, Kentucky.
May 28, 1864.	....	In command of the artillery attached to the 1st corps (Longstreet's), Army of Northern Virginia.
Jan. 25, 1864.	....	Promoted Major-General; resigned January 10, 1864; elected Governor of Louisiana.
June 9, 1864.	Oct. 13, 1862.	Promoted Major-General in the spring of 1865; brigade at first composed of the 1st, 3d, 8th and 10th Confederate regiments, and subsequently of the 1st, 3d, 4th, 9th, 12th and 51st regiments Alabama cavalry, Army of the West.
May, 1864.	....	Held commission in Georgia State forces; commanding the 3d Georgia brigade, composed of the 7th, 8th and 9th regiments.
Sept. 30, 1862.	....	Died October 16, 1862, from the effect of wounds received at Sharpsburg; brigade composed of the 2d, 4th, 14th and 30th North Carolina regiments, D. H. Hill's division, Jackson's corps, Army of Northern Virginia.
Apl. 22, 1863.	....	Brigade composed of the 7th, 8th, 9th and 11th Georgia regiments and the 1st Kentucky regiment; the 59th Georgia regiment was afterwards substituted for the 1st Kentucky, whose term of service had expired; all of the Army of Northern Virginia.
Dec. 13, 1864.	....	Brigade composed of the 14th, 35th, 45th and 49th Georgia regiments and the 3d Louisiana battalion, Army of Northern Virginia; resigned July 19, 1862.
Feb. 10, 1862.	....	Promoted Major-General February 17, 1864; brigade composed of the 1st Florida, 17th Alabama and the 5th and 8th Mississippi regiments; subsequently in command of Major-General Hindman's division, Polk's corps, Army of Tennessee.
Aug. 29, 1861.	....	Promoted Major-General July 14, 1862; brigade composed of Colonel Gladden's 1st Louisiana Regular infantry, Colonel Anderson's 1st Florida regiment, Colonel Jackson's 5th Georgia regiment, the 7th and 8th Mississippi regiments, and Colonel Tyler's battalion of marines; brigade afterwards composed of the 4th, 5th and 6th South Carolina Volunteers and the 2d South Carolina Rifles, Longstreet's corps, Army of Northern Virginia.
....	....	Brigade composed of the 5th Georgia and the 1st, 3d 8th and 10th Confederate regiments cavalry, Army of Tennessee.
Aug. 29, 1861.	....	Resigned May 10, 1862; brigade was composed of the 1st, 7th and 14th Tennessee regiments and one company of cavalry.
Sept. 30, 1862.	....	Brigade composed of the 1st, 14th and 7th Tennessee regiments, the 13th Alabama regiment and the 5th Alabama battalion, Heth's division, A. P. Hill's corps, Army of Northern Virginia.
Apl. 1, 1862.	....	Killed in action at Gettysburg; brigade composed of the 9th, 14th, 38th, 53d and 57th Virginia regiments, Army of Northern Virginia.
Apl. 23, 1963.	....	Commanding brigade in Chalmer's division, Forrest's cavalry corps, Army of the West.

BRIGADIER-GENERALS

	NAME.	STATE.	TO WHOM TO REPORT.	Date of Appointment.	Date of Rank.
20	Ashby, Turner.........	Virginia ...	Gen. T. J. Jackson....	May 23, 1862.	May 23, 1862.
21	Bagby, Arthur P.......	Texas	Lt. Gen. Buckner.....	March, 1864.	....
22	Baker, Alpheus........	Alabama...	Gen. J. E. Johnston..	March 7, 1864.	Mch. 5, 1864.
23	Baker, Lawrence S....	N. Carolina	Gen. R. E. Lee........	July 30, 1863.	July 23, 1863.
24	Baldwin, Wm. E.......	Mississippi.	Gen. Van Dorn.......	Oct. 3, 1862.	Sept. 19, 1862.
25	Barksdale, William....	Mississippi.	Gen. R. E. Lee........	Aug. 12, 1862.	Aug. 12, 1862.
26	Barnes, James W......	Texas......		.. ..	....
27	Barringer, Rufus......	N. Carolina	Gen. R. E. Lee........	June 1, 1864.	June 1, 1864.
28	Barry, William S......	Mississippi.			
29	Barton, Seth M.......	Virginia ...	Gen. E. K. Smith.....	Mch. 18, 1862.	Mch. 11, 1862.
30	Bartow, Francis S.....	Georgia....	Gen. Beauregard.....	July, 1861.	July, 1861.
31	Bate, William B.......	Tennessee.	Gen. B. Bragg........	Oct. 3, 1862.	Oct. 3, 1862.
32	Battle, C. A............	Alabama...	Gen. R. E. Lee........	Aug. 25, 1863.	Aug. 20, 1863.
33	Baylor, John R........	Texas......	....	....	....
34	Beale, Richard L. T....	Virginia ...	Gen. R. E. Lee........	Febr'y, 1865.	Febr'y, 1865.
35	Beall, W. N. R.........	Arkansas ..	Gen. Van Dorn.......	Apl. 17, 1862.	Apl. 11, 1862.
36	Beauregard, G. T......	Louisiana..	{ Commanding Charleston Harbor. }	Mch. 1, 1861.	Mch. 1, 1861.
37	Bee, Barnard E........	S. Carolina.	Gen. J. E. Johnston..	June 17, 1861.	June 17, 1861.
38	Bee, Hamilton P.......	Texas......	Gen. P. O. Hebert....	March 6, 1862.	March 4, 1862.
39	Bell, Tyree H..........	Tennessee.	Maj. Gen. Forrest....	Nov., 1863.	Nov., 1863.
40	Benning, Henry L......	Georgia....	Gen. R. E. Lee........	Apl. 23, 1863.	Jan. 17, 1863.
41	Benton, Samuel........	Mississippi.	Gen. J. B. Hood......	July 26, 1864.	July 26, 1864.

—CONTINUED.

Date of Confirmation.	Date of Acceptance.	REMARKS.
....	....	Killed June 6th, 1862, near Harrisonburg, Virginia; command composed of twenty-six companies; subsequently constituting Robertson's brigade, and organized into the 6th, 7th and 11th Virginia regiments, and the 16th Virginia battalion, Colonel Funsten.
....	....	Brigade composed of Texas cavalry; in autumn of 1864 commanded a division composed of his old brigade and the brigades of DeBray and Brent.
May 11, 1864.	....	Brigade composed of the 37th, 40th, 42d and 54th Alabama regiments.
Feb. 16, 1864.	....	Commanding Second Military District, Department of North Carolina and South Virginia.
Oct. 3, 1862.	....	Died February 19, 1864: commanding brigade, District of Mobile; brigade, at the capture of Fort Donelson, consisted of the 20th and 26th Mississippi and the 26th Tennessee regiments.
Sept. 30, 1862.	....	Killed in action at Gettysburg; brigade composed of the 21st, 13th, 17th and 18th Mississippi regiments, McLaw's division, Longstreet's corps, Army of Northern Virginia.
June 1, 1864.	....	Brigade composed of the 1st, 2d, 3d and 5th North Carolina cavalry regiments, Major-General W. H. F. Lee's division, Army of Northern Virginia.
....	....	Commanding brigade, Army of the Mississippi.
Mch. 18, 1862.	....	Commanded brigade, Army of Northern Virginia, composed of the 9th, 14th, 38th, 53d and 57th Virginia regiments.
....	....	Killed at the Battle of First Manassas July 21, 1861; commanding brigade, Army of the Potomac, composed of the 7th and 8th Georgia regiments.
Oct. 3, 1862.	....	Promoted Major-General February 23, 1864; brigade composed of the 2d, 10th, 15th, 20th, 30th and 37th Tennessee and the 37th Georgia regiments, and the 4th battalion Georgia sharp-shooters; Army of Tennessee.
Feb. 17, 1864.	....	Brigade [formerly Rodes'] composed of the 3d, 5th, 6th, 12th, 26th and 61st Alabama regiments, infantry.
....	....	Commanding brigade, Trans-Mississippi Department; also in command of Confederate forces in Arizona.
....	....	Commanding brigade in Major-General W. H. F. Lee's cavalry division, Army of Northern Virginia, composed of the 9th, 10th and 13th Virginia cavalry regiments; the 14th Virginia cavalry regiment was subsequently added; General Beale succeeded General Chambliss in command of his brigade.
Apl. 17, 1862.	....	Commanding Second Sub-District, District of Mississippi. .
Mch. 1, 1861.	{	Promoted General Confederate States Army July 21, 1861; commanding at Charleston, South Carolina, and afterwards at Manassas.
Aug. 29, 1861.	....	Killed at Manassas July 21, 1861; commanding brigade, Army the Potomac, composed of the 2d and 11th Mississippi, the 6th North Carolina and the 4th Alabama regiments.
Mch. 6, 1862.	....	Brigade composed of DeBray's, Buchell's, Wood's, Terrell's, Gould's and Likin's Texas regiments.
....	....	Commanding 12th Tennessee regiment and acting Brigadier-General; brigade composed of the regiments of Colonels Russell, Greer, Newsom, Wilson and Barteau; afterwards promoted Brigadier-General, and assigned to command of a brigade in Jackson's division, Forrest's cavalry corps.
Apl. 23, 1863.	....	Brigade composed of the 2d, 15th, 17th and 20th Georgia regiments, Hood's division, Longstreet's corps, Army of Northern Virginia.
....	....	Died of wounds, received in action at Atlanta, Georgia, July 28, 1864; commanded a brigade composed of the 27th, 29th, 30th and 34th Mississippi regiments.

BRIGADIER-GENERALS

	NAME.	STATE.	TO WHOM TO REPORT.	Date of Appointment.	Date of Rank.
42	Blanchard, A. G.......	Louisiana..	Gen. Huger...........	Sept. 21, 1861.	Sept. 21, 1861.
43	Boggs, William R......	Georgia....	Lt. Gen. E. K. Smith..	Nov. 4, 1862.	Nov. 4, 1862.
44	Bonham, M. L.........	S. Carolina.	Gen. Beauregard.....	Apl. 23, 1861.	Apl. 23, 1861.
45	Bowen, John S.........	Missouri...	Gen. Beauregard.....	Mch. 18, 1862.	Mch. 14, 1862.
46	Bowles, Pinckney D...	Alabama...	Brig. Gen. Walker....	ApL 2, 1865.	April 2, 1865.
47	Bragg, Braxton........	Louisiana..	{ Commanding at Pensacola, Fla. }	Mch. 7, 1861.	Mch. 7, 1861.
48	Branch, L. O. B........	N. Carolina	Lt. Gen. A. P. Hill....	Nov. 16, 1861.	Nov. 16, 1861.
49	Brandon, Wm. L.......	Mississippi.	Maj. Gen. D. H. Hill..	June 18, 1864.	June 18, 1864.
50	Brantly, W. F..........	Mississippi.	Gen. J. B. Hood......	July 26, 1864.	July 26, 1864.
51	Bratton, John..........	S. Carolina.	Gen. R. E. Lee........	June 9, 1864.	May 6, 1864.
52	Breckinridge, John C..	Kentucky..	Gen. A. S. Johnston..	Nov. 2, 1861.	Nov. 2, 1861.
53	Brent, Joseph L........	Louisiana..	Lt. Gen. S. B. Buckner	October, 1864.	October, 1864.
54	Brown, John C........	Tennessee.	Gen. B. Bragg........	Sept. 30, 1862.	Aug. 30, 1862.
55	Browne, Wm. M.......	....	Gen. A. R. Wright....	Dec'r, 1864.	Dec'r, 1864.
56	Bryan, Goode..........	Georgia....	Gen. R. E. Lee........	Aug. 31, 1863.	Aug. 29, 1863.
57	Buckner, Simon B.....	Kentucky..	Gen. A. S. Johnston..	Sept. 14, 1861.	Sept. 14, 1861.

—CONTINUED.

Date of Confirmation.	Date of Acceptance.	REMARKS.
Dec. 13, 1861.	....	Brigade composed of the 3d, 4th and 22d Georgia regiments, the 3d Alabama regiment, 3d Louisiana battalion and Colonel Williams' North Carolina battalion, Girardey's Louisiana Guard artillery, Grimes' Portsmouth artillery, and the Sussex cavalry.
Apl. 22, 1863.	Oct. 13, 1862.	Chief of Staff to General E. Kirby Smith, commanding Trans-Mississippi Department.
Aug. 29, 1861.	....	Resigned; reappointed October 21, 1861; brigade at first composed of the 7th, 2d, 3d and 8th South Carolina Volunteers, infantry, constituting First brigade, First corps, Army of the Potomac; upon reappointment, ordered to the command of the 1st, 2d and 3d regiments South Carolina cavalry and Lieutenant-Colonel Trenholm's battalion South Carolina cavalry.
Mch. 18, 1862.	....	Promoted Major-General May 25, 1863; commanding 14th, 16th, 17th and 18th Arkansas regiments, Adams' Arkansas infantry regiment, and Jones' Arkansas infantry battalion; assigned, in 1861, to the command of the 4th division, Western Department, embracing the brigades of Martin and Bonham; again in command of the 3d brigade, 1st division, Army of the District of Mississippi.
....	....	Brigade composed of the 21st Virginia battalion, the 2d and 6th Virginia reserves, and the 1st and 2d Confederate [mixed] regiments. Walker's division.
Mch. 7, 1861.	....	Promoted Major-General September 12, 1861; assigned to command at Pensacola, Florida, of the troops there assembled, consisting of the brigades of Colonels Chalmers, Clayton and Gladden, and the troops under Major Bradford.
Dec. 13, 1861.	....	Killed at Sharpsburg; brigade composed of the 7th, 18th, 28th, 33d and 37th North Carolina regiments, A. P. Hill's division, Army of Northern Virginia.
....	....	Assigned to the command of a brigade of cavalry in Mississippi.
....	....	Brigade composed of the 24th, 27th, 29th, 30th and 34th Mississippi regiments.
June 9, 1864.	....	Brigade composed of the 1st regiment South Carolina Volunteers [Hagood's], the 2d regiment South Carolina Rifles, the 5th and 6th regiments South Carolina Volunteers, and the Palmetto Sharpshooters, Longstreet's corps, Army of Northern Virginia.
Dec. 13, 1861.	....	Promoted Major-General April 14, 1862; afterwards Secretary of War.
....	....	Brigade composed of the 2d, 5th, 7th and 8th regiments Louisiana cavalry, Bagby's division, Army of West Louisiana, Lieutenant-General Buckner commanding.
Sept. 30, 1862.	....	Promoted Major-General August 4, 1864; brigade composed of the 18th, 26th, 32d and 45th regiments Tennessee infantry and Newman's battalion Tennessee infantry, Stewart's division, Army of Tennessee; to these the 3d regiment Tennessee infantry was subsequently added.
....	....	Commanding brigade under General H. W. Mercer at the siege of Savannah, in December, 1864; served previously as A. D. C. to President Davis, with rank of Colonel.
Feb. 17, 1864.	....	Brigade composed of the 53d, 55th, 50th and 10th Georgia regiments infantry, McLaw's division, Longstreet's corps, Army of Northern Virginia.
Dec. 13, 1861.	....	Promoted Major-General August 16, 1862; commanding division at Bowling Green, Kentucky, and subsequently at Fort Donelson.

CONFEDERATE ROSTER.

BRIGADIER-GENERALS

	NAME.	STATE.	TO WHOM TO REPORT.	Date of Appointment.	Date of Rank.
58	Buford, A.............	Kentucky..	Gen. J. E. Johnston..	Nov. 29, 1862.	Sept. 2, 1862.
59	Butler, M. Calvin......	S. Carolina.	Gen. R. E. Lee........	Sept. 2, 1863.	Sept. 1, 1863.
60	Cabell, Wm. L.........	Virginia....	Gen. E. K. Smith.....	Apl. 23, 1863.	Jan. 20, 1863.
61	Campbell, Alex'r W....	....	Gen. L. Polk..........	..........1864.	....1864.
62	Canty, James..........	Alabama...	Maj. Gen. Buckner...	Jan. 8, 1863.	Jan. 8, 1863.
63	Capers, E.............	S. Carolina.	Gen. Hood..	Nov. 30, 1864.	Nov. 30, 1864.
64	Carroll, Wm. H.......	Tennessee.	....	Oct. 26, 1861.	Oct. 26, 1861.
65	Carter, John C.........	Tennessee.	Gen. J. E. Johnston..	July 8, 1864.	July 7, 1864.
66	Chalmers, James R....	Mississippi.	Gen. A. S. Johnston..	Feb. 13, 1862.	Feb. 13, 1862.
67	Chambliss, John R., Jr.	Virginia ...	Gen. R. E. Lee..	Jan. 27, 1864.	Dec. 19, 1863.
68	Cheatham, B. F........	Tennessee.	Gen. B. Bragg........	July 9, 1861.	July 9, 1861.
69	Chestnut, James, Jr...	S. Carolina.	Maj. Gen. Sam. Jones	Apl. 23, 1864.	Apl. 23, 1864.
70	Chilton, R H..........	Virginia....	Gen. R. E. Lee........	Oct. 20, 1862.	Oct. 20, 1862.
71	Churchill, T. J.........	Arkansas ..	Gen. Van Dorn.......	Mch. 6, 1862.	Mch. 4, 1862.
72	Clanton, James H......	Alabama...	Gen. D. H. Maury....	Nov. 18, 1863.	Nov. 16, 1863.

—CONTINUED.

Date of Confirmation.	Date of Acceptance.	REMARKS.
Apl. 22, 1863.	....	Assigned to the command of the 2d division of Forrest's cavalry, composed of the brigades of Colonels Thompson and Bell; Lyon's brigade subsequently constituted a part of this command; in 1865 command consisted of the brigades of Roddy, Clanton and Armistead.
Feb. 17, 1864.	....	Promoted Major-General 1864; brigade composed of the 4th, 5th and 6th regiments South Carolina cavalry and "Keitt Squadron" South Carolina cavalry; also of the 1st and 2d South Carolina cavalry; Army of Northern Virginia.
Apl. 23, 1863.	....	Commanding brigade composed of four regiments Arkansas cavalry and one battery of Light artillery; at one time in command of the 18th, 19th, 20th and 21st regiments Arkansas infantry; in 1862 commanding 1st brigade, 2d division, Army of the West.
..........1865.	....	Commanding brigade in Jackson's division, Forrest's cavalry corps.
Apl. 22, 1863.	....	In command of Mobile and its vicinity, the garrison then consisting of the 17th, 21st and 29th Alabama regiments, the 4th and 19th Louisiana regiments, the 30th Louisiana battalion, and various artillery companies, heavy and light.
Nov. 30, 1864.	....	Succeeded Brigadier-General Gist in command of his brigade, composed of the 24th South Carolina, the 16th South Carolina, the 46th and 65th Georgia regiments, the 8th Georgia battalion of infantry, and the 1st battalion Georgia Sharpshooters.
Dec. 20, 1861.	....	Resigned February 1, 1863; commanding brigade in General Polk's Department, Mississippi river defences.
Feb. 13, 1862, and Feb. 17, 1864.	....	Commanding brigade, Brown's division, Cheatham's corps, Army of Tennessee. First command, at Pensacola, Florida, consisted of the 1st and 2d Mississippi regiments, the Quitman artillery company, the Vicksburg artillery company and the Judson artillery company; assigned in January, 1864, to the command of the cavalry brigades of Forrest and McCulloch, constituting the 1st division of Forrest's cavalry; Rucker's brigade subsequently constituted a part of this command; in 1862 commanded 2d brigade, Reserve corps, Army of the Mississippi, composed of the 5th, 7th, 9th, 10th, 29th and Blythe's Mississippi regiments, and Ketchum's Light battery.
Jan. 27, 1864.	Oct. 13, 1862.	Killed in action, below Richmond, August 16, 1864; commanded cavalry brigade in General W. H. F. Lee's division, Army of Northern Virginia.
Aug. 29, 1861.	....	Promoted Major-General March 14, 1862; brigade was composed of the 154th, 6th and 9th regiments Tennessee Volunteers and Blythe's Mississippi battalion; assigned in 1861 to command of 2d division of the Western Department, embracing the brigades of Smith and Stevens.
June 9, 1864.	....	A. D. C. to President Davis, with rank of Colonel; in 1864 in command of a brigade on the coast of South Carolina.
....	....	Chief of Staff, Army of Northern Virginia; Senate refused to confirm nomination as Brigadier-General April 11, 1863; re-appointed February 16, 1864; confirmed same day, to take rank from December 21, 1863; resigned April 1, 1864.
Mch. 6, 1862.	....	Commanding 2d cavalry brigade, General Van Dorn's army; in 1862 commanding 2d brigade, 2d division, Army of the West, composed of the 4th Arkansas infantry regiment, the 1st and 2d Arkansas Riflemen, dismounted, the 4th Arkansas infantry battalion, Turnbull's Arkansas battalion, Humphrey's Light battery, and Reve's Missouri Scouts.
Feb. 17, 1864.	....	Commanding cavalry brigade in the Department of Alabama, Mississippi and East Louisiana.

BRIGADIER-GENERALS

	NAME.	STATE.	TO WHOM TO REPORT.	Date of Appointment.	Date of Rank.
73	Clark, Charles.........	Mississippi.	{ Department of Mississippi. }	May 22, 1861.	May 22, 1861.
74	Clarke, John B., Jr....	Missouri ...	Gen. E. K. Smith.....	Moh. 12, 1864.	Moh. 8, 1864.
75	Clayton, H. D..........	Alabama...	Gen. S. B. Buckner...	Apl. 25, 1863.	Apl. 22, 1863.
76	Cleburne, P. R.........	Arkansas..	Gen. Van Dorn.......	March 6, 1862.	March 4, 1862.
77	Clingman, Thos. L.....	N. Carolina	Gen. T. H. Holmes...	May 17, 1862.	May 17, 1862.
78	Cobb, Howell..........	Georgia....	Maj. Gen. Magruder..	Feb. 13, 1862.	Feb. 13, 1862.
79	Cobb, Thos. R. R......	Georgia....	Gen. Longstreet......	Nov. 1, 1862.	Nov. 1, 1862.
80	Cocke, Phillp St. Geo..	Virginia ...	Gen. J. E. Johnston..	Oct. 21, 1861.	Oct. 21, 1801.
81	Cockrell, Francis M....	Missouri...	Gen. Pemberton......	July 23, 1863.	July 18, 1863.
82	Colquitt, Alfred H....	Georgia....	Gen. R. E. Lee.......	Sept. 30, 1862.	Sept. 1, 1862.
83	Colston, R. E..........	Virginia ...	Maj. Gen. Huger......	Dec. 24, 1861.	Dec. 24, 1861.
84	Conner, James.........	S. Carolina.	Gen. R. E. Lee.......	June 1, 1864.	June 1, 1864.
85	Cook, Phil.............	Georgia....	Gen. R. E. Lee.......	Aug. 8, 1864.	Aug. 5, 1864.
86	Cooke, John R.........	N. Carolina	Gen. Longstreet......	Nov. 1, 1862.	Nov., 1, 1862.
87	Cooper, Douglas H....	Mississippi.	Gen. E. K. Smith.....	June 23, 1863.	May 2, 1863.

—CONTINUED.

Date of Confirmation.	Date of Acceptance.	REMARKS.
Aug. 29, 1861.	....	Resigned October 21, 1863 ; succeeded Brigadier- General Longstreet in command temporarily of his brigade, composed of the 1st, 7th, 11th and 17th Virginia regiments.
May 11, 1864.	....	Commanding brigade in Marmaduke's cavalry division ; previously in command of the Third District, Missouri State Guards.
Apl. 25, 1863.	....	First command, at Pensacola, Florida, composed of the 1st Alabama and the 1st Georgia regiments, and the 2d Alabama battalion ; subsequently his brigade composed of the 1st, 36th, 38th, 32d and 58th Alabama regiments ; promoted Major-General July 8, 1864.
Mch. 6, 1862.	....	Promoted Major-General December 13, 1862 ; brigade composed of the 2d, 5th, 24th and 48th Tennessee and the 15th Arkansas regiments and Calvert's Light Battery, constituting Second brigade, Third corps, Army of the Mississippi.
Sept. 30, 1862.	....	Brigade composed of the 8th, 31st, 51st and 61st North Carolina regiments.
Feb. 13, 1862.	....	Promoted Major-General September 9, 1863 ; brigade composed of the 15th North Carolina, the 2d Louisiana and the 16th and 24th Georgia regiments and Cobb's Legion, Army of Northern Virginia.
....	....	Killed at Fredericksburg ; brigade composed of the 18th, 24th and 16th Georgia regiments, the Legions of Cobb and Phillips and the 3d battalion Georgia Sharpshooters, McLaw's division, Longstreet's corps, Army of Northern Virginia.
Dec. 13, 1861.	....	Brigade composed of the 11th, 18th, 19th and 28th Virginia regiments ; as at first constituted, his brigade was composed of the 18th, 19th, 28th and 49th Virginia regiments, and formed the Fifth brigade, First corps, Army of the Potomac.
Feb. 17, 1864.	....	Brigade composed of the 1st, 2d, 3d, 4th, 5th and 6th regiments Missouri infantry and the 1st regiment and the 3d battalion Missouri cavalry, dismounted, Bowen's division, Army of the West.
Sept. 30, 1862.	....	Brigade composed of the 6th, 19th, 23d, 27th and 28th Georgia regiments, D. H. Hill's division, Jackson's corps, Army of Northern Virginia.
Dec. 24, 1861, and Feb. 17, 1864.	....	Assigned to the command of the First brigade, Department of Norfolk, consisting of the 3d Virginia, the 13th and 14th North Carolina regiments, and several unattached artillery and cavalry companies ; brigade at one time in 1862 composed of the 13th and 14th North Carolina regiments and Manley's Light Battery ; at the Battle of Chancellorsville, brigade composed of the 10th, 23d and 37th Virginia regiments and the 1st and 3d North Carolina regiments, Trimble's division, Army of Northern Virginia.
June 1, 1864.	Oct. 13, 1862.	Brigade composed of the 2d, 3d, 7th, 8th, 15th and 20th regiments South Carolina infantry and James' battalion, Longstreet's corps, Army of Northern Virginia.
....	....	Succeeded General Doles in command of his brigade, composed of the 4th, 12th, 21st and 44th Georgia regiments, infantry, Army of Northern Virginia.
Apl. 22, 1863.	....	Brigade composed of the 15th, 27th, 46th and 48th North Carolina regiments, Heth's division, A. P. Hill's corps, Army of Northern Virginia.
Feb. 17, 1864.	....	Commanding Indian brigade, composed of the 1st Choctaw and Chickasas regiment, 2d Choctaw regiment, Choctaw battalion, 1st and 2d Cherokee and 1st and 2d Creek regiments, Seminole battalion, Osage battalion, and Howell's Texas Light Battery ; subsequently assigned to command of District "Indian Territory."

BRIGADIER–GENERALS

	NAME.	STATE.	TO WHOM TO REPORT.	Date of Appointment.	Date of Rank.
88	Cooper, Samuel........	Virginia ...	President Davis......	Mch. 14, 1861.	Mch. 14, 1861.
89	Corse, M. D............	Virginia ...	Gen. Longstreet......	Nov. 1, 1862.	Nov. 1, 1862.
90	Cosby, George B.......	Kentucky..	Gen. J. E. Johnston..	Apl. 23, 1863.	Jan. 20, 1863.
91	Cox, William R........	N. Carolina	Gen. R. E. Lee........	June 2, 1864.	May 31, 1864.
92	Cox, John Z............	....	....	....	....
93	Crews, C. C............	Georgia....	Gen. Wheeler	..........1864.	...........1864.
94	Crittenden, George B..	Kentucky..	....	Aug. 15, 1861.	Aug. 15, 1861.
95	Cumming, Alfred......	Georgia....	Gen. Forney..........	Oct. 29, 1862.	Oct. 29, 1862.
96	Dahlgren, Chas. G.....	Mississippi.	Gen. Beauregard.....	....	....
97	Daniel, Junius.........	N. Carolina	Gen. G. W. Smith.....	Sept. 30, 1862.	Sept. 1, 1862.
98	Davidson, H. B........	Tennessee.	Gen. S. B. Buckner...	Aug. 18, 1863.	Aug. 18, 1863.
99	Davis, Joseph R........	Mississippi.	Gen. G. W. Smith. ..	Oct. 8, 1862.	Sept. 15, 1862.
100	Davis, Reuben.........	Mississippi.	Gen. A. S. Johnston..	....	....
101	Davis, W. G. M........	Florida	Gen. E. K. Smith.....	Nov. 4, 1862.	Nov. 4, 1862.
102	Dearing, James........	Virginia....	Maj. Gen. Pickett....	....1864.	...........1864.
103	Deas, Zach. C..........	Alabama...	Gen. J. E. Johnston..	Dec. 20, 1862.	Dec. 13, 1862.
104	DeBray, X. B..........	Texas......	Gen. E. K. Smith.....	Apl. 13, 1864.	Apl. 8, 1864.
105	Deshler, James........	Georgia....	Gen. B. Bragg........	July 28, 1863.	July 28, 1863.
106	Dibrell, George G......	Tennessee.	Gen. Jos. Wheeler....	July 26, 1864.	July 26, 1864.
107	Dickison, J. J..........	Florida	Gen. Beauregard.....	....	....
108	Dobbins, Arch. J.......	Arkansas ..	Maj. Gen. Fagan.....	..........1864.	..........1864.
109	Dockery, T. P..........	Arkansas ..	Gen. E. K. Smith.....	Aug. 10, 1863.	Aug. 10, 1863.

—CONTINUED.

Date of Confirmation.	Date of Acceptance.	REMARKS.
Mch. 14, 1861.	....	Adjutant and Inspector-General; promoted General August 31, 1861, to take rank from May 16, 1861.
Apl. 22, 1863.	....	Brigade composed of the 15th, 17th, 29th, 30th and 32d Virginia regiments infantry, Longstreet's corps, Army of Northern Virginia.
Apl. 23, 1863.	....	Commanding cavalry brigade in General Stephen D. Lee's division, Department of Alabama, Mississippi and East Louisiana.
June 2, 1864.	....	Brigade composed of the 2d, 4th, 14th and 30th North Carolina regiments and such portions of the 1st and 3d North Carolina regiments as escaped capture on the 12th May, 1864.
....	....	Colonel Commanding 12th Confederate cavalry; acting Brigadier General.
....	....	Commanding brigade composed of the 1st, 2d, 3d, 4th and 6th Georgia cavalry.
Aug. 15, 1861.	....	Promoted Major-General November 9, 1861; brigade composed of the 16th Mississippi, 21st Georgia, 21st North Carolina and 15th Alabama regiments and Captain Courtney's Light Battery, Longstreet's corps, Army of Northern Virginia.
Apl. 22, 1863.	....	Brigade composed of the 34th, 39th, 36th and 56th Georgia regiments, Stevenson's division, Army of the West.
....	....	Brigadier-General State forces of Mississippi; never mustered into the Confederate service, except temporarily.
Sept. 30, 1862.	....	Killed in action May 12, 1864; brigade composed of the 32d, 43d, 45th and 53d North Carolina regiments infantry and the 2d North Carolina battalion, Army of Northern Virginia.
Feb. 17, 1864.	....	Commanding cavalry brigade, Wheeler's corps, Army of the West.
Oct. 8, 1862.	....	Brigade composed of 1st Confederate battalion, the 2d, 11th, 26th and 42d Mississippi regiment, the 55th North Carolina regiment and the Madison Light Artillery; A. D. C. to President Davis, &c., with rank of Colonel.
....	....	In command of sixty-day troops from Mississippi, at Bowling Green, Kentucky.
Apl. 22, 1863.	....	Brigade composed of 1st regiment Florida cavalry and 6th and 7th regiments of Florida infantry, and Martin's [afterwards McCant's] Light Battery; in spring of 1863 commanded the Department of East Tennessee; resigned the latter part of 1863.
..........1864.	....	In command of a cavalry brigade, Army of Northern Virginia; Killed at High Bridge.
Apl. 22, 1863.	....	Brigade composed of the 19th, 22d, 25th, 26th, 39th and 50th Alabama regiments and Dent's Light Battery; Withers' division, Polk's corps, Army of Tennessee.
....	....	Brigade composed of the 23d, 26th and 32d regiments Texas cavalry.
....	....	Killed at Chickamauga September 20th, 1863; brigade composed of the Texas regiments of Colonels Wilkes' and Mills, the Arkansas regiment of Lieutenant-Colonel Hutchinson, and Douglas' Texas Light Battery; brigade at one time composed of the 17th, 18th, 24th and 25th Texas regiments, consolidated; the 6th, 10th and 15th Texas regiments, consolidated, and the 19th and 24th Arkansas.
....	....	Brigade composed of the 4th, 8th, 9th, 10th and 11th Tennessee regiments cavalry and Shaw's battalion, Army of the West.
....	....	In command of East and South Florida; acting Brigadier-General.
....	....	Commanding brigade in Fagan's division.
June 10, 1864.	....	Commanding middle Sub-District of Arkansas; in 1862 in command of the 1st brigade, 3d division, Army of the West, composed of the 18th, 19th and 20th Arkansas regiments and the Arkansas battalions of McCairns and Jones.

BRIGADIER-GENERALS

	NAME.	STATE.	TO WHOM TO REPORT.	Date of Appointment.	Date of Rank.
110	Doles, George.........	Georgia....	Gen. Longstreet......	Nov. 1, 1862.	Nov. 1, 1862.
111	Donelson, Daniel S....	Tennessee.	....	July 9, 1861.	July 9, 1861.
112	Drayton, Thomas F....	S. Carolina.	....	Sept. 25, 1861.	Sept. 25, 1861.
113	DuBose, Dudley M.. ..	Georgia....	Gen. R. E. Lee........	Nov., 1864.	Nov., 1864.
114	Duke, Basil W...... ..	Kentucky..	....	....	....
115	Duncan, J. K.........	Louisiana..	....	Jan. 7, 1862.	Jan. 7, 1862.
116	Dunnovant, John......	S. Carolina.	Gen. R. E. Lee........	July, 1864.	July, 1864.
117	Early, Jubal A..	Virginia ...	....	Aug. 28, 1861.	July 21, 1861.
118	Echols, John..........	Virginia ...	Gen. Heth...........	Apl. 18, 1862.	Apl. 16, 1862.
119	Ector, M. D...........	Texas......	Gen. B. Bragg........	Sept. 27, 1862.	Aug. 23, 1862.
120	Elliott, Stephen, Jr....	S. Carolina.	Gen. Beauregard.....	May 28, 1864.	May 28, 1864.
121	Elzey, Arlold..........	Maryland..	....	Aug. 28, 1861.	July 21, 1861.
122	Evans, C. A...........	Georgia....	Gen. R. E. Lee........	May 20, 1864.	May 19, 1864.
123	Evans, N. G...........	S. Carolina.	Gen. J. E. Johnston..	Oct. 21, 1861.	Oct. 21, 1861.
124	Ewell, Richard S.......	Virginia ...	Gen. Beauregard.....	June 17, 1861.	June 17, 1861.
125	Fagan, J. F...........	Arkansas ..	Gen. T. H. Holmes...	Oct. 3, 1862.	Sept. 12, 1862.

—CONTINUED.

Date of Confirmation.	Date of Acceptance.	REMARKS.
Apl. 22, 1863.	....	Brigade composed of the 4th, 12th, 21st and 44th Georgia regiments infantry, D. H. Hill's division, Army of Northern Virginia; killed in action at Bethesda Church.
Aug. 29, 1861.	....	Promoted Major-General January 17, 1863; commanded 1st brigade, 2d division, 1st corps. Army of Mississippi, composed of the 8th, 15th, 16th, 21st and 51st Tennessee regiments and Carnes' Light Battery.
Dec. 13, 1861.	....	At first in command of a military district, Coast of South Carolina; subsequently transferred to the Trans-Mississippi Department, where brigade was composed of the 8th and 9th Missouri infantry and Ruffner's Missouri Light Battery.
....	....	Brigade composed of the 18th, 24th and 16th Georgia regiments, the Georgia legions of Cobb and Phillips and the 3d battalion Georgia Sharpshooters, Army of Northern Virginia.
....	....	Succeeded General John H. Morgan in command of his cavalry forces, Department of Southwest Virginia.
Jan. 14, 1862.	....	In command of River Defences below New Orleans; died December 18, 1862, at Knoxville, Tennessee.
....	....	Killed at Vaughn Road October 1, 1864.
Aug. 29, 1861.	....	Promoted Major-General January 17, 1863; brigade composed of the 5th and 23d North Carolina regiments, the 24th Virginia and the 20th Georgia regiments; as at first constituted, his brigade was composed of the 5th, 13th and 24th North Carolina regiments, and formed the 6th brigade, 1st corps, Army of the Potomac; at the Battle of Fredericksburg Early's brigade was composed of the 13th, 25th, 31st, 44th, 49th, 52d and 58th Virginia regiments, Ewell's division, Jackson's corps, Army of Northern Virginia.
Apl. 18, 1862.	....	Brigade composed of the 50th, 60th and 63d Virginia regiments and Edgar's and Derrick's battalions, the 22d Virginia regiment being subsequently added.
Sept. 27, 1862.	....	Brigade composed of the 10th, 11th, 14th and 32d Texas dismounted cavalry regiments and the 15th Arkansas infantry regiment; afterwards commanding brigade in McCown's division, Polk's army corps, Army of Tennessee.
May 28, 1864.	Oct. 13, 1864.	Died of wounds received in front of Petersburg, Virginia; brigade composed of the 17th, 18th, 22d, 23d and 26th regiments South Carolina Volunteers and the Holcombe Legion.
Aug. 29, 1861.	....	Promoted Major-General December 4, 1862; commanding brigade in Ewell's division; brigade at one time composed of the 12th Georgia and the 13th, 25th, 31st, 44th, 52d and 58th Virginia regiments, Jackson's corps, Army of Northern Virginia.
May 20, 1864.	....	Brigade composed of the 13th, 26th, 31st, 38th, 60th and 61st Georgia regiments infantry, Army of Northern Virginia; the 12th Georgia battalion was subsequently added.
Dec. 19, 1861.	....	Brigade composed of the 17th, 18th, 22d, 23d and 26th regiments South Carolina Volunteers and the Holcombe Legion; as at first constituted, his brigade was composed of the 13th, 17th and 18th Mississippi regiments, and formed the 7th brigade, 1st corps, Army of the Potomac; at the Battle of Leesburg his brigade consisted of the 13th, 17th and 18th Mississippi regiments and the 8th Virginia regiments; in June, 1862, in command on James Island, South Carolina.
Aug. 29, 1861.	....	Promoted Major-General January 24, 1862; brigade composed of the 5th, 6th and 13th Alabama and the 12th Mississippi regiments, constituting 2d brigade, 1st corps, Army of the Potomac; afterwards in command of brigade composed of the 1st, 7th, 11th and 17th Virginia regiments.
Oct. 3, 1862.	....	Promoted Major-General April 25, 1864; commanding division in General Price's army.

BRIGADIER–GENERALS

	NAME.	STATE.	TO WHOM TO REPORT.	Date of Appointment.	Date of Rank.
126	Fauntleroy, T. T.......	Virginia....	....	May 18, 1861.	May 18, 1861.
127	Featherston, Wm. S...	Mississippi.	Gen. J. E. Johnston..	Mch. 6, 1862.	March 4, 1862.
128	Ferguson, Sam'l W....	Mississippi.	Gen. J. E. Johnston..	July 28, 1863.	July 23, 1863.
129	Field, Charles W......	Kentucky..	Gen. J. E. Johnston..	Mch. 14, 1862.	Mch. 9, 1862.
130	Finegan, Joseph.......	Florida	....	Apl. 5, 1862.	April 5, 1862.
131	Finley, J. J...........	Florida	Gen. B. Bragg........	Nov. 18, 1863.	Nov. 16, 1863.
132	Fizer, John C..........	Mississippi.	Maj. Gen. McLaws...	..........1865.	..........1865.
133	Floyd, John B.........	Virginia....	Army of Kanawha....	May 23, 1861.	May 23, 1861.
134	Forney, John H........	Alabama...	Gen. Sam. Jones......	Mch. 14, 1862.	Mch. 10, 1862.
135	Forney, W. H..........	Alabama...	Gen. R. E. Lee........	Nov. 9, 1864.	Nov. 9, 1864.
136	Forrest, Nathan B.....	Tennessee.	Gen. E. K. Smith.....	July 21, 1862.	July 21, 1862.
137	Fraser, John W........	Alabama...	Gen. B. F. Cheatham.	May 3, 1863.	May 3, 1863.
138	Frazier, C. W..........	Mississippi.	Gen. Buckner........	May 19, 1863.	May 19, 1863.
139	French, S. G..........	Mississippi.	Gen. R. E. Lee........	Oct. 23, 1861.	Oct. 23, 1861.
140	Frost, D. M...........	Missouri...	Gen. T. H. Holmes....	Oct. 10, 1862.	Mch. 3, 1862.
141	Fry, B. D.............	Alabama...	Gen. R. E. Lee........	May 24, 1864.	May 24, 1864.
142	Gano, Richard M......	Kentucky..	Gen. J. H. Morgan....	April, 1865.	....
143	Gantt, E. W...........	Missouri...	Gen. Polk	....	....
144	Gardner, Frank........	Louisiana..	Gen. Beauregard.....	Apl. 19, 1862.	Apl. 11, 1862.
145	Gardner, Wm. M......	Georgia....	Gen. J. E. Johnston..	Nov. 14, 1861.	Nov. 14, 1861.
146	Garland, Sam'l, Jr.....	Virginia ...	Gen. J. E. Johnston..	May 23, 1862.	May 23, 1862.

—CONTINUED.

Date of Confirmation.	Date of Acceptance.	REMARKS.
....	....	Rank of Brigadier-General conferred by the State of Virginia; resigned October 8th, 1861.
Mch. 6, 1862.	....	Brigade composed of the 12th, 16th, 19th and 48th Mississippi regiments and Smith's Light Battery.
Feb. 17, 1864.	....	Brigade consisted of the 2d Tennessee regiment of cavalry, the 56th and 2d regiments Alabama cavalry, the 17th battalion Tennessee cavalry, the 12th Mississippi battalion of cavalry and Watie's South Carolina Light Battery.
Mch. 14, 1862.	....	Promoted Major-General February 12, 1864; brigade was composed of the 40th, 47th, 55th and 60th Virginia regiments, the 22d Virginia battalion and Captain Pegram's Light Battery, Heth's division, A. P. Hill's corps, Army of Northern Virginia.
Apl. 5, 1862.	....	Commanding East and Middle Florida; afterwards in command of a brigade, Army of Northern Virginia, composed of the 2d, 5th, 9th, 10th and 11th Florida regiments.
Feb. 17, 1864.	....	Brigade composed of the 1st, 3d, 4th, 6th and 7th regiments Florida infantry and the 1st regiment Florida cavalry, dismounted.
....	....	Commanding mixed brigade in Lieutenant-General Hardee's corps, on the retreat through the Carolinas.
Aug. 29, 1861.	....	Relieved; commanding forces in Kanawha Valley; brigade, early in 1862, composed of the 20th Mississippi and the 36th, 50th and 51st Virginia regiments.
Mch. 14, 1862.	....	Promoted Major-General October 27, 1862; commanding Department of Alabama and West Florida; headquarters at Mobile, Alabama; brigade at first corposed of the 9th, 10th and 11th Alabama, the 19th Mississippi and the 38th Virginia regiments. Army of Northern Virginia.
Jan'y, 1865.	....	Brigade composed of the 8th, 9th, 10th, 11th, 13th and 14th Alabama regiments.
Sept. 30, 1862.	....	Promoted Major-General December 4, 1863; assigned by General Bragg to command of a cavalry brigade composed of the 4th, 8th and 9th Tennessee regiments, Russell's 4th Alabama regiment and Freeman's Light Battery.
....	....	Brigade composed of the 55th Georgia, the 62d and 64th North Carolina regiments and Kain's Light Battery.
....	....	Senate refused to confirm.
Dec. 13, 1861.	....	Promoted Major-General August 31, 1862; in command at Evansport, Virginia, blockading the Potomac river; afterwards in command of the District of Cape Fear, North Carolina.
Oct. 10, 1862.	....	Dropped December 9, 1863; S. O. 109; also Brigadier-General Missouri State Guard.
May 24, 1864.	Oct. 13, 1864.	Commanding Walker's and Archer's brigades; at one time in command of the District of Augusta, Georgia.
....	....	Commanding 2d brigade, Morgan's cavalry division; afterwards in command of a brigade of Texas cavalry operating in Indian Territory and Arkansas, composed of the regiments of Colonels DeMorse, Martin, Gurley, Duff and Hardeman, Lieutenant-Colonel Showalter's battalion, the light batteries of Captains Howell and Krumbhar, and Captain Welch's company, known as the "Gano Guards."
....	....	Commanding Fort Thompson, Missouri.
Apl. 19, 1862.	....	Promoted Major-General December 13, 1862; commanding 1st brigade, reserve division, Army of the Mississippi, composed of the 19th, 22d, 25th, 26th and 29th Alabama regiments and Robertson's Light Battery; afterwards in command at Mobile.
Dec. 13, 1861.	....	Commanded post at Richmond, Virginia, &c.; at one time in command of a military district in Florida, &c., &c.
Sept. 50, 1862.	....	Killed at South Mountain September 14th, 1862; brigade composed of the 5th, 12th, 13th, 20th and 23d North Carolina regiments.

BRIGADIER–GENERALS

	NAME.	STATE.	TO WHOM TO REPORT.	Date of Appointment.	Date of Rank.
147	Garnett, R. B..........	Virginia ...	Adj't and Insp. Gen..	Nov. 14, 1861.	Nov. 14, 1861.
148	Garnett, Robt. S......	Virginia ...	....	June 6, 1861.	June 6, 1861.
149	Garrott, Isham W......	Alabama...	Gen. J. E. Johnston..	May 29, 1863.	May 28, 1863.
150	Gartrell, Lucius J......	Georgia....	Gen. Howell Cobb....	..........1864.	..........1864.
151	Gary, M. W............	S. Carolina.	Gen. R. E. Lee........	June 14, 1864.	May 19, 1864.
152	Gatlin, R. C............	N. Carolina	....	Aug. 15, 1861.	July 8, 1861.
153	Gholson, S. J..........	Missouri....	....	June 1, 1864.	May 6, 1864.
154	Gibbs, George C.......	N. Carolina	....	..........1864.	..........1864.
155	Gibson, R. L............	Louisiana..	Gen. J. E. Johnston..	Feb. 1, 1864.	Jan. 11, 1864.
156	Girardey, Victor J. B..	Georgia....	Gen. R. E. Lee........	Aug. 3, 1864.	July 30, 1864.
157	Gist, S. R..............	S. Carolina.	Gen. Pemberton......	Mch. 20, 1862.	Mch. 20, 1862.
158	Gladden, A. H.........	Louisiana..	Gen. B. Bragg........	Sept. 30, 1861.	Sept. 30, 1861.
159	Godwin, A. C..........	N. Carolina	Gen. R E. Lee........	Aug. 9, 1864.	Aug. 5, 1864.
160	Gordon. G. W........	Tennessee.	Gen. J. B. Hood......	Aug. 16, 1864.	Aug. 15, 1864.
161	Gordon, James B......	N. Carolina	Gen. R. E. Lee........	Sept. 28, 1863.	Sept. 28, 1863.
162	Gordon, John B........	Georgia....	Gen. R. E. Lee........	May 11, 1863.	May 7, 1863.
163	Gorgas, Josiah..........	... .	Gen. S. Cooper.......	....1864.	..........1864.

—CONTINUED.

Date of Confirmation.	Date of Acceptance.	REMARKS.
Dec. 13, 1861.	....	Killed at Gettysburg; succeeded General T. J. Jackson in command of the "Stonewall Brigade," composed of the 2d, 4th, 5th, 27th and 33d Virginia regiments; brigade at one time composed of the 8th, 18th, 19th, 28th and 56th Virginia regiments, D. R. Jones' division, Army of Northern Virginia.
Aug. 29, 1861.	....	Killed at Craddock's Ford, Virginia, July 13, 1861.
....	....	Killed at Vicksburg June 17, 1863; at the time of his death he was in command of the 20th Alabama regiment, of S. D. Lee's brigade, and fell before his commission as Brigadier-General was received; commanded Tracy's brigade, after his death, for a few days, until Brigadier-General S. D. Lee was assigned to its command by order of General Pemberton.
....	....	Commanded 2d brigade Georgia Reserves, composed of 1st, 2d, 3d and 4th regiments.
June 14, 1864.	....	Promoted Major-General of cavalry shortly after the Battle of Darbytown; brigade composed of the "Hampton Legion," the 7th South Carolina cavalry, the 7th Georgia cavalry, the 24th Virginia cavalry and Captain Harkerson's Virginia battery of Light artillery, Army of Northern Virginia.
Aug. 29, 1861.	....	Resigned September 8, 1862; commanding Southern Department, Coast Defense of North Carolina; Adjutant-General of North Carolina, with the rank of Major-General.
June 1, 1864.	....	Commanding brigade of cavalry, Department of Alabama, Mississippi and East Louisiana.
....	....	Acting Brigadier-General; commanding post, &c., at Macon, Georgia.
Feb. 1, 1864.	Oct. 13, 1862.	Brigade composed of the 1st, 4th, 11th, 13th, 16th, 19th, 20th, 25th and 30th Louisiana regiments, the 4th Louisiana battalion and Austin's battalion of Sharpshooters; afterwards in command of a division at Spanish Fort, near Mobile, consisting of the brigades of Campbell, Holtzclaw, Ecktor and Thomas, and Patton's regiment of artillery.
....	....	Killed in action in front of Petersburg, Virginia, at the time being in command of A. R. Wright's old brigade.
Mch. 20, 1862.	....	Killed in action, at the Battle of Franklin, November 30, 1864; in command of a brigade composed of the 16th and 24th South Carolina, the 46th and 65th Georgia regiments infantry, the 8th Georgia infantry battalion and the 1st battalion Georgia Sharpshooters.
Dec. 13, 1861.	....	Killed at Shiloh; brigade at Pensacola composed of Lieutenant-Colonel Adam's Louisiana battalion, Lieutenant-Colonel Coppen's battalion of Zouaves, Major Lary's Georgia battalion, Colonel Anderson's 1st Florida regiment and Captain Lee's artillery company.
....	....	First Provost-Marshal of Richmond; afterwards in command of Hoke's brigade, composed of the 6th, 54th and 57th North Carolina regiments, Early's division, Army of Northern Virginia.
....	....	Brigade composed of the 11th and 29th, 12th and 47th, 13th and 154th Tennessee regiments.
Feb. 17, 1864.	Oct. 13, 1862.	Killed in action at Yellow Tavern, Virginia; brigade composed of the 1st, 2d, 3d, 4th and 5th North Carolina regiments, cavalry.
Jan. 25, 1864.	....	Promoted Major-General May 14, 1864; brigade composed of the 13th, 26th, 31st, 38th, 60th and 61st Georgia regiments [originally Lawton's brigade], the 6th Georgia, and the 12th Georgia battalion, Early's division, Army of Northern Virginia.
..........1864.	....	Chief of Ordnance.

BRIGADIER-GENERALS

	NAME.	STATE.	TO WHOM TO REPORT.	Date of Appointment.	Date of Rank.
164	Govan, D. C............	Arkansas ..	Gen. J. E. Johnston..	Feb. 5, 1864.	Dec. 29, 1863.
165	Gracie, A., Jr..........	Alabama...	Lt. Gen. E. K. Smith..	Nov. 4, 1862.	Nov. 4, 1862.
166	Granberry, H. B.......	Texas......	Gen. J. E. Johnston..	Mch. 5, 1864.	Feb. 29, 1864.
167	Grayson, John B.......	Louisiana..	....	Aug. 15, 1861.	Aug. 15, 1861.
168	Gregg, John...........	Texas......	Gen. B. Bragg........	Sept. 27, 1862.	Aug. 29, 1862.
169	Gregg, Maxey..........	S. Carolina.	Gen. R. E. Lee........	Dec. 14, 1861.	Dec. 14, 1861.
170	Green, Martin E.......	Missouri...	Gen. S. Price.........	July 23, 1862.	July 21, 1862.
171	Green, Thomas........	Texas	Gen. E. K. Smith.....	May 23, 1863.	May 20, 1863.
172	Greene, Colton........	....N. Y....	....	....	....
173	Greer, E..............	Texas......	Gen. T. H. Holmes...	Oct. 8, 1862.	Oct. 8, 1862.
174	Griffith, Richard......	Mississippi.	Gen. J. E. Johnston..	Nov. 2, 1861.	Nov., 2, 1861.
175	Grigsby, J. Warren....	Kentucky..	....	....	....
176	Grimes, Bryan.........	N. Carolina	Gen. R. E. Lee.......	June 1, 1864.	May 19, 1864.
177	Hagan, James..........	Alabama...	Gen. Wheeler	Febr'y, 1865.	Febr'y, 1865.
178	Hagood, Johnson......	S. Carolina.	Gen. Pemberton......	July 21, 1862.	July 21, 1862.
179	Hampton, Wade.......	S. Carolina.	Gen. J. E. Johnston..	May 23, 1862.	May 23, 1862.
180	Hannon, M. W.........	....	Gen. Wheeler	..........1865.	..........1865.
181	Hanson, R. H..........	Kentucky..	Gen. J. E. Johnston..	Dec. 20, 1862.	Dec. 13, 1862.

—CONTINUED.

Date of Confirmation.	Date of Acceptance.	REMARKS.
Feb. 5, 1864.	....	Brigade composed of the 1st, 2d, 5th, 6th, 7th and 8th Arkansas regiments, commanded in turn by Generals Hardee, Hindman and Liddell.
Apl. 22, 1863.	....	Killed in the trenches in front of Petersburg December 2, 1864; brigade composed of the 63d Tennessee and the 43d Alabama regiments, and the 1st, 2d, 3d and 4th battalions of the Alabama Legion, Longstreet's corps.
May 11, 1864.	Oct. 13, 1862.	Brigade composed of the 7th, 10th, 6th and 15th, 17th and 19th 24th and 25th Texas regiments.
Aug. 15, 1861.	....	Died at Tallahassee, Florida, October 21, 1861.
Sept. 27, 1862.	....	Brigade composed of the 7th Texas, the 3d, 10th, 34th, 41st and 50th Tennessee regiments and Bledsoe's Light Battery; brigade at one time composed of the 1st, 4th and 5th Texas and the 3d Arkansas regiments, Longstreet's corps, Army of Northern Virginia.
Dec. 24, 1861.	....	Killed at Fredericksburg; brigade composed of the 1st, 12th, 13th and 14th South Carolina infantry regiments and "Orr's Rifles" (1st South Carolina Rifles), A. P. Hill's division, Jackson's corps, Army of Northern Virginia.
Sept. 30, 1862.	....	Killed in action during the siege of Vicksburg; commanded 3d brigade, 1st division, Army of the West, composed of the 4th Missouri regiment, battalion Missouri infantry, battalion Missouri cavalry, dismounted, Confederate Rangers, and King's Light Battery; during the siege of Vicksburg, General Green commanded a brigade in Bowen's division, composed of the remnants of the 2d and 6th Missouri infantry regiments, the 1st and 3d Missouri cavalry regiments, dismounted, and the Light Batteries of Landis and King.
June 25, 1864.	....	Killed in action at the Battle of Mansfield, April 12, 1864; commanding Texas cavalry brigade under General Marmaduke, in the Trans-Mississippi Department; in the assault upon Donaldsville, June 28, 1863, his command consisted of the 4th, 5th and 7th Texas cavalry regiments and the regiments of Phillips and Stone.
....	....	Commanding cavalry brigade, Marmaduke's division, Trans-Mississippi Department.
Oct. 8. 1862.	....	Chief of Bureau of Conscription, Trans-Mississippi Department.
Dec. 13, 1861.	....	Mortally wounded at Savage Station; brigade was composed of the 13th, 17th, 18th and 21st Mississippi regiments.
....	....	Commanding cavalry brigade, Army of Tennessee.
June 1, 1864.	....	Promoted Major-General February 23, 1865; brigade composed of the 32d, 43d, 45th and 53d North Carolina regiments infantry and the 2d North Carolina battalion; General Daniel formerly commanded this brigade.
....	....	Brigade composed of the 1st, 3d, 4th, 12th and 51st Alabama cavalry regiments, Wheeler's cavalry corps, Army of the West.
Sept. 30, 1862.	....	Brigade composed of the 11th, 21st, 25th and 27th South Carolina regiments and Lieutenant-Colonel Rion's South Carolina battalion.
Sept. 30, 1862.	....	Promoted Major-General September 3d, 1863; brigade composed of the 1st, 2d, 4th, 5th and 6th regiments South Carolina cavalry, Jeff. Davis Legion and Cobb Legion, Georgia cavalry, Army of Northern Virginia.
....	....	Commanding brigade in Wheeler's cavalry corps, Martin's division, composed of the 53d Alabama and the 24th Alabama battalion.
Apl. 22, 1863.	....	Killed at Murfreesboro'; commanded brigade composed of the 2d, 4th, 6th and 9th Kentucky regiments and the 41st Alabama regiment, Breckinridge's division, Polk's corps, Army of Tennessee.

BRIGADIER-GENERALS

	NAME.	STATE.	TO WHOM TO REPORT.	Date of Appointment.	Date of Rank.
182	Hardee, Wm. J........	Georgia....	....	June 17, 1861.	June 17, 1861.
183	Hardeman, Wm. P....	....	Maj. Gen. Magruder..	....	....
184	Harris, D. B............	Virginia....	Gen. Beauregard.....	....	....
185	Harris, N. H...........	Mississippi.	Gen. R. E. Lee........	Feb. 17, 1864.	Jan. 20, 1864.
186	Harris, Thos. A........	Missouri...	Gen. Price............	....	....
187	Harrison, Geo. P., Jr..	Georgia....	Gen. Hardee..........	Febr'y, 1865.	Febr'y, 1865.
188	Harrison, Jas. E.......	Texas......	Lt. Gen. E. K. Smith..	Dec'r, 1864.	Dec'r, 1864.
189	Harrison, Richard.·....	Texas......	Maj. Gen. Loring.....	..........1865.	..........1865.
190	Harrison, Thomas.....	Texas......	Gen. B. Bragg........	Jan'y, 1865.	Jan'y, 1865.
191	Hatton, R..............	Tennessee.	Gen. J. E. Johnston..	May 23, 1862.	May 23, 1862.
192	Hawes, J. M...........	Kentucky..	Gen. Beauregard.....	Mch. 14, 1862.	Mch. 5, 1862.
193	Hawthorn, A. T........	Arkansas..	Gen. T. H. Holmes...	Feb. 23, 1864.	Feb. 18, 1864.
194	Hays, Harry T.........	Louisiana..	Gen. R. E. Lee........	July 25, 1862.	July 25, 1862.
195	Hebert, Louis..........	Louisiana..	Gen. Beauregard.....	May 26, 1862.	May 26, 1862.
196	Hebert, Paul O........	Louisiana..	....	Aug. 17, 1861.	Aug. 17, 1861.
197	Helm, Benj. H.........	Kentucky..	Gen. Beauregard.....	Mch. 18, 1862.	Mch. 14, 1862.
198	Heth, Henry...........	Virginia ...	Gen. R. E. Lee........	Jan. 6, 1862.	Jan. 6, 1862.
199	Higgins, Edward.......	Louisiana..	Gen. D. H. Maury....	Nov. 2, 1863.	Oct. 29, 1863.
200	Hill, A. P..............	Virginia....	Gen. J. E. Johnston..	Feb. 26, 1862.	Feb. 26, 1862.
201	Hill, B. J..............	Tennessee.	Gen. B. Bragg........	Oct. 15, 1864.	Oct. 15, 1864.
202	Hill, D. Harvey........	N. Carolina	Gen. J. E. Johnston..	July 10, 1861.	July 10, 1861.
203	Hindman, T. C.........	Arkansas ..	....	Sept. 28, 1861.	Sept. 28, 1861.

—CONTINUED.

Date of Confirmation.	Date of Acceptance.	REMARKS.
Aug. 29, 1861.	....	Promoted Major-General October 7, 1861; brigade composed of the 1st, 2d, 5th, 6th, 7th and 8th Arkansas regiments.
....	....	Commanding brigade, District of Texas, under Major-General Magruder.
....	....	Chief Engineer in charge of Confederate defences during the siege of Charleston, &c.
Feb. 17, 1864.	....	Brigade composed of the 12th, 16th, 19th and 48th regiments Mississippi Volunteers.
....	....	Commissioned Brigadier-General in Missouri State Guard June 10, 1861; resigned in September, 1861, to occupy a seat in the Confederate Congress.
....	....	Brigade composed of the 1st Georgia Regulars, the 32d, 47th and 5th regiments Georgia Volunteers, and the 5th regiment Georgia Reserves.
....	....	Brigade composed of the 15th, 17th and 31st Texas regiments, and Stephen's Texas regiment, Polignac's division, Trans-Mississippi Department,
....	....	Was Colonel of Terry's Texas cavalry regiment and succeeded General J. A. Wharton in command of his brigade of Texas cavalry; afterwards in command of brigade in Stewart's corps.
....	....	Brigade composed of the 8th and 11th Texas, the 4th Tennessee, the 3d Arkansas and the 1st Kentucky regiments cavalry, Wharton's command.
....	....	Killed at Edwards' Farm June 1, 1862; commanded 5th brigade, 1st division, 1st corps, Army of Virginia.
Mch. 14, 1862.	....	Assigned to the command of the cavalry of General A. S. Johnston's army just prior to the Battle of Shiloh.
May 11, 1864.	....	Brigade composed of the 17th, 21st and 28d Tennessee and the 3d Alabama regiments and Austin's Light Battery, constituting the 5th brigade, 3d corps, Army of the Mississippi.
Sept. 30, 1862.	....	Brigade composed of the 5th, 6th, 7th, 8th and 9th Louisiana regiments, Early's division, Jackson's corps, Army of Northern Virginia; promoted Major-General April, 1865.
May 30, 1862.	....	Commanding brigade in Maury's division, Army of the West; also Chief Engineer, Department of North Carolina; in 1862, commanding 2d brigade, 1st division, Army of the West, composed of the 3d Louisiana, the 14th and 17th Arkansas regiments, Whitfield's Texas Legion, Greer's regiment dismounted cavalry, and McDonald's Light Battery.
Aug. 17, 1861.	....	In command of the Department of Texas, New Mexico and Arizona.
Mch. 18, 1862.	....	Killed at Chickamauga September 20, 1863; brigade composed of the 2d, 4th, 6th and 9th Kentucky and 41st Alabama regiments and Cobb's Light Battery, Breckinridge's division, Army of the Tennessee.
Jan. 14, 1862.	....	Promoted Major-General May 24, 1863; brigade composed of the 40th, 47th and 55th Virginia regiments and the 22d Virginia battalion, A. P. Hill's division, Army of Northern Virginia.
Feb. 17, 1864.	....	Assigned to the command of the forts and batteries for the defence of Mobile, Alabama.
Feb. 26, 1862.	....	Promoted Major-General May 26, 1862; brigade composed of the 1st, 7th, 11th and 17th Virginia regiments and Roger's Light Battery, Army of Northern Virginia.
....	....	Commanding brigade, Smith's division, Cheatham's corps, Army of Tennessee.
Aug. 29, 1861.	....	Promoted Major-General March 26, 1862.
Dec. 13, 1861.	....	Promoted Major-General April 14, 1862; brigade composed of the 1st, 2d, 5th, 6th, 7th and 8th Arkansas regiments, Army of the West.

BRIGADIER-GENERALS

	NAME.	STATE.	TO WHOM TO REPORT.	Date of Appointment.	Date of Rank.
204	Hodge, George B......	Kentucky..	....	Nov. 21, 1863.	Nov. 20, 1863.
205	Hogg, Joseph L........	Texas......	Maj. Gen. S. Price....	Feb. 14, 1862.	Feb. 14, 1862.
206	Hoke, Robert F........	N. Carolina	Gen. R. E. Lee........	Apl. 23, 1863.	Jan. 17, 1863.
207	Hoke, W. I.............	N. Carolina	Gen. B. Bragg........	....	....
208	Holmes, Theop. H.....	N. Carolina	....	June 5, 1861.	June 5, 1861.
209	Holtzclaw, J. T........	Alabama...	Gen. J. E. Johnston..	July 8, 1864.	July 7, 1864.
210	Hood, John B..........	Texas......	Gen. T. H. Holmes....	March 6, 1862.	March 3, 1862.
211	Huger, Benjamin......	S. Carolina.	....	June 17, 1861.	June 17, 1861.
212	Humes, W. Y. C.......	Tennessee.	Gen. B. Bragg........	Nov. 17, 1863.	Nov. 16, 1863.
213	Humphries, B. G......	Mississippi.	Gen. R. E. Lee........	Aug. 14, 1863.	Aug. 12, 1863.
214	Hunton, Eppa.........	Virginia ...	Gen. R. E. Lee........	Aug. 12, 1863.	Aug. 9, 1863.
215	Imboden, J. D..........	Virginia ...	....	Apl. 13, 1863.	Jan. 28, 1863.
216	Iverson, Alfred, Jr....	N. Carolina	Gen. T. J. Jackson....	Nov. 1, 1862.	Nov. 1, 1862.
217	Jackman, Sidney D....	Missouri...	Gen. G. O. Shelby....	Febr'y, 1865.	Feb. 9, 1865.
218	Jackson, Alfred E......	Tennessee.	Gen. E. K. Smith.....	Apl. 22, 1863.	Febr'y, 1863.
219	Jackson, Henry R......	Georgia....	Adjt. and Inspt. Gen.	June 4, 1861.	June 4, 1861.

—Continued.

Date of Confirmation.	Date of Acceptance.	REMARKS.
....	....	Brigade composed of the 1st, 2d and 3d battalions Kentucky cavalry, the 27th Virginia Partisan Rangers and Lieutenant Logan's section of Light artillery; at one time in command of the District of "South Mississippi and East Louisiana."
Feb. 14, 1862.	....	Died May 16, 1862; brigade composed of 10th, 11th and Major Crump's regiments Texas dismounted cavalry, Major Mc-Cray's battalion Arkansas infantry, and Captain Goode's Light Battery, constituting 1st brigade, 2d division, Army of the West.
Apl. 23, 1863.	....	Promoted Major-General April 20, 1864; commanded District of North Carolina; at one time in command of brigade composed of the 6th, 21st, 24th and 57th North Carolina regiments and the 1st North Carolina battalion, Early's division, Longstreet's corps, Army of Northern Virginia.
....	....	Acting Brigadier-General and in command of post at Charlotte, North Carolina.
Aug. 29, 1861.	....	Promoted Major-General October 7, 1861; commanding brigade, Army of the Potomac.
....	....	Brigade composed of the 18th, 36th and 38th, and the 32d and 58th (consolidated) Alabama regiments; subsequently the 21st Alabama regiment and Major Williams' battalion (the Pelham Cadets) were added.
Mch. 6, 1862.	....	Promoted Major-General October 10, 1862; commanding Texas brigade, Longstreet's division, Army of Northern Virginia, composed of the 1st, 4th and 5th Texas and the 18th Georgia regiments and the Hampton Legion.
Aug. 20, 1861.	....	Promoted Major-General October 7, 1861; assigned to command at Norfolk, Virginia, and of the forces concentrated in that vicinity.
May 25, 1864.	....	Promoted Major-General 1865; commanding brigade in General Wheeler's cavalry; subsequently in command of a division in Wheeler's cavalry corps, composed of the brigades of Ashby, Harrison and Williams.
Jan. 25, 1864.	....	Brigade composed of the 21st, 13th, 17th and 18th Mississippi regiments. McLaws' division, Longstreet's corps, Army of Northern Virginia.
Feb. 17, 1864.	....	Brigade composed of the 8th, 18th, 19th, 28th and 56th Virginia regiments, Longstreet's corps, Army of Northern Virginia.
Apl. 13, 1863.	....	In command of the "Valley District," Virginia; brigade composed of the 18th, 23d and 25th Virginia cavalry, the 62d Virginia infantry, mounted, and McClanahan's Battery of Horse Artillery.
June 10, 1864.	....	Brigade composed of the 5th, 12th, 20th and 23d North Carolina regiments, D. H. Hill's division, Jackson's corps, Army of Northern Virginia; in 1864, brigade composed of the 1st, 2d, 3d, 4th and 6th Georgia cavalry regiments, Martin's division, Wheeler's corps.
....	....	Brigade composed of his own regiment and those of Colonels Benj. F. Elliott and D. A. Williams—all Missouri troops.
Apl. 22, 1863.	....	Assigned to the command of the 4th Military District of East Tennessee.
Aug. 29, 1861.	....	At first on duty in Western Virginia; resigned December 2, 1861, and subsequently reappointed September 21, 1863; brigade composed of the 1st Confederate, the 66th, 29th, 30th and 25th Georgia regiments and Major Shaaf's battalion; brigade in May, 1862, composed of the 3d Arkansas, 31st Virginia and 1st and 12th Georgia regiments and Hansborough's battalion.

4

BRIGADIER–GENERALS

	NAME.	STATE.	TO WHOM TO REPORT.	Date of Appointment.	Date of Rank.
220	Jackson, John K.......	Georgia....	Gen. B. Bragg........	Feb. 13, 1862.	Feb. 14, 1864.
221	Jackson, Thomas J....	Virginia....	....	June 17, 1861.	June 17, 1861.
222	Jackson, William H....	Tennessee.	Lt. Gen. Pemberton..	Jan. 9, 1863.	Dec. 29, 1862.
223	Jackson, William L....	Virginia....	Gen. R. E. Lee........	Sept'r, 1864.	Sept'r, 1864.
224	Jenkins, Albert G......	Virginia ...	Gen. W. W. Loring...	Aug. 5, 1862.	Aug. 5, 1862.
225	Jenkins, M..............	S. Carolina.	Gen. R. E. Lee........	July 22, 1862.	July 22, 1862.
226	Johnson, A. R..........	Texas......	Gen. Morgan..........	Aug. 4, 1864.	Aug. 4, 1864.
227	Johnson, Bradley T....	Maryland..	Gen. R. E. Lee........	June 28, 1864.	June 28, 1864.
228	Johnson, Bushrod R...	Tennessee.	....	Jan. 24, 1862.	Jan. 24, 1862.
229	Johnson, Edward......	Virginia ...	Brig. Gen. Loring....	Dec. 13, 1861.	Dec. 13, 1861.
230	Johnston, George D....	Mississippi.	Gen. J. B. Hood......	July 26, 1864.	July 26, 1864.
231	Johnston, Albert S....	....	....	....	....
232	Johnston, George H...	Alabama...	....	....	....
233	Johnston, Joseph E....	....	....	....	....
234	Johnston, Robert D....	N. Carolina	Gen. R. E. Lee........	Sept. 2, 1863.	Sept. 1, 1863.
235	Jones, A. C.............	....	....	....	....
236	Jones, D. R.............	Georgia....	Gen. Beauregard.....	June 17, 1861.	June 17, 1861.
237	Jones, John M.........	Virginia ...	Gen. R. E. Lee........	May 16, 1863.	May 15, 1863.
238	Jones, John R..........	Virginia ...	Gen. R. E. Lee........	June 25, 1862.	June 23, 1862.
239	Jones, Samuel.........	Virginia ...	....	Aug. 28, 1861.	July 21, 1861.

—CONTINUED.

Date of Confirmation.	Date of Acceptance.	REMARKS.
Feb. 14, 1862, and Feb. 17, 1864.	....	Brigade composed of the 5th and 8th Mississippi and the 5th Georgia regiments, the 1st Confederate regiment, 2d Georgia battalion of Sharpshooters, and Scogins' Light Battery; in 1862 in command of the 3d brigade, Reserve corps, Army of the Mississippi, composed of the 17th, 18th, 21st and 24th Alabama and the 5th Georgia regiments, and Bortwell's Light Battery.
Aug. 29, 1861.	....	Promoted Major-General October 7, 1861; commanded 1st brigade, Army of the Shenandoah, composed of the 2d, 4th, 5th, 27th and 33d Virginia regiments and Pendleton's Light Battery.
Apl. 22, 1863.	....	Commanding cavalry brigade, Forrest's command; subsequently commanded cavalry division, Department of Alabama, Mississippi and East Louisiana.
....	....	Brigade composed of the 19th, 20th and 46th regiments Virginia cavalry, the 37th battalion Virginia cavalry and the 1st Maryland cavalry.
Sept. 30, 1862.	....	Commanding cavalry brigade, Army of Northern Virginia.
Sept. 30, 1862.	....	Killed at the Battle of the Wilderness May 6, 1864; brigade composed of the 1st, 4th, 5th and 6th regiments South Carolina Volunteers, the 2d regiment South Carolina Rifles and the Palmetto Sharpshooters, Hood's division, Longstreet's corps, Army of Northern Virginia.
....	....	Commanding 2d brigade, General Morgan's cavalry; subsequently in command of Tennessee and Kentucky, after those States passed into the hands of the United States forces.
......:........	....	Commanded Maryland Line, Army of Northern Virginia; in August, 1862, command composed of the 2d brigade, Taliaferro's division, Army of the Valley, comprising the 21st, 42d and 48th Virginia regiments, the 1st Virginia battalion and two light batteries.
Jan. 24, 1862.	....	Promoted Major-General May 21, 1864; brigade composed of the 17th, 23d, 25th, 37th and 44th Tennessee regiments and Captain Darden's Light Battery; in 1862 commanding 3d brigade, 3d division, Army of the Mississippi.
Dec. 24, 1861.	....	Promoted Major-General February 28, 1863; commanded "Stonewall" Jackson's old division.
....	....	Brigade composed of the 19th, 22d, 25th, 39th and 50th Alabama regiments, formerly of Hindman's (afterwards Brown's) division, Army of Tennessee.
....	....	Promoted General August 31, 1861, to take rank from May 30, 1861.
....	....	Commanded brigade in Major-General Edw'd Johnson's division.
....	....	Promoted General August 31st, 1861, to take rank from July 4, 1861; assigned to command at Harper's Ferry.
Feb. 16, 1864.	....	Brigade composed of the 5th, 12th, 20th and 23d North Carolina regiments infantry and the 2d North Carolina battalion.
....	....	Promoted Major-General October 11, 1862; brigade composed of the 4th, 5th, 6th and 9th South Carolina regiments, constituting the 3d brigade, 1st corps, Army of the Potomac; brigade afterwards composed of the 17th and 18th Mississippi and the 5th South Carolina regiments.
Aug. 29, 1861.	....	
Feb. 17, 1864.	....	Killed at battle of Wilderness May '64; commanded a brigade in Johnson's division, Ewell's corps, Army of Northern Virginia.
....	....	Brigade composed of the 44th, 42d, 21st, 25th and 50th Virginia regiments and the 1st battalion Virginia Regulars, Trimble's division, Army of Northern Virginia.
Aug. 29, 1861.	....	Promoted Major-General March 14, 1862; brigade composed of the 7th, 8th, 9th and 11th Georgia regiments, the 1st Kentucky regiment and Alburti's Virginia Light Battery.

BRIGADIER–GENERALS

	NAME.	STATE.	TO WHOM TO REPORT.	Date of Appointment.	Date of Rank.
240	Jones, Thomas M......	....	....	..........1862.	....
241	Jones, W. E............	Virginia ...	Comd'g at Winchester	Oct. 3, 1862.	Sept. 19, 1862.
242	Jordon, Thomas.......	Virginia ...	Gen. Beauregard.....	Sept. 26, 1862.	April 14, 1862.
243	Kelley, J. H............	Alabama...	Gen. B. Bragg........	Nov. 17, 1863.	Nov. 16, 1863.
244	Kemper, J. L..........	Virginia ...	Gen. R. E. Lee........	June 3, 1862.	June 3, 1862.
245	Kennedy, J. D.........	S. Carolina.	....	Dec. 22, 1864.	Dec. 22, 1864.
246	Kershaw, J. B.........	S. Carolina.	Gen. J. E. Johnston..	Feb. 15, 1862.	Feb. 13, 1862.
247	King, Wm. H..........	....	....	July 15, 1864.	Apl. 8, 1864.
248	Kirkland, Wm. W.....	N. Carolina	Gen. R. E. Lee........	Aug. 31, 1863.	Aug. 29, 1863.
249	Lagnel, J. A. de.......	Virginia....	Gen. Huger..........	Apl. 18, 1862.	Apl. 15, 1862.
250	Lane, James H........	N. Carolina	Gen. T. J. Jackson....	Nov. 1, 1862.	Nov. 1, 1862.
251	Lane, Walter P........	Texas......	Maj. Gen. Wharton...	Mch. 18, 1865.	Mch. 18, 1865.
252	Law, E. M..............	Alabama...	Gen. R. E. Lee........	Oct. 3, 1862.	Oct. 3, 1862.
253	Lawton, Alex'r R......	Georgia....	{ Commanding Department of Georgia. }	Apl. 13, 1861.	Apl. 13, 1861.
254	Leadbetter, D..........	Alabama...	Gen. E. K. Smith.....	Mch. 6, 1862.	Feb. 27, 1862.
255	Lee, Edwin G..........	Virginia ...	Gen. J. E. Johnston..	Sept. 23, 1864.	Sept. 23, 1864.
256	Lee, Fitzhugh.........	Virginia ...	Gen. R. E. Lee........	July 25, 1862.	July 24, 1862.
257	Lee, G. W. C..........	Virginia ...	Gen. R. E. Lee........	June 25, 1863.	June 25, 1863.
258	Lee, Robert E.........	Virginia ...	....	....	....

—CONTINUED.

Date of Confirmation.	Date of Acceptance.	REMARKS.
....	....	Commanding brigade in the Department of Alabama and Western Florida.
Oct. 3, 1862.	....	Killed in action; commanding cavalry brigade, Army of Northern Virginia; also in command of Valley District, Virginia.
Sept. 26, 1862.	....	Chief of Staff to General Beauregard.
Feb 17, 1864.	....	Commanding brigade in Wheeler's cavalry; brigade composed of the 63d Virginia, the 58th North Carolina, the 5th Kentucky and the 65th Georgia regiments; subsequently in command of a division in Wheeler's corps, composed of the brigades of Allen, Dibrell and Hannon.
Sept. 30, 1862.	....	Promoted Major-General March 1, 1864; brigade composed of the 1st, 3d, 7th, 11th and 17th Virginia regiments, Pickett's division, Longstreet's corps, Army of Northern Virginia; for a time the 24th Virginia regiment was attached to this brigade.
....	....	Brigade composed of the 2d, 3d, 7th, 8th, 15th, and 20th South Carolina regiments and James' 3d South Carolina battalion, Longstreet's corps, Army of Northern Virginia.
Feb. 13, 1862.	....	Promoted Major-General May 18, 1864; brigade composed of the 2d, 3d, 7th, 8th, 15th and 20th South Carolina regiments, McLaws' division, Longstreet's corps, Army of Northern Virginia.
....	....	Assigned to the command of "Walker's division of infantry," Trans-Mississippi Department; afterwards in command of a Texas brigade in General Polignac's division.
Feb. 16, 1864.	....	Brigade composed of the 26th, 44th, 47th, 52d and 11th North Carolina infantry regiments, and subsequently of the 17th, 66th. 50th and 42d regiments North Carolina infantry, Army of Northern Virginia.
Apl. 18, 1862.	....	On duty in the Ordnance Bureau at Richmond.
Apl. 23, 1863.	....	Brigade composed of the 7th, 18th, 28th, 33d and 37th North Carolina regiments, Pender's division, A. P. Hill's corps, Army of Northern Virginia.
....	....	Commanding brigade of Texas cavalry in Major-General John A. Wharton's division, Trans-Mississippi Department.
Oct. 3, 1862.	....	Promoted Major-General April 9, 1865; brigade composed of the 15th, 44th, 47th and 48th and 4th Alabama regiments, Hood's division, Longstreet's corps, Army of Northern Virginia; at the Battle of Fredericksburg, his brigade composed of the 6th, 54th and 57th North Carolina and the 4th and 44th Alabama regiments.
Aug. 29, 1861.	....	Subsequently Quartermaster-General of the Confederacy; brigade consisted of the 13th, 26th, 31st, 38th, 60th and 61st Georgia regiments, Ewell's division, Jackson's corps, Army of Northern Virginia; at one time in command of Ewell's division.
March 6, 1862.	....	Commanding in Knoxville, Tennessee, in February, 1862; afterwards in command of a brigade composed of the 20th and 23d Alabama regiments and Colonel Vaughn's Tennessee regiment.
....	....	In command at Staunton, Virginia; subsequently detailed on secret service of the Confederacy.
Sept. 30, 1862.	....	Promoted Major-General September 3, 1863; brigade composed of the 1st, 3d, 4th, 5th and 9th Virginia cavalry regiments, Army of Northern Virginia.
....	....	Commanding brigade of local troops for the defence of Richmond; previously was an aid-de-camp to President Davis, with the rank of Colonel; promoted Major-General early in 1865.
....	....	Promoted General August 31, 1861, to take rank from June 14, 1861.

BRIGADIER-GENERALS

	NAME.	STATE.	TO WHOM TO REPORT.	Date of Appointment.	Date of Rank.
259	Lee, Stephen D........	S. Carolina.	Maj. Gen. M. L. Smith	Nov. 6, 1862.	Nov. 6, 1862.
260	Lee, Wm. H. F........	Virginia....	Gen. J. E. B. Stuart..	Oot. 3, 1862.	Sept. 15, 1862.
261	Leventhorpe, C........	N. Carolina	........................1865.	........1865.	.........1865.
262	Lewis, Joseph H.......	Kentucky..	Gen. B. Bragg........	Oct. 1, 1863.	Sept. 30, 1863.
263	Lewis, W. G..........	N. Carolina	Gen. R. E. Lee........	June 2, 1864.	May 31, 1864.
264	Liddell, St. John R....	Louisiana..	Gen. B. Bragg........	July 17, 1862.	July 12, 1862.
265	Lilley, R. D.....	Virginia ...	Gen. R. E. Lee........	June 2, 1864.	May 31, 1864.
266	Little, Henry..........	Missouri ...	Gen. Van Dorn.......	Apl. 16, 1862.	Apl. 16, 1862.
267	Logan, T. M..........	S. Carolina.	Gen. R. E. Lee........	Feb. 23, 1865.	Feb. 15, 1865.
268	Lomax, L. L..........	Virginia ...	Gen. R. E. Lee........	July 20, 1863.	July 23, 1863.
269	Long, A. L...........	Virginia ...	Gen. R. E. Lee........	Sept. 21, 1863.	Sept. 21, 1863.
270	Longstreet, James.....	Alabama...	Gen. Beauregard.....	June 17, 1861.	June 17, 1861.
271	Loring, W. W..........	Florida	Army of the N. West.	May 20, 1861.	May 20, 1861.
272	Lovell, Mansfield......	Maryland..	....	....	....
273	Lowry, M. P..........	Mississippi.	Gen. B. Bragg........	Oct. 6, 1863.	Oct. 4, 1863.
274	Lowry, Robert........	Mississippi.	....	.........1864.	..........1864.
275	Lyon, H. B...........	Kentucky..	....	June 14, 1864.	June 14, 1864.
276	Mabry, H. P..........	Texas......			
277	Mackall, W. W........	Maryland..	Gen. Beauregard.....	March 6, 1862.	Feb. 28, 1862.
278	MacLay, R. P.........				
279	MacRae, William......	N. Carolina	Gen. R. E. Lee........	June 23, 1864.	June 23, 1864.
280	Magruder, J. B........	Virginia ...	....	June 17, 1861.	June 17, 1861.
281	Mahone, William......	Virginia ...	Maj. Gen. Huger......	Nov. 16, 1861.	Nov. 16, 1861.

—CONTINUED.

Date of Confirmation.	Date of Acceptance.	REMARKS.
Apl. 22, 1863.	....	Promoted Major-General August 3, 1863; brigade composed of the 17th, 19th, 22d and 27th Louisiana regiments, the 2d and 46th Mississippi regiments, the 1st Louisiana Heavy Artillery and the 1st Tennessee Heavy Artillery, the last two regiments garrisoning the fixed batteries at Vicksburg.
Oct. 3, 1862.	....	Promoted Major-General April 23, 1864; brigade composed of the 13th and 9th regiments Virginia cavalry, the 2d regiment North Carolina cavalry and McGreggor's Battery of Horse Artillery, Army of Northern Virginia.
Jan. 25, 1864.	....	Brigade composed of the 2d, 4th, 5th, 6th and 9th Kentucky and 41st Alabama regiments, Army of Tennessee; succeeded General Helm in the command of this brigade.
June 2, 1864.	....	Commanding brigade, Army of Northern Virginia, composed of the 6th, 21st, 54th and 57th North Carolina regiments.
Sept. 30, 1862.	....	Brigade composed of the 2d and 15th, 5th and 13th, 6th, 7th and 8th Arkansas regiments, a Pioneer company and Roberts' Light Battery, constituting 1st brigade, 3d corps, Army of the Mississippi.
June 2, 1864.	....	Brigade composed of the 13th, 31st, 49th, 52d and 58th Virginia regiments infantry [formerly Pegram's brigade], Army of Northern Virginia.
Apl. 16, 1862.	....	Killed in action; Commanded 1st division, Army of the West, composed of the brigades of Gates, Hebert and Green.
....	....	Brigade composed of the 4th, 5th and 6th regiments South Carolina cavalry, the Keitt South Carolina Squadron and the 1st regiment [Colonel Black] South Carolina cavalry, Army of Northern Virginia.
Feb. 17, 1864.	....	Promoted Major-General August 10, 1864; brigade composed of the 5th, 6th and 15th Virginia cavalry regiments and the 1st Maryland cavalry, Army of Northern Virginia.
Feb. 17, 1864.	....	Brigadier-General of Artillery and Chief of Artillery of General Ewell's corps, Army of Northern Virginia.
Aug. 29, 1861.	....	Promoted Major-General October 7, 1861; brigade composed of the 1st, 7th, 11th and 17th Virginia regiments, and constituted the 4th brigade, 1st corps, Army of the Potomac.
Aug. 29, 1861.	....	Promoted Major-General February 15, 1862; in command in Western Virginia.
....	....	Promoted Major-General October 7, 1861, and assigned to command at New Orleans.
Feb. 17, 1864.	....	Brigade composed of the 32d and 45th Mississippi regiments, the 16th, 33d and 45th Alabama regiments, the 18th Alabama battalion and Semples' Light Battery, Cleburne's division, Army of Tennessee; the 5th and 8th Mississippi regiments were subsequently added.
....	....	Brigade composed of the 6th, 14th, 15th, 20th, 23d and 43d Mississippi regiments infantry; succeeded General John Adams in the command of this brigade.
June 14, 1864.	....	In command of a brigade composed of the 3d, 7th, 8th and 12th regiments Kentucky cavalry, Forrest's division; subsequently in command of the Department of Kentucky.
Mch. 6, 1862.	....	Chief of Staff to General Bragg.
....	....	Brigade composed of the 11th, 26th, 42d, 47th and 52d North Carolina infantry regiments.
Aug. 29, 1861.	....	Promoted Major-General October 7, 1861; on duty on the Peninsula; afterwards in command of the District of Texas, New Mexico and Arizona.
Dec. 13, 1861, and Feb. 17, 1864.	....	Promoted Major-General July 30, 1864; brigade composed of the 3d Alabama, the 6th, 12th, 16th and 41st North Carolina regiments, the 2d (afterwards 12th) North Carolina regiments, Anderson's division, A. P. Hill's corps, Army of Northern Virginia.

CONFEDERATE ROSTER.

BRIGADIER–GENERALS

	NAME.	STATE.	TO WHOM TO REPORT.	Date of Appointment.	Date of Rank.
282	Major, J. P.	Louisiana..	Gen. R. Taylor	July 25, 1863.	July 21, 1863.
283	Maney, George	Tennessee.	Gen. Beauregard	Apl. 18, 1862.	Apl. 16, 1862.
284	Manigault, A. M.	S. Carolina.	Gen. J. E. Johnston..	Apl. 30, 1863.	Apl. 26, 1863.
285	Marmaduke, J. S.	Missouri...	Gen. T. H. Holmes....	May 25, 1863.	Nov. 15, 1862.
286	Marshall, Humphrey...	Kentucky..		Oct. 30, 1861.	Oct. 30, 1861.
287	Marshall, John	Texas......			
288	Martin, John D	Mississippi.			
289	Martin, James G.	N. Carolina	Gen. T. H. Holmes...	May 17, 1862.	May 15, 1862.
290	Martin, Wm. T.	Mississippi.	Lt. Gen. Pemberton..	Dec. 2, 1862.	Dec. 2, 1862.
291	Maury, Dabney H.	Virginia ...	Gen. Van Dorn	Mch. 18, 1862.	Mch. 12, 1862.
292	Maxey, S. B.	Texas	Gen. A. S. Johnston..	Mch. 7, 1862.	Mch. 4, 1862.
293	McCausland, John.	Virginia ...	Gen. Breckinridge....	May 24, 1864.	May 18, 1864.
294	McComb, Wm.	Tennessee.			
295	McCown, John P.	Tennessee.	Gen. A. S. Johnston..	Oct. 12, 1861.	Oct. 12, 1861.
296	McCray, T. H.	Arkansas ..	Gen. L. Polk	...........1863.	..........1863.
297	McCulloch, Benj.	Texas......		May 1, 1861.	May 1, 1861.
298	McCulloch, Henry E...	Texas......	Gen. Van Dorn	Mch. 18, 1862.	Mch. 14, 1862.
299	McGowan, Samuel.	S. Carolina.	Gen. R. E. Lee	Apl. 23, 1863.	Jan. 17, 1863.
300	McIntosh, James M.	Florida		Jan. 24, 1862.	Jan. 24, 1862.
301	McLaws, Lafayette.	Georgia....	Gen. Magruder	Sept. 25, 1861.	Sept. 25, 1861.
302	McMurry, J. A.	Tennessee.			

—CONTINUED.

Date of Confirmation.	Date of Acceptance.	REMARKS.
Feb. 17, 1864.	....	Commanded 2d cavalry brigade, District of Western Louisiana.
Apl. 18, 1862.	....	Brigade composed of the 1st and 27th Tennessee, the 4th, 6th and 9th Tennessee Confederate regiments, Maney's battalion and Smith's Light Battery, constituting 2d brigade, 2d division, 1st corps, Army of the Mississippi; the 14th and 50th Tennessee regiments were subsequently added.
Apl. 30, 1863.	....	Brigade composed of the 10th and 19th South Carolina, the 24th, 28th and 34th Alabama regiments and Waters' Light Battery; in 1862 brigade known as 4th brigade, Reserve corps, Army of the Mississippi.
Feb. 17, 1864.	....	Promoted Major-General ——, 1864; in command of all the cavalry in North Arkansas; brigade composed of the 3d Confederate, the 25th, 29th and 37th Tennessee regiments and Sweet's Light Battery, constituting the 4th brigade, 3d corps, Army of the Mississippi.
Dec. 13, 1861.	....	Resigned June 17, 1863; at the affair at Princeton, Virginia, in May, 1862, command consisted of the 54th and 29th Virginia regiments, the 5th Kentucky regiment, Dunn's battalion, Bradley's Mounted Kentucky Rifles and Jeffree's Light Battery.
....	....	Killed June 27, 1862, in charge at Gaines' Mill.
Sept. 30, 1862.	....	Brigade consisted of the 17th, 42d, 50th and 66th North Carolina regiments.
Apl. 22, 1863.	....	Promoted Major-General November 10, 1863; assigned to the command of the cavalry brigades of Roddy and Crosby.
Mch. 18, 1862.	....	Promoted Major-General November 4, 1862; commanding Moore's, Ross' and Cabell's brigades; in 1862 commanding 3d division, Army of the West, composed of the brigades of Dockery, Moore and Phifer.
Mch. 6, 1862.	....	Superintendent of affairs in the Indian Territory; commanded brigade in the Army of the Mississippi composed of the 41st Georgia, 24th Mississippi and 9th Texas regiments and Eldridge's Light Battery.
May 24, 1864.	....	Brigade composed of the 14th, 16th, 17th, 21st and 22d regiments Virginia cavalry and Jackson's Battery of Horse Artillery.
....	....	Commanding Tennessee brigade, Heath's division, 3d corps, Army of Northern Virginia.
Dec. 13, 1861.	....	Promoted Major-General March 10, 1862; commanding brigades of Cabell and Churchill, Army of the West; assigned in 1861 to the command of the 3d division, Western Department, embracing the brigades of Marks and Neely.
..........1863.	....	Commanding 3d brigade, McCown's division, Army of Tennessee.
May 14, 1861.	....	Died from wounds received at Pea Ridge; commanding division in Van Dorn's army.
Mch. 18, 1862.	....	In command of Texas; also at one time of a brigade composed of the regiments of Colonels Waterhouse, Flournoy, Fitzhugh and Allen.
ApL 23, 1863.	....	Brigade composed of the 1st, 12th, 13th and 14th South Carolina regiments and "Orr's Rifles" [succeeded General Maxy Gregg in the command], Pender's division, A. P. Hill's corps, Army of Northern Virginia.
Jan. 24, 1863.	....	Killed March 7, 1862, at Pea Ridge; commanding Missouri brigade, Price's division, Van Dorn's army.
Dec. 13, 1861.	....	Promoted Major-General May 23, 1862; brigade composed of the 15th and 32d Virginia, the 5th and 10th Louisiana and the 10th, 50th, 53d and 57th Georgia regiments and Manly's Light Battery, Army of Northern Virginia.
....	....	Commanding Maney's brigade, 2d division, 1st corps, Army of the Mississippi.

BRIGADIER-GENERALS

	NAME.	STATE.	TO WHOM TO REPORT.	Date of Appointment.	Date of Rank.
303	McNair, E...............	Arkansas ..	Lt. Gen. E. K. Smith..	Nov. 4, 1862.	Nov. 4, 1862.
304	McRae, D..............	Arkansas ..	Gen. T. H. Holmes...	Nov. 5, 1862.	Nov. 5, 1862.
305	Mercer, Hugh W......	Georgia....	Brig. Gen. Lawton....	Oct. 29, 1861.	Oct. 29, 1861.
306	Miles, W. R............	Mississippi.	Maj. Gen. Gardner....	...........1864.	...........1864.
307	Miller, William........	Florida	To com'd Fla. reserves	Aug. 5, 1864.	Aug. 2, 1864.
308	Moody, T. M...........	Alabama...	....	....	....
309	Moore, John C.........	Texas......	Gen. Beauregard.....	May 26, 1862.	May 26, 1862.
310	Moore, P. T...........	Virginia....	Maj. Gen. Kemper....	May, 1864.	May, 1864.
311	Morgan, John H.	Tennessee.	Gen. J. E. Johnston..	Dec. 11, 1862.	Dec. 11, 1862.
312	Morgan, John T.......	Alabama...	Gen. B. Bragg........	Nov. 17, 1863.	Nov. 16, 1863.
313	Moulton, Alfred........	Louisiana..	Gen. Beauregard.....	Apl. 18, 1862.	Apl. 16, 1862.
314	Munford, Thomas T...	Virginia ...	Gen. R. E. Lee........	Nov., 1864.	Nov., 1864.
315	Nelson, Allison........	Texas......	Gen. T. H. Holmes...	Sept. 26, 1862.	Sept. 12, 1862.
316	Nichols, Francis T.....	Louisiana..	Gen. R. E. Lee........	Oct. 14, 1862.	Oct. 14, 1862.
317	O'Neal, E. A...........	Alabama...	....	....	....
318	Page, R. L.............	Virginia ...	Gen. D. H. Maury....	Mch. 7, 1864.	Mch. 1, 1864.
319	Palmer, J. B...........	Tennessee.	Gen. J. B. Hood......	...........1864.	Sept'r, 1864.
320	Palmer, S. B...........	....	....	....	....
321	Parsons, M. M.........	Arkansas ..	Gen. T. H. Holmes...	Nov. 5, 1862.	Nov. 5, 1862.

—Continued.

Date of Confirmation.	Date of Acceptance.	REMARKS.
Apl. 22, 1863.	....	Brigade composed of the 1st, 2d, 4th, 31st and 25th Arkansas and the 39th North Carolina regiments and Culpeper's Light Battery; his brigade at one time formed part of McCown's division, Polk's corps, Army of Tennessee.
Apl. 22, 1863.	....	Brigade composed of the regiments of Colonels Glenn, Gause and Hart, and the Light Battery of Captain Marshall.
Dec. 20, 1861.	....	In command at Savannah, Georgia; when in the field, brigade consisted of the 1st, 54th, 57th and 63d Georgia regiments, Army of Tennessee.
....	....	Assigned to the command of Northeast Mississippi; afterwards with General D. H. Maury, at Mobile, Alabama.
....	....	Assigned to the command of the District of Florida.
Apl. 11, 1863.	....	Resigned February 3, 1864; brigade composed of the 2d Texas, the 35th Mississippi and the 37th, 40th and 42d Alabama regiments; in 1862 in command of the 2d brigade, 3d division, Army of the West.
....	....	Commanding and organizing reserve forces in and around Richmond, Virginia.
Apl. 22, 1863.	....	Commanding 3d cavalry brigade, Wheeler's division, Army of Tennessee, composed of the 2d, 3d, 4th, 5th, 10th, Breckinridge's and Ward's Kentucky regiments, Hamilton's battalion, Quirk's company of scouts, escort under Murphy and Bryne's Light Battery.
Feb. 17, 1864.	....	Commanding cavalry brigade composed of the 1st, 3d, 4th, 7th and 51st Alabama regiments, Martin's division, Wheeler's cavalry corps.
Apl. 18, 1862.	....	Killed at the Battle of Mansfield; brigade composed of the 18th and 28th Louisiana regiments, the Cresent Louisiana regiment and the 8th Louisiana battalion.
....	....	Brigade composed of the 1st, 2d, 3d, 4th and 5th Virginia regiments cavalry and the Maryland battalion of cavalry, Army of Northern Virginia.
Sept. 26, 1862.	....	Died at camp near Austin, Texas, October 7, 1862; brigade composed of the 10th regiment Texas infantry and the 15th, 17th and 18th regiments Texas cavalry.
Apl. 22, 1863.	....	Commanding District of Lynchburg, Virginia; brigade, at the Battle of Chancellorsville, composed of the 1st, 2d, 10th, 14th and 15th Louisiana regiments, Trimble's division, Army of Northern Virginia.
....	....	Commanding Rodes' brigade, composed of the 3d, 5th, 6th, 12th and 26th Alabama regiments, D. H. Hill's division, Army of Northern Virginia.
June 9, 1864.	....	Assigned to command of Fort Morgan and the Outer Defences of Mobile Bay; brigade composed of the 21st regiment Alabama infantry, 1st battalion Alabama artillery, 1st battalion Tennessee Heavy Artillery, 5 companies of the 7th regiment Alabama cavalry and a portion of the 1st Alabama Confederate regiment.
....	....	Brigade composed of the 3d, 18th, 26th, 32d and 45th Tennessee regiments, the 23d Tennessee battalion, the 54th and 63d Virginia regiments and the 58th and 60th North Carolina regiments; in December, 1862, Colonel commanding brigade in Breckinridge's division, Polk's corps, Army of Tennessee.
Apl. 30, 1863.	....	Brigade composed of the regiments of Colonels Pickett, Hunter, Poulter and Caldwell, Lieutenant-Colonel Pindall's battalion and Captain Tilden's Light Battery; commanded 4th brigade, Price's division.

BRIGADIER–GENERALS

	NAME.	STATE.	TO WHOM TO REPORT.	Date of Appointment.	Date of Rank.
322	Parsons, W. H.........	Texas......	....	....	....
323	Payne, Wm. H.........	Virginia ...	Gen. R. E. Lee........	Nov. 4, 1864.	Nov. 1, 1864.
324	Paxton, E. F..........	Virginia ...	Gen. T. J. Jackson....	Nov. 1, 1862.	Nov. 1, 1862.
325	Pearce, N. B..........	Arkansas ..	....	....	....
326	Pegram, John..........	Virginia ...	Gen. E. K. Smith.....	Nov. 10, 1862.	Nov. 7, 1862.
327	Pemberton, J. C.......	Virginia....	....	June 17, 1861.	June 17, 1861.
328	Pender, W. D..........	N. Carolina	Gen. R. E. Lee........	July 22, 1862.	June 3, 1862.
329	Pendleton, Wm. N.....	Virginia ...	Gen. J. E. Johnston..	Mch. 26, 1862.	Mch. 26, 1862.
330	Perrin, A..............	S. Carolina.	Gen. R. E. Lee........	Sept. 17, 1863.	Sept. 10, 1863.
331	Perry, E. A............	Florida ...	Gen. R. E. Lee........	Sept. 30, 1862.	Aug. 28, 1862.
332	Perry, W. F............	....	Gen. Longstreet......	Apl. 9, 1865.	Apl. 9, 1865.
333	Pettigrew, J. J.........	N. Carolina	Gen. T. H. Holmes...	Feb. 26, 1862.	Feb. 26, 1862.
334	Pettus, Edmund W....	Alabama...	Gen. J. E. Johnston..	Sept. 19, 1863.	Sept. 18, 1863.
335	Phifer, Charles W......	Texas......	....	Spring 1862.	Spring 1862.
336	Pickett, George E......	Virginia....	Gen. J. E. Johnston..	Feb. 13, 1862.	Jan. 14, 1862.
337	Pike, Albert...........	Arkansas ..	....	Aug. 15, 1861.	Aug. 15, 1861.
338	Pillow, Gideon J.......	Tennessee.	....	July 9, 1861.	July 9, 1861.
339	Polignac, C. J..........	France.....	Gen. E. K. Smith.....	Jan. 10, 1863.	Jan. 10, 1863.
340	Polk, Lucius E.........	Arkansas ..	Gen. J. E. Johnston..	Dec. 20, 1862.	Dec. 13, 1862.
341	Posey, Carnot..........	Mississippi.	Gen. Longstreet......	Nov. 1, 1862.	Nov. 1, 1862.

—Continued.

Date of Confirmation.	Date of Acceptance.	REMARKS.
....	....	Acting Brigadier-General in command of a brigade composed of the 12th, 19th and 21st Texas cavalry, Major Morgan's battalion of Texas cavalry and Pratt's Battery of Light Artillery.
....	....	Brigade composed of 5th, 6th, 8th and 15th regiments Virginia cavalry and the 36th battalion Virginia cavalry, Army of Northern Virginia.
Apl. 22, 1863.	....	Killed at Chancellorsville; brigade composed of the 2d, 4th, 5th, 27th and 33d Virginia regiments, Trimble's division, Jackson's corps, Army of Northern Virginia.
....	....	Commissioned Brigadier-General May, 1861, by the Secession Convention of Arkansas; command composed of Carrol's cavalry regiment, the 3d and 5th, regiments Arkansas infantry, Woodruff's infantry battalion and Reid's Light Battery.
Apl. 25, 1863.	....	Promoted Major-General ——, 1864; Killed at Hatcher's Run; Brigade composed of the 13th, 31st, 49th, 52d and 58th Virginia regiments infantry, Army of Northern Virginia.
Aug. 29, 1861.	....	Promoted Major-General January 14, 1862; as Brigadier-General, commanded Confederate forces north of the Nansemond, on the east bank of James river; brigade at one time in 1861 composed of the 13th and 14th North Carolina regiments and Manley's North Carolina Light Battery.
Sept. 30, 1862.	....	Promoted Major-General May 27, 1863; brigade composed of the 13th, 16th, 22d, 34th and 38th North Carolina regiments infantry, Anderson's division, A. P. Hill's corps, Army of Northern Virginia.
Mch. 26, 1862.	....	Chief of Artillery, Army of Northern Virginia.
Feb. 17, 1864.	Oct. 13, 1862.	Killed at Spottsylvania May 12, 1864; in command of Wilcox's old brigade.
Sept. 30, 1862.	.	Brigade composed of the 2d, 5th and 8th Florida regiments, Anderson's division, A. P. Hill's corps, Army of Northern Virginia.
....	....	Brigade composed of the 15th, 44th, 47th and 48th Alabama regiments, Longstreet's corps, Army of Northern Virginia.
Feb. 26, 1862.	....	Died July 17, 1873, of wounds received July 14th, 1863, at bridge near Falling Waters; brigade composed of the 26th, 44th, 47th, 17th, 52d, 42d and 11th North Carolina regiments, Heth's division, A. P. Hill's corps, Army of Northern Virginia.
Feb. 17, 1864.	....	Brigade composed of the 20th, 23d, 30th, 31st and 46th Alabama regiments, Stevenson's division, Army of Tennessee.
....	....	Brigade composed of the 6th and 9th Texas cavalry, the 3d Arkansas cavalry and the battalions of Stevenson and Bridges.
Jan. 14, 1862.	....	Promoted Major-General October 11, 1862; brigade composed of the 8th, 18th, 19th, 28th and 56th Virginia regiments, Army of Northern Virginia.
Aug. 15, 1861.	....	In command of the Indian Territories and forces there raised; resigned November 1, 1862.
Aug. 29, 1861, and Feb. 17, 1864.	....	Assigned to command of 1st division, Army of the Western Department, composed of Walker's and Russell's brigades.
Apl. 23, 1863.	....	Promoted Major-General April 8th, 1864; commanding 2d Texas brigade.
Apl. 22, 1863.	....	Brigade composed of the 3d and 5th Confederate, the 1st Arkansas, the 2d, 48th and 35th Tennessee regiments and Calvert's Light Battery, Cleburne's division, Army of Tennessee.
Apl. 22, 1863.	....	Killed in action; brigade composed of the 12th, 16th, 19th and 48th Mississippi regiments, Anderson's division, A. P. Hill's corps, Army of Northern Virginia.

BRIGADIER–GENERALS

	NAME.	STATE.	TO WHOM TO REPORT.	Date of Appointment.	Date of Rank.
342	Preston, John S........	S. Carolina.	....	June 10, 1864.	June 10, 1864.
343	Preston, William......	Kentucky..	Gen. Beauregard.....	Apl. 18, 1862.	Apl. 14, 1862.
344	Price, Sterling.........	Missouri ...	....	....	....
345	Pryor, Roger A........	Virginia ...	Gen. J. E. Johnston..	Apl. 16, 1862.	Apl. 16, 1862.
346	Quarles, Wm. A........	Tennessee.	Gen. J. E. Johnston..	Sept. 5, 1863.	Aug. 25, 1863.
347	Raines, Gabriel J......	N. Carolina	....	Sept. 23, 1861.	Sept. 23, 1861.
348	Raines, James E......	Tennessee.	Lt. Gen. E. K. Smith..	Nov. 4, 1862.	Nov. 4, 1862.
349	Ramseur, Stephen D...	N. Carolina	Gen. T. J. Jackson....	Nov. 1, 1862.	Nov. 1, 1862.
350	Randall, Horace.......	....	....	....	....
351	Randolph, George W..	Virginia ...	Maj. Gen. Magruder..	Feb. 13, 1862.	Feb. 13, 1862.
352	Ransom, Matt. W......	N. Carolina	Gen. R. E. Lee........	June 15, 1863.	June 13, 1863.
353	Ransom, Robert, Jr....	N. Carolina	Maj. Gen. Huger......	Mch. 6, 1862.	Mch. 1, 1862.
354	Reid, John C..........	Alabama...	Gen. J. E. Johnston..	...........1864.	....1864.
355	Reynolds, A. E.	Mississippi.	Gen. R. E. Lee........	March, 1865.	March, 1865.
356	Reynolds, A. W........	Virginia ...	Gen. J. E. Johnston..	Sept. 17, 1863.	Sept. 14, 1863.
357	Reynolds, D. H........	Arkansas ..	Gen. L. Polk..........	Mch. 12, 1864.	Mch. 5, 1864.
358	Richardson, R. V......	Tennessee.	Gen. J. E. Johnston..	Dec. 3, 1863.	Dec. 1, 1863.
359	Ripley, Roswell S......	S. Carolina.	....	Aug. 15, 1861.	Aug. 15, 1861.
360	Roane, J. Selden.......	Arkansas ..	Gen. Van Dorn.......	Mch. 20, 1862.	Mch. 20, 1862.

—CONTINUED.

Date of Confirmation.	Date of Acceptance.	REMARKS.
June 10, 1864.	Oct. 13, 1862.	In charge of the Bureau of Conscription.
Apl. 18, 1862.	....	Promoted Major-General 1865; commanded the 3d brigade in Major-General John C. Breckinridge's division, composed of the 20th Tennessee, the 60th North Carolina, the 1st, 3d and 4th Florida regiments and Mebane's Light Battery.
....	....	In command of the Missouri State Guard, and received into Confederate service with the rank of Major-General.
Apl. 16, 1862.	....	Resigned July 19th, 1862; brigade composed of the 14th Louisiana, the 14th Alabama, the 2d Florida and the 3d Virginia regiments and Coppen's Light Battery; brigade at one time composed of the 3d Virginia, 14th Alabama and the 2d, 5th and 8th Florida regiments, Army of Northern Virginia.
Jan. 25, 1864.	....	Commanding brigade in Walthall's division, Stewart's corps, Army of Tennessee, composed of the 42d, 48th, 46th and 55th consolidated, the 53d and 49th Tennessee regiments, the 1st Alabama and the 4th and 30th Louisiana regiments.
Dec. 13, 1861.	....	In charge of the Bureau of Conscription; again, Chief of the Torpedo and Sub-terra Shell Department.
....	....	Killed at the Battle of Stone's River December 31, 1862; brigade composed of the 11th Tennessee, 29th North Carolina and the 41st Georgia regiments, the 3d Georgia battalion and Captain McTyere's Light Battery.
Apl. 22, 1863.	....	Promoted Major-General June 1, 1864; brigade composed of the 2d, 4th, 14th and 30th North Carolina regiments, D. H. Hill's division, Army of Northern Virginia.
....	....	Commanding brigade in Walker's division; killed in action at Jenkins' Ferry.
Feb. 13, 1862.	....	Resigned December 13, 1862; at one time Secretary of War.
Feb. 16, 1864.	....	Brigade composed of the 24th, 25th, 35th, 49th and 56th North Carolina regiments, Longstreet's corps, Army of Northern Virginia.
March 6, 1862.	....	Promoted Major-General May 26, 1863; assigned to command of the 1st brigade, camp near Kingston, North Carolina, numbering some 4,000 men.
....	....	Acting as Brigadier-General in recruiting, mustering into service and brigading cavalry in Northern Alabama.
....	....	Colonel commanding Tilghman's brigade after he was killed at Battle of Baker's Creek; afterwards Senior Colonel commanding brigade of General Jos. R. Davis, during his absence, composed of the 26th, 2d, 11th and 42d Mississippi regiments, the 1st Alabama regiment and the 55th North Carolina regiment.
Feb 17, 1864.	....	Brigade composed of the 54th and 63d Virginia regiments and the 58th and 60th North Carolina regiments, Major-General Stevenson's division.
May 16, 1864.	Oct. 13, 1862.	Brigade composed of the 1st and 2d Arkansas cavalry regiments, dismounted, the 4th, 25th and 31st Arkansas infantry regiments and the 4th Arkansas infantry battalion; the 39th regiment North Carolina infantry was subsequently added, and was afterwards exchanged for the 9th Arkansas infantry regiment.
....	....	Brigade composed of the 12th, 14th and 15th regiments Tennessee cavalry, McDonald's battalion, and the 7th Tennessee regiment was subsequently added.
Aug. 15, 1861.	....	In command at Charleston, South Carolina; brigade, at the Battle of Fredericksburg, composed of the 4th and 44th Georgia and the 1st and 3d North Carolina regiments, D. H. Hill's division, Jackson's corps, Army of Northern Virginia.
Mch. 20, 1862.	....	Assigned to duty at Little Rock, reorganizing the scattered forces, after the withdrawal of Price and Van Dorn; commanded a brigade attached to Major-General Sam. Jones' division, Army of the West.

BRIGADIER-GENERALS

	NAME.	STATE.	TO WHOM TO REPORT.	Date of Appointment.	Date of Rank.
361	Roberts, Wm. P........	N. Carolina	Gen. R. E. Lee........	Feb. 21, 1865.	Feb. 21, 1865.
362	Robertson, B. H........	Virginia ...	Gen. T. J. Jackson....	June 9, 1862.	June 9, 1862.
363	Robertson, E. S. C.....	Texas......	....	....	....
364	Robertson, F. H.......	Texas......	Gen. J. B. Hood......	July 26, 1864.	July 26, 1864.
365	Robertson, J. B........	Texas......	Gen. T. J. Jackson....	Nov. 1, 1862.	Nov. 1, 1862.
366	Roddy, P. D............	Alabama...	Gen. B. Bragg........	Aug. 3, 1863.	Aug. 3, 1863.
367	Rodes, R. E............	Alabama...	Gen. J. E. Johnston..	Oct. 21, 1861.	Oct. 21, 1861.
368	Ross, L. S.............	Texas	Gen. J. E. Johnston..	Feb. 5, 1864.	Dec. 21, 1863.
369	Ross, Reuben R........	....	....	....	....
370	Rosser, Thos. L........	Texas......	Gen. R. E. Lee........	Oct. 10, 1863.	Sept. 28, 1863.
371	Rucker, E. W..........	....	....	....	....
372	Ruggles, Dan'l.........	Virginia ...	....	Aug. 9, 1861.	Aug. 9, 1861.
373	Russell, W. W..........	....	....	....	....
374	Rust, Albert...........	Arkansas ..	Gen. Van Dorn.......	Mch. 6, 1862.	Mch. 4, 1862.
375	Saunders, J. C. C......	Alabama...	Gen. R. E. Lee........	June 7, 1864.	May 31, 1864.
376	Scales, Alfred M.......	N. Carolina	Gen. R. E. Lee.......	June 15, 1863.	June 13, 1863.
377	Scott, Thomas M......	Louisiana..	Lt. Gen. L. Polk......	May 24, 1864.	May 10, 1864.
378	Scurry, W. R..........	Texas......	Gen. T. H. Holmes....	Sept. 26, 1862.	Sept. 12, 1862.
379	Sears, C. W............	Mississippi.	Lt. Gen. L. Polk......	Mch. 7, 1864.	Mch. 1, 1864.
380	Semmes, Paul J........	Georgia....	Gen. J. E. Johnston..	Mch. 18, 1862.	Mch. 11, 1862.
381	Sharp, J. H...........	Mississippi.	Gen. J. B. Hood......	July 26, 1864.	July 26, 1864.
382	Shelby, J. O...........	Missouri...	Gen. E. K. Smith......	Feb. 5, 1864.	Dec. 15, 1863.
383	Shelley, Charles M.....	Alabama...	....	....	....
384	Shingler, Wm. P.......	S. Carolina.	....	....	....

—CONTINUED.

Date of Confirmation.	Date of Acceptance.	REMARKS.
....	....	Assigned to command of Dearing's old brigade, Army of Northern Virginia.
Sept. 30, 1862.	....	Brigade composed of the 2d, 6th, 7th and 11th Virginia regiments and the 16th Virginia battalion, Colonel Funsten.
....	....	Brigadier-General of Texas State forces; commanding the 27th brigade; on staff duty with General H. E. McCulloch.
....	....	Assigned to command of a brigade composed of the 8th and 11th Texas and the 4th Tennessee regiments cavalry.
Apl. 22, 1863.	....	Brigade composed of the 1st, 4th and 5th Texas and the 3d Arkansas regiments, Hood's division, Longstreet's corps, Army of Northern Virginia.
Jan. 25, 1864.	....	Commanded brigade in Forrest's cavalry.
Dec. 13, 1861.	....	Promoted Major-General May 2, 1863; brigade composed of the 3d, 5th, 6th, 12th, 26th and 61st Alabama regiments infantry, D. H. Hill's division, Jackson's corps, Army of Northern Virginia.
Feb. 5, 1864.	... .	
....	....	Commanded Hume's cavalry brigade, Wheeler's corps.
Feb. 17, 1864.	....	Promoted Major-General 1864; brigade composed of the 7th, 11th and 12th regiments Virginia cavalry and the 25th battalion Virginia cavalry, Army of Northern Virginia.
....	....	Commanded brigade in General Forrest's cavalry, composed of the 7th, 12th, 14th and 15th Tennessee regiments, Forrest's old regiment and the 7th Alabama and 5th Mississippi regiments.
Aug. 9, 1861, and Feb. 17, 1864.	....	Brigade consisted of the 9th Mississippi, 10th Mississippi, 1st Alabama and 7th Alabama regiments. Villipigue's battalion, the Quitman Artillery and the Vicksburg Artillery; subsequently in command of other brigades.
....	....	Commanding 2d brigade, General W. T. Martin's cavalry division.
Mch. 6, 1862.	....	Brigade composed of the Arkansas infantry regiments of Colonels Carrol, King and Snead, the Arkansas infantry battalions of Colonels McCarver, Lemoyne and Jones, and a Light Battery; attached to Major-General Samuel Jones' division, Army of the West.
June 7, 1864.	....	Killed in action below Petersburg, Virginia, August 21, 1864; brigade composed of the 8th, 9th, 10th, 11th and 14th Alabama regiments.
Feb. 16, 1864.	....	Brigade composed of the 13th, 16th, 22d, 32d and 38th regiments North Carolina infantry (formerly Pender's brigade), Army of Northern Virginia.
May 24, 1864.	....	Brigade composed of the 12th Louisiana, the 27th, 35th, 49th, 55th and 57th Alabama regiments; the 3d, 7th and 8th Kentucky regiments were detached from this brigade, and mounted.
Sept. 27, 1862.	....	Killed at Jenkins' Ferry.
May 11, 1864.	....	Brigade composed of the 4th, 35th, 36th, 39th and 46th Mississippi regiments and the 7th Mississippi battalion.
Mch. 13, 1862.	....	Died of wounds received at Sharpsburg; brigade composed of the 10th, 50th, 51st and 53d Georgia regiments, McLaw's division, Longstreet's corps, Army of Northern Virginia.
....	....	Brigade composed of the 1st Mississippi battalion Sharpshooters and the 7th, 9th, 10th, 41st and 44th Mississippi regiments infantry, Hindman's division, Polk's corps, Army of Tennessee.
Feb. 5, 1864.	....	Commanded brigade in General Price's army.
....	....	Commanded brigade in Walthall's division, Stewart's corps, Army of Tennessee, composed of the 17th, 26th and 29th Alabama regiments and the 37th Mississippi regiment.
....	....	Acting Brigadier-General.

BRIGADIER–GENERALS

	NAME.	STATE.	TO WHOM TO REPORT.	Date of Appointment.	Date of Rank.
385	Shoup, F. A............	Florida	Gen. S. B. Buckner...	Apl. 11, 1863.	Sept. 12, 1862.
386	Sibley, H. H............	Louisiana..	....	June 17, 1861.	June 17, 1861.
387	Simms, James P......	....	Maj. Gen. Kershaw...	Nov., 1864.	Nov., 1864.
388	Slack, W. Y............	Missouri...	Gen. Van Dorn.......	Apl. 17, 1862.	Apl. 12, 1862.
389	Slaughter, Jas. E......	Virginia ..	Gen. B. Bragg........	Mch. 18, 1862.	Mch. 8, 1862.
390	Smith, E. Kirby........	Florida	Gen. J. E. Johnston..	June 17, 1861.	June 17, 1861.
391	Smith, George A......	....	....	....	....
392	Smith, Gustavus W....	Kentucky..	Gen. J. E. Johnston..	....	....
393	Smith, James A........	Tennessee.	Gen. B. Bragg........	Oct. 1. 1863.	Sept. 30, 1863.
394	Smith, M. L............	Florida	Gen. M. Lovell........	Apl. 11, 1862.	Apl. 11, 1862.
395	Smith, Preston	Tennessee.	Gen. B. Bragg........	Oct. 27, 1862.	Oct. 27, 1862.
396	Smith, T. B............	Tennessee.	Gen. J. B. Hood......	Aug. 2, 1864.	July 29, 1864.
397	Smith, William........	Virginia....	....	Apl. 23, 1863.	Jan. 31, 1863.
398	Smith, William D......	Georgia....	Maj. Gen. Pemberton	Mch. 14, 1862.	Mch. 7, 1862.
399	Snead, John L. T......	Virginia ...	....	....	....
400	Sorrell, G. Moxley.....	Georgia....	Gen. R. E. Lee........	Oct. 31, 1864.	Oct. 27, 1864.
401	Stafford, L. A..........	Louisiana..	Gen. R. E. Lee........	Oct. 8, 1863.	Oct. 8, 1863.
402	Starke, Peter B........	....	Gen. Forrest........	....	....
403	Starke, William E......	Louisiana..	Gen. T. J. Jackson....	Aug. 6, 1862.	Aug. 6, 1862.
404	Steele, William........	Texas......	Gen. T. H. Holmes....	Oct. 3, 1862.	Sept. 12, 1862.

—CONTINUED.

Date of Confirmation.	Date of Acceptance.	REMARKS.
Apl. 11, 1863.	....	In command of the artillery at Mobile; Chief of Artillery of General J. E. Johnston's army in the Dalton campaign; Chief of Staff under General Hood at Atlanta; brigade at one time composed of the 7th, 9th, 10th, 41st and 44th Mississippi regiments and the 9th Mississippi battalion.
Aug. 29, 1861.	....	Commanding brigade; headquarters at San Antonio, Texas.
....	....	Brigade composed of the 10th, 50th, 51st and 53d Georgia regiments, Kershaw's division, Longstreet's corps, Army of Northern Virginia.
Apl. 17, 1862.	....	Killed in action at Pea Ridge; commanding Missouri brigade, Price's division, Van Dorn's army.
Mch. 18, 1862.	....	Inspector-General, Department Number 2, Army of the Mississippi.
Aug. 29, 1861.	....	Promoted Major-General October 11, 1861; as Brigadier-General commanded Elzey's and Forney's brigades; brigade at first composed of the 9th, 10th and 11th Alabama, the 14th Mississippi and the 38th Virginia regiments, Army of the Potomac.
....	....	Acting Brigadier-General; in command at Fort Gaines, &c.
....	....	Promoted Major-General September 19, 1861; first assignment was, as Major-General, to the command of the 2d corps of the Army of the Potomac.
Feb. 17, 1864.	....	Commanding brigade, Cleburne's division, Hardee's corps, Army of Tennessee.
Apl. 11, 1862.	....	Promoted Major-General November 4th, 1862; commanding 3d Sub-District, District of Mississippi.
Apl. 22, 1863.	....	Killed at Chickamauga, September 20, 1863; brigade composed of the 11th, 12th, 13th, 29th, 47th and 154th Tennessee regiments, a battalion of Sharpshooters and Scott's Light Battery, forming part of Cheatham's division, Polk's corps, Army of Tennessee.
....	....	Brigade composed of the 2d and 20th Tennessee, the 37th Georgia, the 15th, 30th and 37th Tennessee (consolidated) regiments and Major Carswell's battalion Georgia Sharpshooters.
Apl. 23, 1863.	....	Promoted Major-General August 12, 1863; brigade composed of the Virginia regiment of Colonel Board, Colonel Harman (the 52d), Colonel Terrell (the 13th), Colonel Hoffman (the 31st) and Colonel Gibson's (the 49th); at the Battle of Chancellorsville his brigade was composed of the 13th, 49th, 52d and 58th and 31st Virginia regiments, Early's division, Army of Northern Virginia.
Mch. 14, 1862.	....	Died at Charleston, South Carolina, October 4, 1862; commanding a district in the Department of South Carolina, Georgia and Florida; headquarters on James Island.
....	....	Commanding River brigade, Department Number 2, Major-General Polk's command.
....	....	Assigned to command of Wright's Georgia brigade, Mahone's division, A. P. Hill's corps, composed of the 2d, 22d, 48th and 64th regiments Georgia Volunteers and the 2d and 10th battalion Georgia Volunteers.
Jan. 25, 1864.	Oct. 13, 1862.	Killed in action; succeeded General Starke in command of his brigade, composed of the 1st, 2d, 9th, 10th and 15th Louisiana regiments and Coppen's Louisiana battalion, Jackson's division, Army of Northern Virginia.
....	....	Commanding brigade in Chalmers' division, Forrest's cavalry, corps.
Sept. 30, 1862.	....	Killed at Sharpsburg September 17, 1862; brigade composed of the 2d, 5th, 9th, 10th, 14th and 15th Louisiana regiments, Jackson's division, Army of Northern Virginia.
Oct. 3, 1862.	....	Brigade composed of the 12th, 19th and 21st regiments Texas cavalry.

BRIGADIER–GENERALS

	NAME.	STATE.	TO WHOM TO REPORT.	Date of Appointment.	Date of Rank.
405	Steuart, George H.....	Maryland..	....	Mch. 18, 1862.	Mch. 6, 1862.
406	Steen, A. E............	Missouri...	Gen. S. Price.........	April, 1862.	April, 1862.
407	Stevens, C. H..........	S. Carolina.	Gen. J. E. Johnston..	Feb. 1, 1864.	Jan. 20, 1864.
408	Stevens, Walter H.....	Virginia....	....		
409	Stevenson, Carter L....	Virginia ...	....	Mch. 6, 1862.	Feb. 27, 1862.
410	Stewart, A. P..........	Tennessee.	....	Nov. 8, 1861.	Nov. 8, 1861.
411	St. John, I. M..........	Georgia....	....	Febr'y, 1865.	Febr'y, 1865.
412	Stovall, M. A...........	Georgia....	Gen. B. Bragg........	Apl. 23, 1863.	Jan. 20, 1863.
413	Strahl, O. F............	Tennessee.	Gen. B. Bragg........	July 28, 1863.	July 28, 1863.
414	Stuart, J. E. B........	Virginia ...	Gen. J. E. Johnston..	Sept. 24, 1861.	Sept. 24, 1861.
415	Tallaferro, Wm. B.....	Virginia....	Gen. J. E. Johnston..	Mch. 6, 1862.	Mch. 4, 1862.
416	Tappan, J. C...........	Arkansas ..	Gen. T. H. Holmes...	Nov. 5, 1862.	Nov. 5, 1862.
417	Taylor, Richard........	Louisiana..	Gen. J. E. Johnston..	Oct. 21, 1861.	Oct. 21, 1861.
418	Taylor, Thomas H.....	Kentucky..	Lt. Gen. E. K. Smith..	Nov. 4, 1862.	Nov. 4, 1862.
419	Terrill, James E. B....	Virginia ...	Gen. R. E. Lee........	June 1, 1864.	May 31, 1864.
420	Terry, William.........	Virginia ...	Gen. R. E. Lee........	May 20, 1864.	May 19, 1864.
421	Terry, William R......	Virginia ...	Gen. R. E. Lee........	June 10, 1864.	May 31, 1864.
422	Thomas, Allen.........	Louisiana..	Gen. E. K. Smith.....	Feb. 17, 1864.	Feb. 4, 1864.

—Continued.

Date of Confirmation.	Date of Acceptance.	REMARKS.
Mch. 18, 1862.	....	Commanding Maryland Line; brigade composed of the 44th, 25th and 58th Virginia and the 1st Maryland regiment, Army of Northern Virginia.
....	....	Brigade composed of the battalions of Colonels Winston and Ceamal, and the companies of Rives and Bennett, and the Light Battery of Kennealy, constituting 3d brigade of the 1st division, Army of the West.
Feb. 1, 1864.	....	Killed in action at Atlanta, Georgia, July, 1864; brigade composed of the 1st Georgia Confederate, the 30th, 66th, 25th and 29th Georgia regiments and the 1st battalion Georgia Sharpshooters.
....	....	On Engineer duty at Richmond, Virginia.
Mch. 6, 1862.	....	Promoted Major-General October 10, 1862; commanding all troops at Cumberland Gap and its vicinity during the early occupation of East Tennessee.
Dec. 13, 1861.	....	Promoted Major-General June 2, 1863; commanded 4th brigade, 1st division, Department of the West, composed of the 4th, 5th, 29th, 31st and 33d Tennessee regiments; also in command of a brigade in Cheatham's division, Polk's corps, Army of Tennessee, composed of the 4th, 5th, 19th, 24th, 31st and 33d Tennessee regiments, and Stanford's Light Battery.
....	....	Chief of the Nitre and Mining Bureau; also Second Commissary General.
Apl. 23, 1863.	....	Brigade composed of the 40th, 41st, 42d and 43d Georgia regiments, to which were added the 52d Georgia and the 1st Georgia State Line, Army of Tennessee.
Jan. 25, 1864.	....	Killed in action; brigade composed of the 4th, 5th, 19th, 24th, 31st and 33d Tennessee regiments and Stanford's Light Battery, Cheatham's division, Polk's corps, Army of the Tennessee.
Dec. 13, 1861.	....	Promoted Major-General July 25, 1862; Chief of Cavalry, Army of Northern Virginia.
Mch. 6, 1862.	....	Promoted Major-General January 1, 1865; commanding brigade in division of General T. J. Jackson; brigade afterwards composed of the 10th, 23d, 37th, 42d, 47th and 48th Virginia regiments, Ewell's corps, Army of Northern Virginia.
Apl. 22, 1863.	....	Brigade composed of the Arkansas regiments of Colonels Thaler, Guirstead, Shaver and Dawson and Etter's Arkansas Light Battery.
Dec. 13, 1861.	....	Promoted Major-General July 28, 1862; brigade composed of the 6th, 7th, 8th and 9th Louisiana regiments, Wheat's battalion and a Virginia Light Battery, Army of Northern Virginia.
....	....	President declined to nominate for confirmation by the Senate.
June 1, 1864.	....	Killed in action, and was at the time, commanding Pegram's old brigade, composed of the 13th, 31st, 49th, 52d and 58th Virginia regiments infantry, Army of Northern Virginia.
May 20, 1864.	Oct. 13, 1862.	Assigned to the command of a brigade composed of the remnants of the "Old Stonewall brigade" and the brigades of Jones and Stuart; thus constituted, this brigade included the 2d, 4th, 5th, 10th, 21st, 23d, 25th, 27th, 33d, 37th, 42d, 44th, 48th and 50th regiments Virginia Infantry, Army of Northern Virginia.
June 10, 1864.	....	Brigade composed of the 1st, 7th, 11th, 24th and 3d Virginia regiments.
Feb. 17, 1864.	....	Brigade composed of the 17th, 26th, 27th, 28th and 31st Louisiana Volunteers, infantry, and Weatherley's battalion of Sharpshooters.

BRIGADIER-GENERALS

	NAME.	STATE.	TO WHOM TO REPORT.	Date of Appointment.	Date of Rank.
423	Thomas, B. M.........	....	....	Aug. 4, 1864.	Aug. 4, 1864.
424	Thomas, Edward L....	Georgia....	Gen. T. J. Jackson....	Nov. 1, 1862.	Nov. 1, 1862.
425	Thompson, M. Jeff.....	....	....	....	....
426	Tilghman, Lloyd.......	Kentucky..	Gen. A. S. Johnston..	Oct. 18, 1861.	Oct. 18, 1861.
427	Toombs, Robert........	Georgia....	....	July 19, 1861.	July 19, 1861.
428	Toon, Thomas F.......	N. Carolina	Gen. R. E. Lee........	June 2, 1864.	May 31, 1864.
429	Tracy, E. D............	Alabama...	Gen. E. K. Smith.....	Aug. 16, 1862.	Aug. 16, 1862.
430	Trapier, J. H.........	S. Carolina.	....	Oct. 21, 1861.	Oct. 21, 1861.
431	Trimble, Isaac R......	Maryland..	....	Aug. 9, 1861.	Aug. 9, 1861.
432	Trudean, J............	....	....	....	....
433	Tucker, W. F..........	Mississippi.	....	Mch. 7, 1864.	Mch. 1, 1864.
434	Tyler, R. C......	Tennessee.	....	Mch. 5, 1864.	Feb 23, 1864.
435	Vance, Robt. B........	N. Carolina	Gen. B. Bragg........	Apl. 23, 1863.	Mch. 4, 1863.
436	Van Dorn, Earl........	Mississippi.	....	June 5, 1861.	June 5, 1861.
437	Vaughn, A. J..........	Tennessee.	Gen. B. Bragg........	Nov. 21, 1863.	Nov. 18, 1863.
438	Vaughn, John C.......	Tennessee.	Gen. E. K. Smith.....	Oct. 3, 1862.	Sept. 22, 1862.
439	Villipigue, J. B........	S. Carolina.	Gen. Beauregard.....	Mch. 18, 1862.	Mch. 13, 1862.
440	Wade, Wm. B.........	....	....	....	....

—CONTINUED.

Date of Confirmation.	Date of Acceptance.	REMARKS.
....	....	Assigned to command of a brigade composed of the 1st, 2d and 3d regiments Alabama Reserves; afterwards known as the 61st, 62d and 63d Alabama regiments.
Apl. 22, 1863.	....	Brigade composed of the 14th, 35th, 45th and 49th Georgia regiments, the 3d Louisiana battalion and Captain Davidson's Light Battery, the Letcher Artillery, Pender's division, A. P. Hill's corps, Army of Northern Virginia.
....	....	Commanding First Military District, Missouri State Guards; afterwards in command of Shelby's old brigade.
Dec. 13, 1861.	....	Killed at Baker's Creek, Mississippi, May 16, 1863; at one time commanding 1st division of the 1st corps, Army of Tennessee.
Aug. 29, 1861.	....	Resigned March 4, 1863; brigade composed of the 2d, 15th, 17th and 20th Georgia regiments and the 1st regiment Georgia Regulars, Longstreet's corps, Army of Northern Virginia.
June 2, 1864.	....	Commanded Johnston's brigade, composed of the 5th, 12th, 20th and 23d North Carolina regiments and Wilson's battalion.
Sept. 30, 1862.	....	Killed near Port Gibson May 1, 1863; brigade composed of the 20th, 23d, 30th, 31st and 46th Alabama regiments, Stevenson's division, Army of Tennessee.
Dec. 13, 1861.	....	In command at Georgetown South Carolina, and also of Fort Moultrie and Sullivan's Island during the iron-clad attack upon Fort Sumter, April 7, 1863.
Aug. 9, 1861.	....	Promoted Major-General January 17, 1863; assigned to command of brigade at Evansport on the Potomac river; afterwards in command of Crittenden's brigade, composed of the 21st Georgia, the 21st North Carolina and the 16th Mississippi regiments and Courtney's Virginia battery, Longstreet's corps, Army of Northern Virginia; at the Battle of Fredericksburg, Trimble's brigade was composed of the 12th and 21st Georgia, the 15th Alabama and the 21st North Carolina regiments, Ewell's division, Jackson's corps, Army of Northern Virginia.
....	....	Never mustered into Confederate service; commanded Louisiana State troops; in charge of water batteries, at Columbus, Kentucky.
May 11, 1864.	....	Brigade composed of the 7th, 9th, 10th, 41st and 44th regiments Mississippi infantry and a battalion of Sharpshooters.
June 9, 1864.	....	In command of military post, West Point, Georgia; afterwards in command of a brigade composed of the 37th Georgia, the 20th, 15th and 37th and 10th and 30th Tennessee regiments, and the 4th battalion Georgia Sharpshooters.
Apl. 23, 1863.	....	Commanding 2d brigade, McCown's division, Polk's corps, Army of Tennessee, composed of the 29th and 39th North Carolina regiments, the 3d and 9th Georgia battalions and McDuffie's Light Battery.
Aug. 29, 1861.	....	Promoted Major-General September 19, 1861; commanding Army of the District of the Mississippi.
Feb. 17, 1864.	....	Succeeded General Preston Smith in command of his brigade, composed of the 154th, 13th, 12th, 47th, 11th and 29th Tennessee regiments, Scott's Light Battery and a battalion of Sharpshooters, Army of Tennessee.
Oct. 3, 1862.	....	Brigade composed of seven regiments and two battalions (all mounted) from East Tennessee and one battalion Georgia cavalry.
Mch. 18, 1862.	....	Died November 9, 1862; commanded 4th Sub-district, District of Mississippi; also in command of the 2d brigade, 1st division, Army of the District of Mississippi.
....	....	Commanded 1st cavalry brigade, 1st division, Forrest's cavalry command.

BRIGADIER–GENERALS

	NAME.	STATE.	TO WHOM TO REPORT.	Date of Appointment.	Date of Rank.
441	Walker, H. H.........	Virginia ...	Gen. R. E. Lee........	July 1, 1863.	July 1, 1863.
442	Walker, James A......	Virginia ...	Gen. R. E. Lee........	May 16, 1863.	May 15, 1863.
443	Walker, John G........	Missouri ...	Maj. Gen. Holmes....	Jan. 9, 1862.	Jan. 9, 1862.
444	Walker, L. M..........	Tennessee.	Gen. Beauregard.....	Apl. 11, 1862.	Mch. 11, 1862.
445	Walker, L. P...........	Alabama...	Gen. A. S. Johnston..	Sept. 17, 1861.	Sept. 17, 1861.
446	Walker, R. Lindsay....	Virginia ...	....	....	....
447	Walker, W. H. T......	Georgia....	Brig. Gen. B. Bragg..	May 25, 1861.	May 25, 1861.
448	Walker, W. S..........	Florida	Gen. Beauregard.....	Oct. 30, 1862.	Oct. 30, 1862.
449	Wallace, W. H.........	S. Carolina.	....	Sept. 30, 1864.	Sept. 30, 1864.
450	Walthall, E. C.........	Mississippi.	Gen. B. Bragg........	Apl. 23, 1863.	Apl. 13, 1862.
451	Waterhouse, R........	Texas......	....	Mch. 17, 1865.	Mch. 17, 1865.
452	Watie, Stand..........	{ Indian } { Territ'y }	Gen. E. K. Smith.....	May 10, 1864.	May 6, 1864.
453	Waul, T. N............	Texas......	....	Sept. 19, 1863.	Sept. 18, 1863.
454	Wayne, Henry C.......	Georgia....	Gen. J. E. Johnston..	Dec. 16, 1861.	Dec. 16, 1861.
455	Weisiger, D. A........	Virginia ...	Gen. R. E. Lee........	June 7, 1864.	May 31, 1864.
456	Wharton, G. C........	Virginia ...	Gen. Sam. Jones......	Sept. 25, 1863.	July 8, 1863.
457	Wharton, John A......	Texas......	Gen. B. Bragg........	Nov. 18, 1862.	Nov. 18, 1862.
458	Wheeler, Joseph.......	Georgia....	Gen. B. Bragg........	Oct. 30, 1862.	Oct. 30, 1862.
459	Whitfield, F. E........	Mississippi.	....	May 9, 1863.	May 9, 1863.
460	Whitfield, J. W........	Texas	Gen. J. E. Johnston..	May 9, 1863.	May 9, 1863.
461	Whiting, W. H. C......	Mississippi.	....	Aug. 28, 1861.	July 21, 1861.
462	Wickham, W. C........	Virginia ...	Gen. R. E. Lee........	Sept. 2, 1863.	Sept. 1, 1863.

—CONTINUED.

Date of Confirmation.	Date of Acceptance.	REMARKS.
Feb. 17, 1864.	....	Brigade composed of the 40th, 47th and 55th Virginia regiments and the 22d Virginia battalion; also in command of Archer's brigade, Army of Northern Virginia.
Feb. 17, 1864.	....	Commanded brigade, Army of Northern Virginia, composed of the 13th, 31st, 58th, 44th, 25th and 52d Virginia and the 12th Georgia regiments; commanded "Stonewall Brigade" from May, 1863, and Pegram's division in 1865.
Jan. 9, 1862.	....	Promoted Major-General November 8, 1862; brigade consisted of the 30th and 40th Virginia, the 1st, 2d and 3d North Carolina and the 3d Arkansas regiments and the Light Batteries of Captains Walker and Cooke.
Apl. 11, 1862.	....	Killed in action; commanding cavalry brigade, General Price's army.
Dec. 13, 1861.	....	Resigned March 31, 1862; at one time Secretary of War.
....	....	Commanding artillery of General A. P. Hill's corps, Army of Northern Virginia.
Aug. 29, 1861.	....	Resigned October 29, 1861; appointed Major-General May 27, 1863; killed in action near Atlanta, Georgia.
Apl. 22, 1863.	....	Commanding 3d Military District of South Carolina; subsequently in command of a brigade composed of the 17th, 18th, 22d, 23d and 26th South Carolina regiments and Colonel Elliott's Holcombe Legion.
....	....	Brigade composed of the 17th, 18th, 22d, 23d and 26th regiments South Carolina Volunteers and the Holcombe Legion.
Apl. 23, 1863.	....	Promoted Major-General June 10, 1864; brigade composed of the 24th, 27th, 29th, 30th and 34th Mississippi regiments, Withers' division, Polk's corps, Army of Tennessee.
....	....	Brigade composed of the 3d, 16th, 17th and 19th Texas infantry regiments and the 16th regiment Texas cavalry, dismounted.
May 10, 1864.	....	Brigade composed of the 1st and 2d Cherokee regiments, the 1st and 2d Creek regiments, a Cherokee battalion, a Seminole battalion, an Osage battalion and a battalion composed of "Volunteers from the States."
June 10, 1864.	....	
Dec. 24, 1861.	....	Declined; accepted appointment of Adjutant-General of the State of Georgia.
June 7, 1864.	....	Commanded Mahone's old brigade, composed of the 6th, 16th, 12th, 61st and 41st Virginia regiments of infantry, Army of Northern Virginia.
Feb. 17, 1864.	....	Brigade composed of the 50th, 51st and 63d Virginia regiments infantry and the 30th Virginia battalion.
Apl. 22, 1863.	....	Promoted Major-General November 10, 1863; commanded cavalry brigade, Army of Tennessee, composed of the 8th Texas, the 2d and 3d Georgia, the 4th Tennessee and the 1st and 3d Confederate regiments, a Tennessee battalion, Gibson's Light Battery, &c.
Apl. 22, 1863.	....	Promoted Major-General January 20, 1863; Chief of Cavalry in General Bragg's army, and commanding brigades of Hagan, Forrest, Wharton and Morgan.
....	....	Acting Brigadier-General.
Jan. 25, 1864.	....	Brigade composed of Whitfield's Legion and the 3d, 6th and 9th Texas cavalry.
Aug. 29, 1861.	....	Promoted Major-General February 28, 1863; brigade in 1861 composed of the 2d and 11th Mississippi, the 4th Alabama and the 6th North Carolina regiments, Army of the Potomac; at one time in command of the 3d brigade, Army of the Shenandoah.
Jan. 25, 1864.	....	Brigade composed of the 1st, 2d, 3d and 4th regiments Virginia cavalry, Army of Northern Virginia.

　CONFEDERATE ROSTER.

BRIGADIER-GENERALS

	NAME.	STATE.	TO WHOM TO REPORT.	Date of Appointment.	Date of Rank.
463	Wigfall, Louis T.......	Texas......	Gen. J. E. Johnston..	Oct. 21, 1861.	Oct. 21, 1861.
464	Wilcox, Cadmus M....	Tennessee.	Gen. J. E. Johnston..	Oct. 21, 1861.	Oct. 21, 1861.
465	Williams, John S......	Kentucky..	Brig. Gen. Marshall..	Apl. 18, 1862.	Apl. 16, 1862.
466	Wilson, Claudius C....	Georgia....	Gen. B. Bragg........	Nov. 18, 1863.	Nov. 16, 1863.
467	Winder, Charles S.....	Maryland..	Gen. J. E. Johnston..	Mch. 7, 1862.	Mch. 1, 1862.
468	Winder, John H.......	Maryland..	....	June 21, 1861.	June 21, 1861.
469	Wise, Henry A.........	Virginia ...	....	June 5, 1861.	June 5, 1861.
470	Withers, Jones M......	Alabama...	....	July 10, 1861.	July 10, 1861.
471	Wood, S. A. M...... ..	Alabama...	....	Jan. 7, 1862.	Jan. 7, 1862.
472	Wofford, W. T.........	Georgia....	Gen. R. E. Lee........	Apl. 23, 1863.	Jan. 17, 1863.
473	Wright, A. R...........	Georgia....	Gen. R. E. Lee........	June 3, 1862.	June 3, 1862.
474	Wright, G. J...........	Georgia....	Gen. R. E. Lee........	....	....
475	Wright, M. H..........	....	....	....	....
476	Wright, Marcus J......	Tennessee.	Gen. J. E. Johnston..	Dec. 20, 1862.	Dec. 13, 1862.
477	York, Zebulon.........	Louisiana..	Gen. R. E. Lee........	June 2, 1864.	May 31, 1864.
478	Young, P. M. B........	Georgia....	Gen. R. E. Lee........	Oct. 10, 1863.	Sept. 28, 1863.
479	Young, Wm. H........	Texas......	Gen. J. B. Hood......	Aug. 16, 1864.	Aug. 15, 1864.
480	Zollicoffer, Felix K....	Tennessee.	....	July 9, 1861.	July 9, 1861.

—CONTINUED.

Date of Confirmation.	Date of Acceptance.	REMARKS.
Dec. 20, 1861.	....	Resigned February 20. 1862; brigade composed of the 1st, 4th and 5th Texas and the 1st Georgia regiments, Army of the Potomac.
Dec. 13, 1861.	....	Promoted Major-General August 13, 1863; brigade composed of the 8th, 9th, 10th, 14th and 11th Alabama regiments, the 19th Mississippi and the 38th Virginia regiments, Anderson's division, A. P. Hill's corps, Army of Northern Virginia.
Apl. 18, 1862.	....	Brigade composed of the 22d, 36th and 45th Virginia infantry regiments, the 8th Virginia cavalry, Bailey's and Edgar's battalions and the Light Batteries of Captains Otey and Lowry; brigade afterwards composed of the 1st, 2d and 9th Kentucky, the 2d Kentucky battalion, Allison's squadron and Hamilton's battalion.
Feb. 17, 1864.	....	Died November 24, 1863; brigade composed of the 13th, 25th, 29th and 30th Georgia regiments, the 1st battalion Georgia Sharpshooters and the 4th Louisiana battalion, Army of Tennessee.
Mch. 6, 1862.	....	Killed at Cedar Run August 9, 1862; brigade composed of the 2d, 4th, 5th, 27th and 33d Virginia regiments, Jackson's division, Army of Northern Virginia.
Aug. 29, 1861.	....	In command of prison camps at Andersonville, Milen, &c., &c.
Aug. 29, 1861, and Feb. 17, 1864.	....	Brigade consisted of the 26th, 34th, 46th and 9th Virginia regiments and the Light Batteries of Captains McComas and Armistead, Army of Northern Virginia.
Aug. 29, 1861.	....	Promoted Major-General April 6, 1862; commanding Reserve corps, Army of the Mississippi, composed of the brigades of Gardner, Chalmers, Jackson and Manigault.
Jan. 14, 1862.	....	Brigade composed of the 7th Alabama, 5th, 7th and 8th Arkansas and 44th Tennessee regiments, the battalions of Majors Kelly and Hardcastle, a company of Georgia cavalry and a company of Mississippi artillery; resigned October 17, 1863; at the Battle of Chickamauga his brigade was composed of the 32d and 45th Mississippi and the 33d, 45th and 16th Alabama regiments, Major Hankin's battalion and Semple's Light Battery.
Apl. 23, 1863.	....	Assigned to command of Cobb's Georgia brigade. McLaw's division, Longstreet's corps, Army of Northern Virginia, composed of the 18th, 24th and 16th Georgia regiments, Cobb's Legion, Phillip's Legion and the 3d battalion Georgia Sharpshooters; afterwards in command of North Georgia.
Sept. 30, 1862.	....	Promoted Major-General November 23, 1864; brigade composed of the 3d, 22d, 46th and 48th Georgia regiments and the 2d Georgia battalion, Anderson's division, A. P. Hill's corps, Army of Northern Virginia.
....	....	Acting Brigadier-General, in command of General P. M. B. Young's brigade.
....	....	Acting Brigadier-General; at one time on ordnance duty at Atlanta, Georgia.
Apl. 22, 1863.	....	Brigade composed of the 16th, 28th, 38th, 8th, 51st and 52d Tennessee regiments. Murray's Tennessee battalion and Carnes' Light Battery, Cheatham's division, Polk's corps, Army of Tennessee.
June 2, 1864.	....	Brigade composed of the 1st, 2d, 3d, 5th, 6th, 7th, 8th, 9th, 10th, 14th and 15th regiments Louisiana infantry.
Feb. 17, 1864.	....	Promoted Major-General December 12, 1864; brigade composed of the "Cobb Legion," the "Jeff. Davis Legion," "Phillip's Legion" and the 7th Georgia—all cavalry commands, Army of Northern Virginia; for the 7th Georgia regiment, the 10th Georgia regiment was afterwards substituted; Millen's battalion was subsequently added.
....	....	Brigade composed of the 9th Texas infantry, the 10th, 14th and 32d Texas, dismounted, and the 29th and 39th North Carolina infantry regiments.
Aug. 29, 1861.	....	Killed at Mill Spring; commanded Camp of Instruction at Trousdale, Tennessee; afterwards assigned to the command of the Department of East Tennessee.

REGIMENTS, &c., IN CONFEDERATE SERVICE.

No.	State	Command	Arm of Service	Commander	Date of Rank	Remarks
1st	Alabama.	Regiment	Cavalry	{ Col. Wm. W. Allen	July 11, 1862.	Promoted Major-General.
				{ Col. L. H. Clanton	1861.	Promoted Brigadier-General.
2d	"	"	"	Col. F. W. Hunter	May 1, 1861.	
3d	"	"	"	Col. James Hagan		Promoted Brigadier-General.
1st	"	"	Infantry	Col. J. W. G. Steedman	Mch. 4, 1861.	
				{ Col. H. D. Clayton	Mch. 28, 1861.	Promoted Major-General July 9, 1864.
2d	"	"	"	{ Col. H. Maury	1861.	
				{ Col. W. S. Goolwyn	May 31, 1861.	Promoted Brigadier-General.
3d	"	"	"	{ Col. C. A. Battle	1861.	
				{ Col. T. Lomax	Oct. 3, 1861.	Promoted Brigadier-General.
4th	"	"	"	{ Col. P. D. Bowles	1861.	
5th	"	"	"	Col. E. McL. Law	July 1, 1861.	
6th	"	"	"	Col. J. M. Hall	1861.	
7th	"	"	"	Col. Jas. N. Lightfoot.	May 7, 1863.	
8th	"	"	"	{ Col. Y. L. Royster	June 16, 1862.	
9th	"	"	"	{ Col. Thos. E. Irby	1861.	
				{ Col. Sam'l Henry	Oct. 21, 1861.	
10th	"	"	"	Col. A. S. Cunningham.		
11th	"	"	"	{ Col. I. L. Woodward	1862.	
				{ Col. J. C. C. Saunders.	Sept. 11, 1862.	Promoted Brigadier-General.
12th	"	"	"	Col. Syd. Moore	Sept. 14, 1861.	
13th	"	"	"	Col. Sam'l B. Pickens.	1861.	
14th	"	"	"	{ Col. R. T. Jones	1861.	
				{ Col. B. D. Fry	July 19, 1861.	Promoted Brigadier-General.
15th	"	"	"	{ Col. L. Pinkard	Oct. 2, 1862.	
				{ Col. Thos. J. Judge	1861.	
15th	"	"	"	Col. A. A. Lowther	Apl. 28, 1863.	Promoted Brigadier-General.
16th	"	"	"	{ Col. James Canty	June 17, 1862.	
				{ Col. A. H. Helvenstein.	1863.	
				{ Col. W. B. Wood	1862.	
17th	"	"	"	Col. Virgil S. Murphy	Apl. 25, 1862.	Promoted Brigadier-General.
18th	"	"	"	Col. J. T. Holtzclaw	May 10, 1862.	
19th	"	"	"	{ Col. A. K. McSpaulding.	Oct. 30, 1861.	
				{ Col. Jos. Wheeler	1861.	Promoted Lieutenant-General.
20th	"	"	"	{ Col. E. W. Pettus	May 28, 1863.	Promoted Brigadier-General.
				{ Col. J. W. Carroll	1862.	Promoted Brigadier-General.

No.	Regiment	Colonel	Date	Remarks
21st	"	Col. C. D. Anderson	May 8, 1862.	Promoted Brigadier-General.
		Col. Jas. Crawford	Dec. 20, 1862.	
22d	"	Col. John C. Marrast		
23d	"	Col. Z. C. Deas	Mch. 18, 1861.	Promoted Brigadier-General.
24th	"	Col. F. K. Beck	June 2, 1861.	
		Col. N. N. Davis		
25th	"	Col. W. A. Buck	Jan. 28, 1862.	
26th	"	Col. J. V. Loomis	Apl. 2, 1862.	Promoted Brigadier-General.
27th	"	Col. E. A. O'Neal	Nov. 2, 1862.	
		Col. James Jackson	Nov. 2, 1862.	
28th	"	Col. A. H. Hughes	Nov. 2, 1862.	Promoted Brigadier-General.
29th	"	Col. J. W. Fraser	Dec. 9, 1862.	
30th	"	Col. Jno. F. Connolly		
31st	"	Col. J. R. F. Tatnall		Promoted Brigadier-General.
32d	"	Col. Chas. M. Shelley	Mch. 22, 1862.	
33d	"	Col. D. R. Hundley	May 8, 1862.	
34th	"	Col. Alex'r McKinstry	Apl. 18, 1862.	
35th	"	Col. Sam'l Adams	Apl. 23, 1862.	
		Col. J. C. B. Mitchell	Mch. 25, 1862.	
36th	"	Col. Ed. Goodwyn	Nov. 12, 1862.	
37th	"	Col. J. W. Robertson	Mch. 16, 1863.	
38th	"	Col. Robt. H. Smith	May 13, 1862.	Delegate to Confederate Congress at Montgomery.
39th	"	Col. Jas. F. Dowdell	June 30, 1862.	
40th	"	Col. Chas. T. Ketchum	May 17, 1862.	
		Col. Henry D. Clayton	Apl. 30, 1862.	Promoted Major-General.
41st	"	Col. Jno. H. Hughley	June 27, 1863.	
42d	"	Col. A. A. Coleman	May 16, 1862.	
43d	"	Col. M. L. Stansel	Nov. 4, 1862.	
		Col. Henry Talbird		
44th	"	Col. Jno. W. Portis	Sept. 1, 1862.	Promoted Brigadier-General.
		Col. T. M. Mordy		Promoted Brigadier-General.
		Col. Arch. Gracie, Jr.		
45th	"	Col. Chas. A. Derby		
46th	"	Col. James Kent	Mch. 25, 1863.	
47th	"	Col. E. B. Breedlove		
		Col. W. S. Goodwin	May 20, 1862.	
48th	"	Col. Mich'l L. Woods	July 15, 1863.	
49th	"	Col. M. J. Bulger		
50th	"	Col. — Oliver		
51st	Partisan Rangers.	Col. Jas L. Sheffield	May 23, 1863.	
52d	Infantry.	Col. Jeptha Edwards	May 8, 1862.	
53d	Partisan Rangers.	Col. J. C. Coltart		
54th	Infantry.	Col. Jno. T. Morgan	Sept. 6, 1862.	Promoted Brigadier-General.
		Col. S. D. Hale		
		Col. M. W. Hannon	Nov. 5, 1862.	Promoted Brigadier-General.
		Col. Alpheus Baker	Jan 28, 1863.	Promoted Brigadier-General.

REGIMENTS, &c.—CONTINUED.

No.	State	Command	Arm of Service	Commander	Date of Rank	Remarks
55th	Alabama	Regiment	Infantry	Col. John Snodgrass	Feb. 25, 1863	
56th	"	"	Partisan Rangers	Col. Wm. Boyle		
57th	"	"	Infantry	Col. Jno. P. W. Amerine	Apl. 13, 1863	
1st	"	Legion	Artillery	Col. Henry W. Hilliard		
1st	"	Battalion	"	Lt. Col. Forsyth		
2d	"	"	Infantry	Major Hollinquist		
5th	"	"	"	Lt. Col. Chadick		
8th	"	"	"	Lt. Col. Blount		
9th	"	"	"	Major Clifton		
10th	"	"	"	Col. Robt. W. Harper	Apl. 14, 1862	
1st	Arkansas	Regiment	Cavalry	Col. Jas. A. Williamson	Nov. 8, 1862	
2d	"	"	"	{ Col. B. T. Embry	...1862	
				Col. Sam'l G. Earl	May 26, 1862	
3d	"	"	"	{ Col. S. Borland		
				Col. N. F. Shnaus	...1862	
4th	"	"	"	Col. John Drew		
1st	Cherokee	"	Mounted Rifles	Col. D. H. Cooper		Promoted Brigadier-General.
2d	Choctaw & Chickasaw	"	"	Col. Stand. Watie		Promoted Brigadier-General.
1st	Cherokee	"	Infantry	Col. D. M. McIntosh		
2d	Creek	"	"	{ Col. J. W. Colquitt	July 11, 1862	
				Col. J. F. Fagan	...1862	Promoted Major-General.
1st	Arkansas	"	"	{ Col. Dan'l C. Govan	Jan. 28, 1862	Promoted Brigadier-General.
				Col. Van. H. Manning	Mch. 11, 1862	
3d	"	"	"	Col. Henry G. Bunn	Nov. 4, 1862	
4th	"	"	"	{ Col. E. McNair	...1862	Promoted Brigadier-General.
				Col. L. Featherstone	May 16, 1862	
5th	"	"	"	Col. D. C. Cross	...1862	
6th	"	"	"	Col. A. T. Hawthorne	May 14, 1862	Promoted Brigadier-General.
7th	"	"	"	{ Col. R. G. Shaver	...1862	
				Col. John H. Kelley	May 5, 1862	Promoted Brigadier-General.
8th	"	"	"	Col. W. K. Patterson	...1862	
9th	"	"	"	Col. J. L. Dunlop	Jan. 12, 1862	
10th	"	"	"	Col. A. R. Witt	May 27, 1862	
11th	"	"	"	{ Col. T. D. Merrick		
				Col. John L. Smith	...1862	

Regiment	Type	Officer	Date	Notes
12th	"	Col. Y. J. Reid	Oct. 2, 1862.	Promoted Brigadier-General.
13th	"	Col. E. W. Gantt	...1862.	Promoted Brigadier-General.
13th	"	Col. J. McNeely	Nov. 5, 1862.	Promoted Brigadier-General.
14th	"	Col. J. C. Tappan	...1862.	
14th	"	Col. Frank P. Powers		
14th	"	Col. — Mitchell.	...1862.	
15th	"	Col. Benj. M. Johnson	Mch. 4, 1862.	Promoted Major-General.
15th	"	Col. P. R. Cleburne		
16th	"	Col. David Province	...1861.	
16th	"	Col. J. F. Hill	...1862.	
17th	"	Col. Judah E. Cravens		
17th	"	Col. F. Hector	Oct. 14, 1862.	
18th	"	Col. R. H. Crockett	...1862.	
18th	"	Col. — McCarver.		
19th	"	Col. C. L. Dawson,		
20th	"	Col. H. P. Johnson	May 13, 1862.	
20th	"	Col. Rich'd Lyon.	...1862.	
21st	"	Col. S. Boone.	Aug. 21, 1862.	
21st	"	Col. D. McRae.	...1862.	Promoted Brigadier-General.
22d	"	Col. H. McCord.		
22d	"	Col. G. W. King.	...1862.	
23d	"	Col. O. P. Lyle.	Sept. 10, 1862.	
23d	"	Col. C. W. Adams.	1862.	Promoted Brigadier-General.
24th	"	Col. E. E. Portlock.	June 6, 1862.	
25th	"	Col. Chas. R. Tunball.	June 13, 1862.	
26th	"	Col. A. S. Morgan.		
27th	"	Col. J. R. Snaylor.		
28th	"	Col. D. McRae		
29th	"	Col. J. C. Pleasants.		Promoted Brigadier-General.
30th	"	Col. Robt. A. Hart.	Nov. 12, 1862.	
31st	"	Col. T. H. McCray.	May 27, 1862.	Promoted Brigadier-General.
32d	"	Col. L. C. Gause,		
1st	Battalion	Major W. H. Brooks.		
2d	"	Major W. D. Barnett.		
3d	"			
4th	"	Lt. Col. Mason.		
5th	"			
6th	"	Major D. G. White.		
7th	"	Major F. W. Desha.		
8th	"			
9th	"	Major John H. Kelley.		
10th	"	Lt. Col. R. Scott.		
11th	"	Major Trumbull.		
1st Seminole Indians	"	Lt. Col. Jumper.		
1st Florida	Regiment	Col. G. T. Maxwell.	Nov. 4, 1862.	
"	Cavalry	Col. W. G. M. Davis.	...1861.	
2d	"	Col. Carruway Smith.	Nov. 4, 1862.	Promoted Brigadier-General.

REGIMENTS, &c.—Continued.

No.	State	Command	Arm of Service	Commander	Date of Rank	Remarks
1st	Florida	Regiment	Infantry	Col. W. K. Beard	Nov. 22, 1862	
2d	"	"	"	Col. L. G. Pyles	1861	Promoted Brigadier-General.
3d	"	"	"	Col. E. A. Perry	July 25, 1861	
4th	"	"	"	Col. W. S. Dilworth	Sept. 2, 1862	
	"	"	"	Col. W. L. L. Bowen	1861	
5th	"	"	"	Col. J. P. Hunt	1861	
	"	"	"	Col. T. B. Lamar	July 6, 1863	
6th	"	"	"	Col. John G. Hately	1862	
7th	"	"	"	Col. J. J. Finley	Apl. 14, 1862	Promoted Brigadier-General.
8th	"	"	"	Col. Robert Bullock	June 2, 1863	
9th	"	"	"	Col. David Lang	Oct. 2, 1862	
	"	"	"	Col. R. B. Thomas		
1st	"	Battalion	"	Lt. Col. Holland		
	"	"	"	Lt. Col. E. H. Hopkins	1862	
	"	"	"	Lt. Col. Martin		
	"	Light Battery	Artillery	Captain Dunham		
	"	"	"	Captain Gamble		
	"	"	"	Captain Villipigue		
	"	"	"	Captain Abell		
1st	Georgia	Regiment	Cavalry	Col. J. J. Morrison	May 21, 1862	
	"	"	"	Col. C. A. Whaley	Nov. 2, 1862	
2d	"	"	"	Col. C. C. Crews	1862	Brigadier-General by brevet.
	"	"	"	Col. W. J. Lawton	1861	
3d	"	"	"	Col. A. E. Kennon	Mch. 13, 1863	
	"	"	"	Col. J. Thompson	1862	
4th	"	"	"	Col. M. J. Crawford	1861	Delegate to Confederate Congress at Montgomery.
	"	"	"	Col. Duncan L. Clinch	Jan. 16, 1863	
5th	"	"	"	Col. Isaac W. Avery	Jan. 20, 1863	Promoted Brigadier-General.
6th	"	"	"	Col. Robt. H. Anderson	Mch. 6, 1863	
7th	"	"	"	Col. John K. Hart		
8th	"	"	"	Col. E. C. Anderson, Jr.		
9th	"	"	"	Col. J. L. McAllister		
10th	"	"	"	Col. Taliaferro		
1st	"	"	Partisan Rangers	Col. A. A. Hunt	Feb. 6, 1862	
1st	"	"	Enlisted Men	Col. Wm. J. Magill		
	"	"	Infantry	Col. Chas. H. Olmstead	Dec. 26, 1861	

Regiment	Colonel	Date	Remarks
2d	Col. E. M. Burt	Apl. 25, 1862.	Promoted Major-General.
3d	Col. Edwl J. Walker	July 1, 1862.	Promoted Brigadier-General.
4th	Col. A. R. Wright	Nov. 1, 1862.	Promoted Brigadier-General.
	Col. Philip Cook	1862.	
5th	Col. George Doles	Dec. 31, 1862.	
6th	Col. Chas. P. Daniels	Sept. 17, 1862.	
	Col. J. T. Lofton	1862.	
7th	Col. A. H. Colquitt	Aug. 31, 1862.	Promoted Brigadier-General.
	Col. W. W. White	1862.	
8th	Col. W. T. Wilson	Dec. 16, 1862.	
	Col. John R. Towers	1862.	
9th	Col. L. M. Lamar	1862.	
	Col. John C. Mounger	July 23, 1862.	
10th	Col. J. B. Weems	Oct. 29, 1862.	
	Col. Alfred Cumming	Nov. 8, 1862.	Promoted Brigadier-General.
11th	Col. F. H. Little	1862.	
12th	Col. G. T. Anderson	Jan. 22, 1863.	Promoted Brigadier-General.
	Col. Ed. Wills	1862.	
13th	Col. Z. T. Conner	1862.	
	Col. Jas. M. Smith	1862.	
14th	Col. M. Douglass	1862.	
	Col. R. W. Folsom	Oct. 23, 1862.	
15th	Col. Felix Price	1862.	
	Col. Wm. M. McIntosh	Nch. 25, 1862.	
16th	Col. T. W. Thomas	1862.	
	Col. Goode Bryan	Feb. 15, 1862.	Promoted Brigadier-General.
17th	Col. H. C. Hedges	Jan. 17, 1863.	Promoted Brigadier-General.
	Col. H. L. Benning	1862.	
18th	Col. S. Z. Ruff	Jan. 17, 1862.	
	Col. W. T. Wofford	Jan. 12, 1862.	Promoted Brigadier-General.
19th	Col. Andrew J. Hutchins	1862.	
	Col. W. W. Boyd	May 29, 1862.	
20th	Col. John A. Jones	1862.	
	Col. J. B. Cumming	Sept. 27, 1861.	
21st	Col. John T. Mercer	Apl. 22, 1863.	
22d	Col. James Wasden	Sept. 17, 1862.	
	Col. R. H. Jones	1862.	
23d	Col. D. F. Best	1862.	
	Col. Thos. Hutchinson	Aug. 19, 1861.	
24th	Col. Robt. McMillen	Sept. 2, 1861.	
25th	Col. C. C. Wilson	May 8, 1862.	Promoted Brigadier-General.
26th	Col. W. H. Atkinson	1862.	
	Col. C. W. Styles	Sept. 17, 1862.	
27th	Col. C. T. Zachary	1862.	
	Col. L. B. Smith		
28th	Col. Tully Graybill	Nov. 3, 1862.	
	Col. T. J. Warthen		

6

REGIMENTS, &c.—CONTINUED.

No.	STATE.	COMMAND.	ARM OF SERVICE.	COMMANDER.	DATE OF RANK.	REMARKS.
29th	Georgia	Regiment	Infantry	Col. Wm. J. Young	May 10, 1862.	
30th	"	"	"	Col. Thos. W. Maughan	Dec. 16, 1862.	
31st	"	"	"	Col. David J. Bailey		Promoted Brigadier-General.
32d	"	"	"	Col. C. A. Evans	May 13, 1862.	Promoted Brigadier-General.
33d	"	"	"	Col. Geo. P. Harrison, Jr.	May 15, 1862.	
34th	"	"	"	Col. A. Littlefield		
	"	"	"	Col. J. A. W. Johnston	May 17, 1862.	
35th	"	"	"	Col. Bolling Holt	Nov. 1, 1862.	
	"	"	"	Col. E. L. Thomas		Promoted Brigadier-General.
36th	"	"	"	Col. Jesse A. Glen	Apl. 24, 1862.	
37th	"	"	"	Col. A. F. Rudler	May 6, 1863.	
38th	"	"	"	Col. J. D. Matthews	Dec. 13, 1862.	
	"	"	"	Col. Geo. W. Lee		
39th	"	"	"	Col. J. T. McConnell	Mch. 20, 1862.	
40th	"	"	"	Col. Abda Johnson		
41st	"	"	"	Col. Chas. A. McDaniel	Mch. 20, 1862.	
42d	"	"	"	Col. R. J. Henderson		
43d	"	"	"	Col. Skidmore Harris	Mch. 20, 1862.	
	"	"	"	Col. P. H. Colquitt		
44th	"	"	"	Col. Sam'l P. Lumpkin	May 26, 1862.	
	"	"	"	Col. Robt. A. Smith		
45th	"	"	"	Col. Thos. J. Simons	Oct. 13, 1862.	
	"	"	"	Col. T. Hardeman		
46th	"	"	"	Col. Peyton H. Colquitt	Mch. 17, 1862.	
47th	"	"	"	Col. G. W. Williams	May 12, 1862.	
48th	"	"	"	Col. Wm. Gibson	Mch. 12, 1862.	
49th	"	"	"	Col. S. T. Player	June 9, 1863.	
	"	"	"	Col. A. J. Lane		
50th	"	"	"	Col. F. Kearse	July 31, 1863.	
	"	"	"	Col. W. R. Manning		
51st	"	"	"	Col. E. Ball	May 2, 1863.	
	"	"	"	Col. W. M. Slaughter		
52d	"	"	"	Col. S. D. Phillips	Nov. 25, 1862.	
	"	"	"	Col. Wier Boyd		
53d	"	"	"	Col. Jas. P. Sims	Oct. 8, 1862.	
	"	"	"	Col. L. T. Doyal		
54th	"	"	"	Col. Charlton H. Way	May 16, 1862.	
55th	"	"	"	Col. C. B. Harkie	May 17, 1864.	

No.	State	Organization	Arm	Commander	Date	Remarks
56th			"	Col. E. P. Watkins	May 15, 1862.	See post; promoted Brigadier-General.
57th			"	Col. Wm. Barkuloo		See post.
58th			"	Col. Jack Brown	June 16, 1862.	
59th			"	Col. William H. Stiles	July 15, 1862.	
60th			"	Col. John H. Lamar		
61st			"	Col. J. R. Griffin	Aug. 1, 1862.	
62d			"	Col. George A. Gordon	Dec. 23, 1862.	
63d			"	Col. Jno. W. Evans	May 26, 1862.	
64th			"	Col. John S. Fain	Apl. 28, 1863.	
65th			"	Col. Thos. R. R. Cobb		
1st		Legion	"	Col. Wm. Phillips		
2d		Battalion	"	Lt. Col. Villipigue		
3d		"	"	Major Hardeman		
4th		"	"	Lt. Col. Stovall		
5th		"	"	Lt. Col. Stiles		
6th		"	"	Lt. Col. Lamar		
7th		"	Artillery	Lt. Col. Leyden		
8th		"	"	Major Rylander		
9th		"	"	Lt. Col. A. S. Cutts		
10th		"	"	Lt. Col. H. D. Capers		
11th		"	"	Maj. Geo. A. Gordon		
12th		"	"	Maj. J. T. Montgomery		
13th		"	Partisan Rangers	Maj. J. R. Griffin		
14th		"	"			
15th		"	"			
16th		"	Infantry	Maj. Wm. S. Basinger	May 10, 1863.	Known as "The Savannah Volunteer Guards."
17th		"	"			
18th		"	"			
19th		"	"	Lt. Col. Spaulding		
20th		"	Cavalry	Lt. Col. M. Cumming		
21st		"	"			
22d		"	"			
1st		"	"	Col. Thos. Woodward	Mch. 11, 1862.	
2d	Kentucky	Regiment	Infantry	Col. Ben. Hardin Helm		
2d		"	"	Col. John H. Morgan	Apl. 4, 1862.	Promoted Brigadier-General.
3d		"	"	Col. J. R. Butler	Sept. 2, 1862.	Promoted Brigadier-General.
4th		"	"	Col. H. L. Giltner	Oct. 5, 1862.	
5th		"	"	Col. D. Howard Smith	Sept. 2, 1862.	
6th		"	"	Col. J. Warren Grigsby	Sept. 1, 1862.	Promoted Brigadier-General.
7th		"	"	Col. R. N. Gano	Sept. 1, 1862.	Promoted Brigadier-General.
8th		"	"	Col. R. S. Clarke	Sept. 10, 1862.	
9th		"	"	Col. W. C. Breckinridge	Dec. 11, 1862.	
1st		"	Infantry	Col. Blanton Duncan		

[handwritten marginalia: "1512"]

REGIMENTS, &c.—CONTINUED.

No.	State.	Command.	Arm of Service.	Commander.	Date of Rank.	Remarks.
2d	Kentucky	Regiment	Infantry	Col. James W. Hewitt	Apl. 21, 1863.	Promoted Brigadier-General.
	"	"	"	Col. R. H. Hanson		
3d	"	"	"	Col. A. P. Thompson		
4th	"	"	"	Col. Joseph P. Kuckolds.	Feb. 29, 1863.	
	"	"	"	Col. Robt. P. Trabue	Nov. 14, 1862.	
5th	"	"	"	Col. Hiram Hawkins		
	"	"	"	Col. And. J. May		
6th	"	"	"	Col. Joseph H. Lewis	Jan. 14, 1862.	Promoted Brigadier-General.
7th	"	"	"	Col. Ed. Crossland		
8th	"	"	"	Col. H. B. Lyon	Feb. 3, 1862.	Promoted Brigadier-General.
9th	"	"	"	Col. J. W. Caldwell	Apl. 22, 1863.	
	"	"	"	Col. F. H. Hunt		
10th	"	"	"	Col. A. R. Johnson	Aug. 13, 1862.	
11th	"	"	Partisan Rangers.	Col. B. E. Caudill		
1st	"	Battalion	Cavalry	Maj. John Shawhan	May 4, 1861.	
1st	Louisiana	Regiment	Artillery	Col. John S. Scott	Aug. 14, 1861.	
1st	"	{ Crescent City } Regiment.	Infantry	Col. C. A. Fuller		
	"	Enlisted Men.	"	Col. M. J. Smith	May 31, 1862.	
	"		"	Col. Jas. Strawbridge	Feb. 16, 1863.	
1st	"	Regiment	"	Col. Dan'l W. Adams	June 16, 1862.	Promoted Brigadier-General.
	"	"	"	Col. A. R. Harrison		
2d	"	"	"	Col. J. M. Williams	June 6, 1862.	
3d	"	"	"	Col. W. M. Levy		
	"	"	"	Col. J. B. Gilmor	Nov. 5, 1862.	
4th	"	"	"	Col. A. C. Hunt'r	Mch. 29, 1863.	
	"	"	"	Col. R. J. Barrow		
5th	"	"	"	Col. Henry Forno	July 31, 1862.	
	"	"	"	Col. T. G. Hunt		
6th	"	"	"	Col. Wm. Monaghan	Nov. 7, 1862.	
	"	"	"	Col. J. G. Seymour		
7th	"	"	"	Col. David Penn	July 20, 1862.	Promoted Major-General.
	"	"	"	Col. Harry T. Hays	June 10, 1861.	
8th	"	"	"	Col. H. B. Kelley		
9th	"	"	"	Col. Leroy A. Staff rd.	Apl. 24 1862.	
10th	"	"	"	Col. Eugene Waggaman.	Oct. 1, 1862.	Promoted Brigadier-General.
	"	"	"	Col. M. Marigny		

				Date	Remarks
11th	"	"	Col. S. F. Marks........	Aug. 2, 1861.	Promoted Brigadier-General.
12th	"	"	Col. Thos. M. Scott......	Aug. 9, 1861.	Promoted Brigadier-General.
13th	"	"	Col. R. L. Gibson........	Sept. 16, 1861.	Promoted Brigadier-General.
14th	"	"	Col. Z. York............	Aug. 15, 1862.	Promoted Brigadier-General.
			Col. R. W. Jones........		
15th	"	"	Col. Edmund Pendleton...	Oct. 14, 1862.	Preston Pond
16th	"	"	Col. Dan'l Gober........	May 8, 1862.	
17th	"	"	Col. Robt. Richardson....	May 23, 1862.	
			Col. S. S. Heard.........		
18th	"	"	Col. L. L. Arnaud........	Sept. 26, 1862.	Promoted Brigadier-General.
			Col. A. Mouton..........		
19th	"	"	Col. W. P. Winans.......	July 17, 1862.	
20th	"	"	Col. B. L. Hodge........	July 7, 1862.	
			Col. Leon Van Zinken...		
			Col. Aug. Reichard......		
21st	"	"	Col. Isaac W. Patton....	May 15, 1862.	
			Col. M. L. Smith.........		
22d	"	"	Col. Edward Higgins.....	May 26, 1862.	
23d	"	"	Col. Charles H. Herrick..		
24th	"	"	Col. Paul E. Theard.....		
25th	"	"	Col. J. C. Lewis●........	Dec. 31, 1862.	Delegate to Provisional Congress at Montgomery.
26th	"	"	Col. Winchester Hall....	Nov. 25, 1862.	
			Col. Alex't DeClovet....		
27th	"	"	Col. Leon D. Marks......	Apl. 19, 1862.	
28th	"	"	Col. Henry Gray........	May 1, 1862.	
29th	"	"	Col. Allen Thomas.......	May 3, 1862.	Promoted Brigadier-General.
30th	"	"	Col. G. A. Breaux......	June 16, 1862.	
31st	"	"	Col. Chas. H. Morrison...		
32d	"	"	Col. J. C. D.unis........		
33d	"	"	Lt. Col. W. G. Vincent...	Sept. 1, 1862.	
1st	Partisan Rangers.	"	Lt. Col. J. B. Walton...		+
1st	Artillery......	"	Lt. Col. Leighton.......		
1st	Infantry.......	"	Lt. Col. Coppens........		
2d	Zouaves......	"	Major Wh..at..........		Afterwards changed to 15th regiment.
3d	Infantry......	"			
4th		"	Lt. Col. J. McEnery.....		
5th		"	Lt. Col. Kennedy.......		
6th		"	Lt. Col. C. H. Morrison..		

REGIMENTS, &c.—CONTINUED.

No.	State	Command	Arm of Service	Commander	Date of Rank	Remarks
1st	Maryland	Regiment	Infantry	Col. R. T. Johnson		Promoted Brigadier-General. It is believed that the State of Maryland gave to the military service of the Confederacy about fifteen thousand of her sons. They were not, however, organized into Maryland regiments, and becoming attached as individual soldiers to various commands, their services were necessarily credited to organizations from other States in which they enlisted from time to time, either singly or in squads.
1st	Mississippi	Wirt Adams' Regiment	Cavalry	Col. Wirt Adams	Oct. 15, 1861.	Promoted Brigadier-General.
1st	"	Regiment	"	Col. R. A. Pinson	June 10, 1862.	
2d	"	"	"	Col. Jas. Gordon		
3d	"	"	"	Col. Smith		
1st	"	"	Partisan Rangers	Col. W. C. Faulkner	Aug. 1, 1862.	
2d	"	"	Artillery	Col. J. G. Ballentine		
1st	"	"	Infantry	Col. W. T. Withers	May 14, 1862.	
1st	"	"	"	Col. J. M. Simonton	Sept. 10, 1861.	
2d	"	"	"	Col. J. N. Stone	Apl. 22, 1862.	
	"	"	"	Col. W. C. Faulkner		
3d	"	"	"	Col. T. A. Mellon	May 6, 1862.	
	"	"	"	Col. J. B. Deason		
4th	"	"	"	Col. T. W. Adair	July 16, 1863.	
	"	"	"	Col. Jos. Drake		
5th	"	"	"	Col. John Weer		
	"	"	"	Col. A. E. Fant		
6th	"	"	"	Col. Robert Lowry	May 23, 1862.	Promoted Brigadier-General.
	"	"	"	Col. J. C. Thornton		
7th	"	"	"	Col. W. H. Bishop		
	"	"	"	Col. E. J. Goode		
8th	"	"	"	Col. J. C. Wilkinson	May 7, 1862.	
9th	"	"	"	Col. F. E. Whitfield	Feb. 13, 1862.	Promoted Brigadier-General.
	"	"	"	Col. J. R. Chalmers		Promoted Brigadier-General.
10th	"	"	"	Col. James Barr	Feb. 27, 1863.	
	"	"	"	Col. R. A. Smith		
11th	"	"	"	Col. P. M. Green	Sept. 25, 1862.	
	"	"	"	Col. P. F. Liddell		

Regiment	Colonel	Date	Remarks
12th	Col. W. H. Taylor	Apl. 27, 1862	
	Col. Henry Hughes		
13th	Col. J. W. Carter	Aug. 10, 1862	
	Col. W. T. Barksdale		
14th	Col. George W. Abbott		
	Col. —— Baldwin		
15th	Col. M. Farrell		
	Col. W. S. Statln		
16th	Col. S. E. Baker	Nov. 1, 1862	Promoted Brigadier-General.
17th	Col. Carnot Posey	Apl. 26, 1862	Elected member of Confederate Congress.
	Col. W. D. Holder		Promoted Brigadier-General.
18th	Col. W. S. Featherston	Apl. 26, 1862	
	Col. T. M. Griffin	May 3, 1862	Promoted Brigadier-General.
19th	Col. N. H. Harris		
20th	Col. Chr. H. Mott		
	Col. D. R. Russell	Sept. 11, 1861	Promoted Brigadier-General.
21st	Col. Benj. G. Humphreys	Dec. 4, 1861	
22d	Col. Frank Schaller	Sept. 24, 1862	
23d	Col. J. M. Wells		
24th	Col. T. J. Davidson	Nov. 13, 1861	Promoted Brigadier-General.
25th	Col. W. F. Dowd	Jan. 1, 1863	Promoted Brigadier-General.
26th	Col. Thos. H. Mauum		
	Col. John D. Martin	Sept. 10, 1861	Promoted Brigadier-General.
27th	Col. A. E. Reynolds	Mch. 26, 1863	Promoted Brigadier-General.
	Col. J. A. Campbell		
	Col. Thos. M. Jones		
28th	Cavalry		
	Col. P. B. Starr e	Feb. 24, 1862	Promoted Brigadier-General.
29th	Infantry		
	Col. W. F. Brantly	Dec. 13, 1862	Promoted Brigadier-General.
	Col. E. C. Walthall	June 6, 1863	Promoted Major-General.
30th	Col. James J. Scales		
	Col. G. F. Neill		
31st	Col. J. A. Orr	Apl. 9, 1862	Member of Confederate Congress.
32d	Col. M. P. Lowry	Apl. 3, 1862	Promoted Brigadier-General.
33d	Col. —— Hardcastle	Apl. 19, 1862	
	Col. E. W. Hurst		
34th	Col. Sam'l Benton	Apl. 19, 1862	Promoted Brigadier-General.
35th	Col. W. S. Barry	Jan. 27, 1862	Promoted Brigadier-General.
36th	Col. W. W. Witherspoon	May 11, 1862	
	Col. D. J. Brown		
37th	Col. Orlando Holland	Oct. 4, 1862	
	Col. Rob't McLain		
38th	Col. F. W. Adams		
39th	Col. W. B. Shelby	May 13, 1862	
40th	Col. W. B. Colbert	May 14, 1862	
41st	Col. W. F. Tucker	May 8, 1862	
42d	Col. Hugh R. Miller	May 14, 1862	Promoted Brigadier-General.

REGIMENTS, &c.—CONTINUED.

No.	STATE.	COMMAND.	ARM OF SERVICE.	COMMANDER.	DATE OF RANK.	REMARKS.
43d	Mississippi	Regiment	Infantry	{ Col. Rich'd Harrison... { Col. W. H. Moore....	Nov. 9, 1862.	Promoted Brigadier-General.
44th	"	"	"	Col. A. B. Hardcastle...		
45th	"	"	"	Col. C. W. Sears....	Dec. 11, 1862.	Promoted Brigadier-General.
46th	"	"	"	Col. James Jordan....		
47th	"	"	"	Col. James M. Jayne..		
48th	"	"	"	Col. Jno. W. Balfour..	Jan. 17, 1863.	
49th	"	"	"	Lt. Col. Martin...		
1st	"	Jeff. Davis' Leg'n	Cavalry, &c.	Lt. Col. Wirt Adams...		Promoted Brigadier-General.
2d	"	Wirt Adams' "	"	Lt. Col. A. K. Blythe.		
1st	"	Battalion	"	Lt. Col. Taylor....		
2d	"	"	"	Maj. Hardcastle....		
3d	"	"	"	Lt. Col. Baskerville...		
4th	"	"	"	Maj. Kilpatrick....		
5th	"	"	Infantry			
6th	"	"	"			
7th	"	"	"			
1st	Missouri	Regiment	Cavalry	Lt. Col. Rosser....	Dec. 31, 1861.	
2d	"	"	"	Col. Elijah Gates....		
3d	"	"	"	Col. Robert McCulough.		
4th	"	"	"	Col. Colton Greene ...	Nov. 4, 1862.	Promoted Brigadier-General.
5th	"	"	"	Col. J. Q. Burbridge...	Nov. 13, 1862.	
6th	"	"	"	Col. B. F. Gordon....		
1st	"	"	Infantry	{ Col. G. W. Thompson... { Col. A. C. Riley.... { Col. Lucius L. Rich..	Aug. 9, 1862.	
2d	"	"	"	{ Col. Pembroke Senteny. { Col. J. V. Burbridge...		
3d	"	"	"	{ Col. W. R. Gause.... { Col. Benj. A. Rives....	Aug. 6, 1862.	
4th	"	"	"	Col. A. McFarlane...	Sept. 1, 1862.	
5th	"	"	"	Col. Jas. McCown....		
6th	"	"	"	Col. Eugene Irwin....		
7th	"	"	"	Col. Cyrus Franklin...		
8th	"	"	"	Col. Chas. S. Mitchell..	Aug. 18, 1862.	
9th	"	"	"	Col. John B. Clark, Jr..	June 28, 1862.	Promoted Brigadier-General.
10th	"	"	"	Col. A. C. Pirkett....		
11th	"	"	"	Col. S. C. Hunter....		
12th	"	"	"	Col. J. D. White....		

Regiment	State	Branch	Colonel	Date	Promotion
13th		"	Col. B. A. Rives		
14th		"	Col. S. Jackman		
15th		"	Col. Wm. Jeffers		
1st	North Carolina	"	Col. John A. McDowell	July 8, 1862.	
			Col. Hamilton A. Brown	Dec. 14, 1863.	Promoted Brigadier-General.
2d		"	Col. M. S. Stokes	Mch. 20, 1863.	
			Col. W. R. Cox		
3d		"	Col. C. C. Few	July 1, 1862.	Promoted Major-General.
			Col. W. L. DeRosset	Oct. 3, 1863.	Promoted Brigadier-General.
			Col. Stephen D. Thurston		
4th		"	Col. G. Mears		
			Col. Bryan Grimes	June 19, 1862.	
			Col. G. B. Anderson		
5th		"	Col. Thomas M. Garrett	Jan. 16, 1863.	
			Col. D. K. McRae		
6th		"	Col. Isaac E. Avery	June 3, 1862.	
			Col. Robert F. Webb	July 3, 1863.	Promoted Major-General.
7th		"	Col. W. D. Pender	July 27, 1862.	
			Col. Edward G. Haywood		
8th		"	Col. R. P. Campbell	May 16, 1861.	Promoted Brigadier-General.
			Col. H. M. Shaw	July 23, 1863.	
9th		Cavalry	Col. James B. Gordon	Oct. 17, 1863.	Promoted Major-General.
			Col. William H. Cheek		
10th		Artillery	Col. R. Ransom, Jr.	Aug. 20, 1861.	
			Col. J. A. J. Bradford	Sept. 7, 1863.	
11th		Infantry	Col. Stephen D. Pool	Oct. 26, 1861.	Promoted Brigadier-General.
			Col. Collett Leventhorpe		
12th		"	Col. Henry E. Coleman		
			Col. Sol. Williams	June 13, 1863.	
13th		"	Col. Joseph H. Hyman		Promoted Brigadier-General.
			Col. A. M. Scales		
14th		"	Col. R. T. Bennett		Promoted Brigadier-General.
			Col. W. P. Roberts	Feb. 27, 1861.	Promoted Brigadier-General.
15th		"	Col. Wm. McRae		
			Col. Henry A. Dowd		
16th		"	Col. John S. McElroy	June 1, 1862.	
			Lt. Col. Wm. A. Stowe	May 31, 1862.	
17th		"	Col. Stephen Lee		
			Col. Wm. F. Martin	July 27, 1861.	
18th		"	Col. John P. Barry	May 3, 1863.	
19th		Cavalry	Col. Robt. H. Cowan		
			Col. Wm. G. Robinson	Sept. 1, 1861.	
20th		Infantry	Col. Nelson Slough	Jan. 14, 1863.	Promoted Brigadier-General.
			Col. Thomas F. Toon	Feb. 26, 1863.	Promoted Brigadier-General.
21st		"	Col. Alf. Iverson, Jr.		Promoted Brigadier-General.
			Col. W. W. Kirkland	Apl. 21, 1863.	

REGIMENTS, &c.—CONTINUED.

No.	STATE.	COMMAND.	ARM OF SERVICE.	COMMANDER.	DATE OF RANK.	REMARKS.
22d	North Carolina	Regiment	Infantry	Col. James Connor	June 13, 1862	Acting Brigadier-General; elected Governor of North Carolina.
23d	"	"	"	Col. Thos. S. Galloway, Jr	Sept. 21, 1863	Promoted Brigadier-General.
	"	"	"	Col. Dan'l Chrisle	May 8, 1862	
24th	"	"	"	Col. John F. Hokes		Promoted Brigadier-General.
25th	"	"	"	Col. Wm. I. Clarke	July 18, 1861	Promoted Brigadier-General.
	"	"	"	Col. H. M. Rutlege	May 21, 1862	
26th	"	"	"	Col. Henry K. Burgwynn	Aug. 19, 1862	
	"	"	"	Col. John R. Lane	July 1, 1863	
27th	"	"	"	Col. Z. B. Vance		
	"	"	"	Col. John A. Gilmer, Jr.	Dec. 5, 1862	
28th	"	"	"	Col. John R. Cooke		
	"	"	"	Col. Sam'l D. Lowe	Nov. 1, 1862	
29th	"	"	"	Col. James H. Lane		
	"	"	"	Col. R. B. Vance	Apl. 24, 1861	
30th	"	"	"	Col. Wm. B. Creasman	Mch. 16, 1863	
31st	"	"	"	Col. Francis M. Parker	Oct. 2, 1861	
	"	"	"	Col. John V. Jordan	Sept. 19, 1861	
32d	"	"	"	Col. D. G. Coward	June 18, 1863	
33d	"	"	"	Col. Edmund C. Brabble	May 7, 1862	
	"	"	"	Col. Clark M. Avery	June 17, 1862	
34th	"	"	"	Col. Wm. L. J. Lowrance	Sept. 11, 1862	
	"	"	"	Col. Rich'd H. Riddick		
35th	"	"	"	Col. Jno. G. Jones	July 1, 1862	
	"	"	"	Col. M. W. Ransom		Promoted Brigadier-General.
36th	"	"	Artillery	Col. Wm. Lamb	May 14, 1862	
37th	"	"	Infantry	Col. Wm. M. Barbour	June 30, 1862	
	"	"	"	Col. Charles C. Lee		
38th	"	"	"	Col. Wm. J. Hoke	Jan. 17, 1862	
39th	"	"	"	Col. David Coleman	May 19, 1862	Acting Brigadier-General.
40th	"	"	Artillery	Col. John I. Hedrick	Dec. 1, 1863	
41st	"	"	Cavalry	Col. John A. Baker	Sept. 3, 1863	
42d	"	"	Infantry	Col. Geo. C. Gibbs	Apl. 22, 1862	Acting Brigadier-General.
43d	"	"	"	Col. Thos. S. Kenan	Apl. 21, 1862	
44th	"	"	"	Col. Thos. Singletary	June 28, 1862	
	"	"	"	Col. G. B. Singletary		
45th	"	"	"	Col. J. H. Morehead	Sept. 30, 1862	Promoted Brigadier-General.
	"	"	"	Col. Sam'l H. Boyd		
	"	"	"	Col. Junius Daniel	June 26, 1863	

No.	State	Service	Officer	Date	Notes
46th	"		Col. E. D. Hall	Apl. 4, 1862.	
47th	"		Col. Geo. H. Faribault	Jan. 5, 1863.	
48th	"		Col. S. H. Rogers	Apl. 9, 1862.	
			Col. Robt. C. Hall	Dec. 4, 1863.	
			Col. Sam'l H. Wakup		
49th	"		Col. —— Hill		
			Col. Lee M. McAfee	Nov. 1, 1862.	
50th	"		Col. S. D. Ramseur	Dec. 1, 1862.	Promoted Major-General.
			Col. Jas. A. Washington	Nov. 10, 1863.	
			Col. George Wortham		
51st	"		Col. M. D. Craton		
			Col. Hector McKethan	Jan. 19, 1863.	
			Col. J. L. Cantwell		
52d	"		Col. J. K. Marshall	Apl. 23, 1862.	
53d	"		Col. Wm. A. Owens	May 6, 1862.	
54th	"		Col. K. M. Murchison	May 8, 1862.	
55th	"		Col. Jno. K. Connally	May 19, 1862.	
56th	"		Col. Paul F. Faison	July 31, 1862.	
57th	"		Col. A. C. Godwin	July 17, 1862.	
58th	"	Partisan Rangers.	Col. Jno. B. Palmer	July 29, 1862.	Promoted Brigadier-General.
59th	"	Cavalry.	Col. Dennis D. Ferrebee	Aug. 16, 1862.	
60th	"	Infantry.	Col. W. M. Hardy	May 14, 1863.	
61st	"		Col. J. D. Radcliffe	Aug. 30, 1862.	
62d	"	Partisan Rangers.	Col. R. G. A. Love	July 11, 1862.	
			Lt. Col. Geo. W. Clayton	July 11, 1862.	
63d	"	Cavalry.	Col. Peter G. Evans	Oct. 6, 1862.	
			Lt. Col. Stephen B. Evans	Oct. 1, 1862.	
64th	"	Infantry.	Col. L. M. Allen	July 20, 1862.	
65th	"	Partisan Rangers.	Col. Geo. N. Folk	Aug. 3, 1863.	
66th	"		Col. A. D. Moore	Aug. 3, 1863.	
67th	"	Infantry.	Col. John N. Whitford	Jan. 18, 1864.	
1st	"		Col. James W. Hinton	July 8, 1863.	
1st	"	Heavy Artillery.	Lt. Col. Williams		
1st	"	Sharpshooters.	Maj. Alexander MacRae	Mch. 25, 1863.	
2d	"	Infantry.	Lt. Col. W. J. Green		
			Maj. Jno. M. Hancock	June 29, 1863.	
3d	"	Artillery.	Maj. J. W. Moore	Feb. 24, 1863.	
12th	"	Cavalry.	Adjutant Wm. A. Pugh	May 2, 1863.	
13th	"	Light Artillery.	Lt. Col. Joseph B. Starr	Dec. 1, 1863.	
{Thomas' Leg'n Inf't Reg't}	"	Infantry.	Col. Wm. H. Thomas	Sept. 27, 1862.	
{Thomas' Leg'n Battalion}			Lt. Col. Jas. A. McKamey	Jan. 3, 1864.	
14th Battalion	"	Cavalry.	Lt. Col. Jas. L. Henry	Dec. 25, 1863.	
15th	"		Lt. Col. Jas. M. Wynn	July 22, 1863.	
1st South Carolina Regiment			Col. John L. Black	June 25, 1862.	

REGIMENTS, &c.—CONTINUED.

No.	State	Command	Arm of Service	Commander	Date of Rank	Remarks
2d	South Carolina	Regiment	Cavalry	Col. M. C. Butler	Aug. 22, 1862	Promoted Major-General.
3d	"	"	"	Col. Thos. J. Lipscomb.	Aug. 19, 1862.	
4th	"	"	"	Col. C. I. Colcock.	Aug. 16, 1862.	
5th	"	"	"	Col. B. Huger Rutledge.	Dec. 16, 1862.	
6th	"	"	"	Col. S. W. Ferguson.		Promoted Brigadier-General.
7th	"	"	"	Col. John Dunnovant.	Nov. 1, 1862.	Promoted Brigadier-General.
	"	"	"	Col. H. K. Aiken.		
1st	"	"	Artillery	Col. A. C. Haskell.	Sept. 5, 1862.	
	"	"	"	Col. Alfred Rhett.		
2d	"	"	"	Col. Ransom D. Calhoun.	Oct. 17, 1862.	
3d	"	"	"	Col. A. D. Frederick.	Nov. 8, 1862.	
	"	"	"	Col. Wm. Butler.		
1st	"	"	Palmetto Sharps'rs	Col. Jno. W. Goss.	May 5, 1863.	
2d	"	"	Rifle	Col. F. E. Harrison.	Sept. 3, 1862.	
	"	"	"	Col. T. H. Burgs.	Dec. 14, 1861.	
	"	"	"	Col. D. H. Hamilton.		
1st	"	Reg.— 1st S.C.V.	Infantry	Col. Maxcy Gregg.		Promoted Brigadier-General.
	"		"	Col. C. W. McCreary.		
	"		"	Col. F. W. Kilpatrick.		
2d	"	1st S.C.V.	"	Col. Johnson Hagood.	Jan. 31, 1863.	Promoted Brigadier-General.
	"		"	Col. T. J. Glover.		
3d	"	2d S.C.V.	"	Col. Jas. Hagood.		
	"		"	Col. J. B. Kennedy.	May 13, 1862.	Promoted Major-General.
	"		"	Col. Wm. Wallace.		
4th	"	3d S.C.V.	"	Col. Jas. D. Nance.	May 14, 1862.	
5th	"	4th S.C.V.	"	Col. J. H. Williams.		
6th	"	5th S.C.V.	"	Col. J. R. R. Sloan.		
7th	"	6th S.C.V.	"	Col. A. Cowart.	Aug. 12, 1862.	
	"		"	Col. John Bratton.		
8th	"	7th S.C.V.	"	Col. Jas. H. Rion.		
	"		"	Col. D. Wyatt Aiken.	May 14, 1862.	Promoted Major-General.
9th	"	8th S.C.V.	"	Col. T. G. Bacon.		Promoted Brigadier-General.
	"		"	Col. John W. Hennegan.	May 14, 1862.	
10th	"	9th S.C.V.	"	Col. E. B. Cash.		
	"		"	Col. Jno. D. Blanding.	July 12, 1861.	

		Regiment	Colonel	Date	Note
11th	"	10th S.C.V.	Col. Jno. F. Pressley.....	Apl. 6, 1863.	Promoted Brigadier-General.
			Col. A. M. Manigault.....	Nov. 27, 1862.	
12th	"	11th S.C.V.	Col. F. H. Gantt..........	Feb. 27, 1863.	
			Col. Wm. C. Heyward......		
13th	"	12th S.C.V.	Col. Jno. L. Miller........		
			Col. R. G. M. Dunnovant		
			Col. Dixon Barnes........		
			Col. Cad. Jones..........		
14th	"	13th S.C.V.	Col. J. L. Miller..........		
			Col. E. L. Bookter........		
			Col. B. T. Brockman......		
			Col. O. E. Edwards.......		
			Col. J. F. Hunt..........		
15th	"	14th S.C.V.	Col. Abner Perrin........	Feb. 20, 1863.	Promoted Brigadier-General.
			Col. James Jones.........		
			Col. Sam'l McGowan......		Promoted Brigadier-General.
16th	"	15th S.C.V.	Col. J. N. Brown.........	Sept. 9, 1861.	
			Col. W. D. DeSaussure....		
17th	"	16th S.C.V.	Col. Jos. F. Gist.........		
			Col. W. McCutchen.......		
18th	"	17th S.C.V.	Col. Jas. McCullough.....	Apl. 29, 1862.	
			Col. C. J. Elford.........		
19th	"	18th S.C.V.	Col. Jno. H. Means.......	Dec. 19, 1861.	
			Col. F. W. McMaster.....		
20th	"	19th S.C.V.	Col. Wm. H. Wallace.....		Promoted Brigadier-General.
			Col. J. M. Gadberry......		
			Col. A. J. Lithgoe........		
			Col. W. C. Moraigne......		
21st	"	20th S.C.V.	Col. T. P. Shaw..........	Jan. 11, 1862.	
			Col. L. M. Keitt..........		
22d	"	21st S.C.V.	Col. S. M. Boykin........		
			Col. R. F. Graham........	May 5, 1862.	
23d	"	22d S.C.V.	Col. S. D. Goodlett.......		
			Col. Joseph Abney........		
			Col. O. M. Dantzler......		
24th	"	23d S.C.V.	Col. D. Fleming..........		
			Col. G. W. Bevet.........	Apl. 1, 1863.	
25th	"	24th S.C.V.	Col. H. L. Benbow........		
			Col. L. M. Hatch.........	Apl. 1, 1863.	Promoted Brigadier-General.
			Col. C. H. Stevens........		Promoted Brigadier-General.
26th	"	25th S.C.V.	Col. Ellison Capers.......		
27th	"	26th S.C.V.	Col. R. B. Smith.........		
28th	"	27th S.C.V.	Col. C. H. Simonton......	Aug. 14, 1862.	
			Col. A. D. Smith.........	Sept. 9, 1862.	
			Col. Peter C. Gaillard....		

REGIMENTS, &c.—CONTINUED.

No.	State	Command	Arm of Service	Commander	Date of Rank	Remarks.
29th	South Carolina	Reg. 1st Regulars	Infantry	Col. R. H. Anderson		Promoted Lieutenant-General.
	"			Col. John Dunnovant		Promoted Brigadier-General.
	"			Col. Wm. Butler		
30th	"	Regiment	Orr's 1st Rifles	Col. J. L. Orr		
	"			Col. J. W. Marshall		
	"			Col. J. M. Perrin		
	"			Col. F. E. Harrison		
	"			Col. G. W. D. Miller		
31st	"	"	" 2d "	Col. J. V. Moore		
32d	"	Hampton Legion	Afterw'ds mounted	Col. R. E. Bowen		Promoted Lieutenant-General.
	"			Col. Wade Hampton		Promoted Brigadier-General.
	"			Col. M. W. Gary		Promoted Brigadier-General.
	"			Col. T. M. Logan		
33d	"	Holcombe "	Infantry	Col. P. F. Stevens		Acting Brigadier-General.
	"			Col. W. P. Shingler		
	"			Col. —— Crawley		
34th	"	Regiment	Palmetto Sharpshooters	Col. M. Jenkins		Promoted Brigadier-General.
	"			Col. Jos. A. Walker		
1st	"	Battalion	Cavalry	Lt. Col. Black		
2d	"			Maj. Fender		
3d	"			Maj. J. P. Adams		
1st	"	Palmetto Battal'n	Artillery	Lt. Col. White		
2d	"	Battalion	Infantry	Lt. Col. Gaillard		
3d	"	"	"	Maj. W. Stokes		
4th	"	"	"	Lt. Col. G. S. Jones		
5th	"	"	"	Maj. Easley		
6th	"	"	"	Maj. J. V. Moore		
7th	"	"	"	Maj. Boyd		
8th	"	"	"	Maj. P. H. Nelson		
9th	"	"	"	Lt. Col. Colcock		
	"			Lt. Col. Smith		
1st	"	Lucas Battalion	Artillery	Maj. J. J. Lucas		
2d	"	Palmetto "	"	Maj. E. B. White		
	"	Manigault "		Maj. Edw'd Manigault		
	"	Palmetto Guards Battalion	"	Maj. S. D. Byrd		
	"		"	Maj. G. L. Buist		

No.			Regiment	Officer	Date	Remarks
	"	"	Washington	Capt. S. D. Lee		
	"	"	German (Bachman's)	Capt. J. F. Hart		
	"	"	German A.	Capt. — Halsey		
	"	"	" B.	Capt. W. K. Bachman		
	"	"	Regulars	Capt. Fred. Wagener		
				Capt. Franz Melchers		
				Capt. W. C. Preston, Jr.		
	"	"	McIntosh	Capt. McIntosh		
				Capt. Burnson		
				Capt. McIntosh		
	"	"	Marion	Capt. Edw'd L. Parker		
	"	"	Lafayette	Capt. J. T. Kanapaux		
	"	"	Washington, S.C.	Capt. Geo. H. Walter		
	"	"	Chesterfield	Capt. Cott		
	"	"	McBeth	Capt. R. Boyce		
				Capt. Wm. Munro		
	"	"	Wagner	Capt. C. E. Kanapaux		
	"	"	Ferguson	Capt. T. Ferguson		
	"	"	Waties	Capt. J. W. Waties		
	"	"	Beaufort	Capt. Stephen Elliott		
	"	"	Gist Guard	Capt. C. E. Chichester		
	"	"	Alston	Capt. Chas. Alston		
	"	"	Matthew	Capt. Bonneau		
	"	"	Ward	Capt. Josiah Ward		
	"	"	Garden	Capt. Hugh Garden		
	"	"	Stanley	Capt. Stanley		
	"	"	Gaillard	Capt. Gaillard		
1st	Tennessee	Cavalry	Regiment	Col. Jas. E. Carter	June 9, 1863.	
2d	"	"	"	Col. — Brazelton, Jr.		
3d	"	"	"	Col. H. M. Ashby	May 24, 1862.	
4th	"	"	"	Col. A. C. Kellup		
5th	"	"	"	Col. J. W. Starnes		
6th	"	"	"	Col. J. B. McLinn		
7th	"	"	"	Col. J. S. Wheeler		
8th	"	"	"	Col. J. G. Stockes		
9th	"	"	"	Col. Baxter Smith	Nov. 24, 1862.	
10th	"	"	"	Col. J. D. Bennett		
11th	"	"	"	Col. — Napier		
12th	"	"	"	Col. J. H. Edmundson	Feb. 14, 1863.	Promoted Brigadier-General.
1st	"	Infantry	"	Col. Rob't V. Richardson	May 8, 1861.	Promoted Brigadier-General.
1st	"	"	"	Col. P. Turney		
2d	"	"	"	Col. George Maney		
				Col. H. R. Field		
3d	"	"	"	Col. David Goodall		
				Col. N. J. Lillard		
3d	"	"	"	Col. John C. Brown		
				Col. C. H. Walker	Sept. 26, 1862.	Promoted Major-General.

REGIMENTS, &c.—Continued.

No.	STATE.	COMMAND.	ARM OF SERVICE.	COMMANDER.	DATE OF RANK.	REMARKS.
4th	Tennessee	Regiment	Infantry	Col. J. D. Henry		
5th	"	"	"	Col. H. P. Neely		
6th	"	"	"	Col. Wm. C. Snow	Dec. 7, 1862.	
				Col. W. E. Travis		
				Col. G. C. Porter	May 8, 1862.	
7th	"	"	"	Col. W. H. Stephens	May 8, 1863.	
				Col. J. A. Fite		
8th	"	"	"	Col. John H. Anderson		
				Col. A. S. Fulton		
9th	"	"	"	Col. C. S. Hurt	May 7, 1862.	
				Col. H. L. Douglass		
10th	"	"	"	Col. R. W. McCavock	Nov. 6, 1862.	
				Col. A. Heiman		
				Col. Wm. Thedford		
11th	"	"	"	Col. Jas. E. Raines		Promoted Brigadier-General.
12th	"	"	"	Col. R. M. Russell		Promoted Brigadier-General.
13th	"	"	"	Col. A. J. Vaughn		Promoted Brigadier-General.
14th	"	"	"	Col. Wm. McComb	Sept. 2, 1862.	
				Col. W. A. Forbes		
15th	"	"	"	Col. D. W. Carroll		
				Col. C. M. Carroll		
16th	"	"	"	Col. D. M. Donnell	Feb. 20, 1863.	
				Col. Jno. H. Savage		
17th	"	"	"	Col. T. W. Newman		
18th	"	"	"	Col. J. B. Palmer		Promoted Brigadier-General.
19th	"	"	"	Col. Francis M. Walker	May 8, 1862.	
20th	"	"	"	Col. J. B. Smith	May 8, 1862.	
				Col. Jael A. Barth		
				Edw'd Pickett, Jr.		
21st	"	"	"	Col. A. T. Robertson		
				Col. Thos. J. Freeman		
22d	"	"	"	Col. R. H. Keeble	Dec. 16, 1862.	
				Col. Matt. Martin		
23d	"	"	"	Col. J. A. Wilson	Jan. 4, 1863.	
				Col. R. D. Allison		
24th	"	"	"	Col. Jno. M. Hughes	July 21, 1862.	
25th	"	"	"	Col. S. S. Stanton		

	Col.		Promoted	
26th	Col. J. M. Lillard	Sept. 6, 1862.		
27th	Col. A. W. Caldwell	May 15, 1862.		
28th	Col. C. H. Williams			
29th	Col. J. P. Murray			
30th	Col. Sam'l Powell			
31st	Col. J. W. Head			
	Col. E. E. Tansill	May 8, 1862.		
32d	Col. W. M. Bratford			
33d	Col. E. C. Cook	May 8, 1862.		
	Col. W. P. Jones			
	Col. A. W. Campbell		Promoted Brigadier-General.	
34th	Col. Jas. A. McMurray			
35th	Col. W. M. Churchwell		Promoted Brigadier-General.	
36th	Col. R. J. Hill	Sept. 6, 1861.		
37th	Col. Alex'r K. Alley			
	Col. R. J. Morgan			
38th	Col. Moses White		Promoted Brigadier-General.	
	Col. Jno. C. Carter	May 10, 1862.		
39th	Col. R. F. Looney			
	Col. W. M. Bratford			
	Col. Alpheus Baker		Promoted Brigadier-General.	
40th	Col. L. M. Walker			
41st	Col. Robt. Farquhason	Nov. 27, 1861.		
42d	Col. W. A. Quarles		Promoted Brigadier-General.	
43d	Col. J. W. Gillespie			
44th	Col. Jno. S. Fulton	May 5, 1862.		
	Col. C. A. McDaniel			
45th	Col. A. Searey			
	Col. Addison Mitchell			
46th	Col. Jonathan Dawson	Sept. 30, 1862.		
47th	Col. John M. Clark			
54th	Col. M. R. Hill			
48th	Col. W. M. Voorhies			
49th	Col. G. H. Nixon			
	Col. D. A. Lyman			
	Col. Jas. E. Bailey	Jan. 26, 1862.		
50th	Col. C. A. Sugg			
51st	Col. R. M. Browder			
52d	Col. B. J. Lea			
53d	Col. J. R. White			
54th	Col. A. J. Abernathy			
55th	Col. Wm. Dearing	Sept. 25, 1862.		
	Col. A. J. Brown			
56th	Col. A. J. Brown			
57th	Col. — Morgan			
58th	Col. — Crews			

7

REGIMENTS, &c.—CONTINUED.

No.	State	Command	Arm of Service	Commander	Date of Rank	Remarks
59th	Tennessee	Regiment	Infantry	Col. W. L. Eakin	Mch. 19, 1863.	
60th	"	"	"	Col. Jno. H. Crawford	Sept. 15, 1862.	
61st	"	"	"	Col. F. E. Pitts		
62d	"	"	"	Col. Jno. A. Rowan		
63d	"	"	"	Col. R. G. Fain	July 31, 1862.	
154th	"	"	"	{ Col. A. Fitzgerald		
				{ Col. Preston Smith		Promoted Brigadier-General.
2d	"	"	"	Col. Turney		
3d	"	"	"	Col. W. B. Bate		Promoted Brigadier-General.
1st	"	Battalion	"	Col. Jno. C. Vaughan		Promoted Brigadier-General.
2d	"	"	Cavalry	Lt. Col. McNairy		
3d	"	"	"	Lt. Col. Bitle		Afterwards formed into a regiment [see 1st regiment cavalry].
4th	"	"	"	Lt. Col. Branner		
5th	"	"	"	Lt. Col. McClelland		
6th	"	"	"	Lt. Col. Logwood		
7th	"	"	"	Lt. Col. Bennett		
8th	"	"	"	Lt. Col. J. W. Starnes		
9th	"	"	"	Lt. Col. Gantt		
10th	"	"	"	Lt. Col. E. S. Smith		
11th	"	"	"	Lt. Col. Gordon		
1st	"	Regiment	Infantry	Maj. W. L. Eakin		Afterwards 59th regiment, Col. Cooke.
1st	Texas	"	Cavalry	Col. McCulloch		
2d	"	"	"	Col. E. L. Pyron	Oct. 8, 1862.	
3d	"	"	"	Col. John Pearil		
4th	"	"	"	Col. H. P. Mabry		Promoted Brigadier-General.
5th	"	"	"	Col. James Reilly		
6th	"	"	"	Col. Thos. Green		Promoted Brigadier-General.
				{ Col. L. S. Ross	May 24, 1862.	Promoted Brigadier-General.
7th	"	"	"	{ Col. R. Warren Stone		
				{ Col. A. P. Bagby		
				{ Col. Wm. Steele		Promoted Brigadier-General.
9th	"	"	"	{ Col. Thos. Harrison	Nov. 18, 1862.	
				{ Col. John A. Wharton		Promoted Major-General.
9th	"	"	"	{ Col. Nath'l Townes	May 24, 1862.	
				{ Col. W. H. Sims		

Regiment	Colonel	Date	Remarks
10th	{ Col. C. R. Earp	Mch. 20, 1863.	
	{ Col. M. F. Locke		
11th	Col. J. C. Burks		
12th	Col. W. H. Parsons	Oct. 23, 1861.	Acting Brigadier-General.
13th	{ Col. J. H. Burnett	Mch. 1, 1862.	
	{ Col. M. T. Johnson	May 8, 1862.	
14th	Col. Geo. H. Sweet	May 20, 1862.	
15th	Col. Wm. Fitzhugh		
16th	Col. Jas. R. Taylor	May 24, 1862.	
17th	{ Col. Geo. F. Moore		
	{ Col. Nicholas Darnell, Sr.	Mch. 15, 1862.	
18th	Col. N. H. Darnell, Jr.		
19th	Col. Nath'l M. Burford	Apl. 10, 1862.	
20th	Col. Thos. Coke Bass	Nch. 15, 1862.	
21st	Col. G. W. Carter	Mch. 8, 1862.	
22d	Col. Jas. G. Stevens		
23d	Col. N. C. Gould		
24th	Col. F. C. Wilkes		
25th	Col. C. C. Gillespie		
26th	Col. X. B. DeBray	Apl. 24, 1862.	
27th	Col. J. W. Whitfield	June 1, 1862.	Promoted Brigadier-General.
28th	Col. Horace Randall		Promoted Brigadier-General.
29th	Col. Chas. DeMorse		Promoted Brigadier-General.
30th	Col. E. J. Gurley	June 2, 1862.	
31st	Col. Julius Andrews		
32d	Col. A. T. Rainey	Jan. 2, 1862.	
1st	Col. N. L. McGinniss		
2d	Col. P. N. Luckett		
3d	Col. J. C. G. Key	July 10, 1862.	Promoted Brigadier-General.
4th	Col. John Marshall		
	{ Col. Jas. J. Archer	Nov. 1, 1862.	
5th	{ Col. R. M. Powell		
6th	Col. R. R. Garland	Sept. 3, 1861.	Promoted Brigadier-General.
7th	{ Col. H. B. Granberry	Aug. 29, 1861.	Promoted Brigadier-General.
	{ Col. John Gregg		Promoted Brigadier-General.
8th	Col. W. H. Young	May 13, 1862.	
9th	Col. E. B. Nichols		
10th	{ Col. Roger Q. Mills	Sept. 12, 1862.	Promoted Brigadier-General.
	{ Col. Allison Nelson	June 23, 1862.	
11th	Col. O. M. Roberts		
12th	Col. Overton Young		
13th	Col. J. Bates		
14th	Col. Edward Clark		
15th	Col. J. W. Speight	Apl. 16, 1862.	
16th	Col. George Flournoy		

Infantry.

REGIMENTS, &C.—CONTINUED.

No.	STATE.	COMMAND.	ARM OF SERVICE.	COMMANDER.	DATE OF RANK.	REMARKS.
17th	Texas	Regiment	Infantry	Col. R. T. P. Allen	June 9, 1862.	
18th	"	"	"	Col. David Culberson	Feb. 23, 1863.	
				Col. W. B. Ochiltree		
19th	"	"	"	Col. Rich'd Waterhouse	May 12, 1862.	Promoted Brigadier-General.
20th	"	"	"	Col. H. M. Elmore		
21st	"	"	"	Col. W. H. Griffin		
22d	"	"	"	Col. R. B. Hubbard		
1st	"	Battalion	Cavalry	Lt. Col. R. P. Crump		
2d	"	"	"	Maj. W. O. Yager		
3d	"	Squadron	"	Maj. Whitfield		
4th	"	Battalion	"	Capt. R. M. Gans		
1st	"	Battalion	Infantry	Lt. Col. J. W. Speight		
2d	"	"	"	Maj. J. F. Kirby		
3d	"	"	"	Mnj. Oswald		
4th	"	"	"	Lt. Col. Hubbard		
5th	"	"	"			
1st	Virginia	Regiment	Cavalry	Col. Jas. H. Drake	Oct. 2, 1862.	
				Col. Fitzhugh Lee		Promoted Major-General.
2d	"	"	"	Col. Thos. T. Munford	Apl. 25, 1862.	Promoted Brigadier-General.
3d	"	"	"	Col. Thos. H. Owens	Nov. 18, 1862.	
				Col. R. Johnston		
4th	"	"	"	Col. W. C. Wickham	June 9, 1862.	Promoted Brigadier-General.
5th	"	"	"	Col. G. H. Robertson		
6th	"	"	"	Col. Thos. L. Rosser	June 24, 1862.	Promoted Major-General.
				Col. Jno. S. Green	Oct. 15, 1862.	
7th	"	"	"	Col. R. H. Dulany		
				Col. A. McDonald		
8th	"	"	"	Col. Jas. M. Corns	May 15, 1862.	
				Col. W. H. Jenifer		
9th	"	"	"	Col. R. L. T. Beale		Promoted Brigadier-General.
				Col. J. F. Johnston		
10th	"	"	"	Col. J. Lucius Davis	June 24, 1862.	
11th	"	"	"	Col. O. R. Funsten		
12th	"	"	"	Col. A. W. Harman	June 20, 1862.	
13th	"	"	"	Col. Jno. R. Chambliss	July 13, 1861.	Promoted Brigadier-General.

Regiment		Colonel	Date	Remarks
14th	"	Col. Jas. Cochran	Feb. 12, 1863.	
15th	"	Col. Wm. B. Ball	Sept. 11, 1862.	
16th	"	Col. Milton J. Ferguson	Jan. 15, 1863.	
17th	"	Col. Wm. H. French	Jan. 28, 1863.	
18th	"	Col. G. W. Imboden	Dec. 15, 1862.	
19th	"	Col. W. L. Jackson	Apl. 11, 1863.	Promoted Brigadier-General.
1st	Infantry	Col. Fred'k G. Skinner; Col. Lewis B. Williams	Sept. 16, 1862.	Promoted Brigadier-General.
2d	"	Col. J. N. Adenbousch; Col. J. W. Allen		
3d	"	Col. Roger A. Pryor; Col. Jos. Mayo, Jr.	Apl. 27, 1862.	Promoted Brigadier-General.
4th	"	Col. Chas. A. Ronald	Apl. 22, 1862.	Promoted Brigadier-General.
5th	"	Col. Wm. Terry; Col. J. H. S. Funk; Col. W. H. Harman; Col. W. S. H. Baylor	Aug. 29, 1862.	Killed at Second Manassas.
6th	"	Col. Geo. T. Rogers; Col. J. T. Corprew	May 8, 1862.	
7th	"	Col. J. L. Kemper; Col. W. T. Patton; Col. C. C. Flowerree		Promoted Major-General.
8th	"	Col. Eppa Hunton	June 3, 1862.	Promoted Brigadier-General.
9th	"	Col. J. C. Owens; Col. D. J. Godwin		
10th	"	Col. E. T. H. Warren; Col. S. B. Gibbons	May 8, 1862.	Elected member of Confederate Congress.
11th	"	Col. S. Garland, Jr.		Promoted Brigadier-General.
12th	"	Col. David A. Weisiger		Promoted Brigadier-General.
13th	"	Col. Jas. E. B. Terrill; Col. A. P. Hill		Promoted Brigadier-General. / Promoted Lieutenant-General.
14th	"	Col. Jas. A. Walker; Col. G. A. Goodman	July 1, 1861.	Promoted Brigadier-General.
15th	"	Col. Jas. G. Hodges; Col. W. W. White		
16th	"	Col. Thos. P. August; Col. —— Morrison	July 1, 1861.	Promoted Brigadier-General.
17th	"	Col. Jos. H. Ham; Col. H. T. Parrish	Aug. 30, 1862.	
18th	"	Col. M. D. Corse; Col. Morton Marye		Promoted Brigadier-General.
19th	"	Col. R. E. Withers; Col. Henry Gantt		
20th	"	Col. J. B. Strange		Disbanded.

REGIMENTS, &c.—CONTINUED.

No.	STATE.	COMMAND.	ARM OF SERVICE.	COMMANDER.	DATE OF RANK.	REMARKS.
21st	Virginia	Regiment	Infantry	Col. W. A. Witcher	Dec. 1, 1862.	
22d	"	"	"	Col. John M. Patton	Nov. 3, 1861.	
23d	"	"	"	Col. Geo. S. Patton	Apl. 15, 1862.	Promoted Brigadier-General, Major-General and Lieutenant-General.
24th	"	"	"	Col. Jubal A. Early	May 2, 1861.	Promoted Brigadier-General.
25th	"	"	"	Col. W. R. Terry	Sept. 21, 1861.	
	"	"	"	Col. Richard L. Maury	May 31, 1864.	
26th	"	"	"	Col. J. C. Higginbotan	Jan. 28, 1863.	
	"	"	"	Col. Geo. H. Smith		
27th	"	"	"	Col. P. R. Page	May 13, 1862.	
28th	"	"	"	Col. C. A. Crump		
29th	"	"	"	Col. Jas. K. Edmondson	Nov. 19, 1862.	Promoted Brigadier-General.
	"	"	"	Col. John Echols	Apl. 29, 1862.	
	"	"	"	Col. R. C. Allen	Apl. 10, 1863.	
30th	"	"	"	Col. James Giles		
31st	"	"	"	Col. A. C. Moore	Apl. 18, 1862.	The 30th Virginia regiment (mounted) was the first and only mounted regiment which the State of Virginia organized up to the Battle of First Manassas. It was commanded by Col. R. C. W. Radford.
32d	"	"	"	Col. A. T. Harrison	May 1, 1862.	
33d	"	"	"	Col. Jno. S. Hoffman	May 21, 1862.	
	"	"	"	Col. E. B. Montague	Feb. 1, 1863.	
34th	"	"	"	Col. F. W. Holliday		
35th	"	"	"	Col. A. C. Cummings		
36th	"	"	"	Col. J. H. Ware		
37th	"	"	"	Col. Jno. McCausland	July 16, 1861.	Promoted Brigadier-General.
	"	"	"	Col. T. V. Williams	June 20, 1862.	
38th	"	"	"	Col. — Faulkerson		
39th	"	"	"	Col. E. C. Edmonds	July 1, 1861.	Disbanded.
40th	"	"	"	Col. J. M. Brockenboro'	July 1, 1861.	
41st	"	"	"	Col. Wm. Allen Parham	July 29, 1862.	Promoted Brigadier-General.
42d	"	"	"	Col. J. R. Chambliss		
43d	"	"	"	Col. R. W. Withers	Feb. 24, 1863.	
44th	"	"	"	Col. Jesse Burks		Disbanded,
	"	"	"	Col. J. S. Hubbard		
	"	"	"	Col. W. C. Scott		

Regiment	Colonel	Date	Remarks
45th	Col. Wm. H. Browne	May 14, 1862	
46th	Col. W. E. Peters		
47th	Col. R. T. W. Duke	May 24, 1862	
47th	Col. Rob't M. Mayo		
48th	Col. G. W. Richardson	Oct. 16, 1862	
48th	Col. Thos. S. Garnett		
49th	Col. John A. Campbell		
49th	Col. J. Cattlett Gibson		
50th	Col. Wm. Smith	Jan. 30, 1863	Promoted Brigadier-General.
50th	Col. A. S. Vandeventer		
51st	Col. A. W. Reynolds		Promoted Brigadier-General.
51st	Col. Gabriel C. Wharton	June 6, 1863	Promoted Brigadier-General.
52d	Col. Jas. H. Skinner		
52d	Col. M. T. Harman		
53d	Col. John B. Baldwin	Mch. 5, 1863	Elected member of Confederate Congress.
53d	Col. W. R. Aylett		
54th	Col. H. B. Tomlin		
54th	Col. Robt. C. Trigg	May 2, 1863	
55th	Col. W. S. Christian		
56th	Col. Francis Mallory		
57th	Col. W. D. Stuart		
57th	Col. J. B. Magruder	Jan. 12, 1863	
58th	Col. Geo. W. Carr		
58th	Col. J. H. Board	Oct. 30, 1862	
59th	Col. Sam'l H. Letcher		
59th	Col. Wm. B. Tabb		
60th	Col. —— Henningsen		
60th	Col. B. H. Jones	Aug. 6, 1862	
61st	Col. Wm. E. Starke		
61st	Col. V. D. Groner	Oct. 18, 1862	Partisan Rangers.
62d	Col. Geo. H. Smith		Infantry.
63d	Col. J. J. McMahon	May 24, 1862	
64th	Col. Campbell Slemp	Dec. 14, 1862	
1st	Col. J. Thompson Brown		Artillery.
2d	Col. R. Tansill		
3d	Col. Jno. C. Porter		
4th	Col. J. Thomas Goode		
1st	Major Munford		Enlisted Men. Battalion
2d			
3d			
4th	Lt. Col. Nat. Tyler		Artillery.
5th	Major W. R. Foster		
6th			
7th	Lt. Col. S. M. Wilson		Artillery.
8th	Major Dufficld		
9th	Lt. Col. Hansborough		Transferred to 5th Virginia Cavalry.

REGIMENTS, &c.—CONTINUED.

No.	STATE.	COMMAND.	ARM OF SERVICE.	COMMANDER.	DATE OF RANK.	REMARKS.
10th	Virginia	Battalion	Artillery	Major W. O. Allen		
11th	"	"	Cavalry	Major B. F. Bradley		
12th	"	"	Artillery	Major F. J. Boggs		
13th	"	"	"	Major J. Floyd King		
14th	"	"	Cavalry	Major E. Burroughs		
16th	"	"	"	Major John Critcher		

CONFEDERATE REGIMENTS.

No.	CONFEDERATE.	COMMAND.	ARM OF SERVICE.	COMMANDER.	DATE OF RANK.	REMARKS.
1st	Confederate	Regiment	Infantry	Col. George A. Smith	....	Promoted Brigadier-General.
2d	"	"	"	Col. Thos. H. Mangum	....	
3d	"	"	"	Col. Jas. B. Johnson	....	
4th	"	"	"		....	
5th	"	"	"	Col. C. C. Henderson	Mch. 11, 1863.	
6th	"	"	Partisan Rangers	Col. W. C. Claiborne	May 10, 1862.	Promoted Brigadier-General.
7th	"	"	Cavalry	Col. W. B. Wade	June 15, 1862.	
8th	"	"	Infantry	Col. J. Smith	....	
9th	"	"	Cavalry	Col. C. T. Goode	Dec. 14, 1862.	
10th	"	"	"	Col. Jas. Howard	....	
11th	"	"	"	Col. Jno. T. Cox	May 12, 1862.	
12th	"	"	"	Col. W. N. Estes	....	
13th	"	"	"	Col. F. Dumontell	....	
14th	"	"	"			

LEGIONS IN CONFEDERATE SERVICE.

No.	NAME.	STATE.	ORGANIZATION.	COMMANDER.	DATE OF RANK.	REMARKS.
1st	Hilliard's	Alabama	Legion	Col. Jack Thorlngton	Dec. 1, 1862.	Promoted Brigadier-General.
2d	Clanton's	"	"	Col. J. H. Clanton	....	
3d	Cobb's	Georgia	"	Col. P. M. B. Young	Nov. 1, 1862.	Promoted Major-General.
4th	Phillips'	"	"	Col. E. S. Barkly	Feb. 13, 1863.	
5th	Miles'	Louisiana	"	Col. Wm. R. Miles	....	
6th	Jeff. Davis'	Mississippi	"	Col. J. F. Waring	Dec. 2, 1862.	
7th	Thomas'	North Carolina	"	Col. Wm. H. Thomas	....	
8th	Hampton's	South Carolina	"	Col. W. W. Gary	Aug. 25, 1862.	Promoted Brigadier-General.
9th	Holcombe's	"	"	Col. W. P. Shingler	Oct. 8, 1862.	Promoted Brigadier-General by brevet.
10th	Waul's	Texas	"	Col. T. N. Waul	May 17, 1862.	Promoted Brigadier-General.

COMMISSIONED AND WARRANT OFFICERS OF THE

RANK.	NAME.	STATE WHERE BORN.	STATE FROM WHICH APPOINTED.
Admiral	Franklin Buchanan	Maryland	Maryland
Captain	Lawrence Rousseau	Louisiana	Louisiana
"	French Forrest	Virginia	Virginia
"	Josiah Tattnall	Georgia	Georgia
"	V. M. Randolph	Virginia	Alabama
"	George N. Hollins	Maryland	Maryland
"	D. N. Ingraham	South Carolina	South Carolina
"	Samuel Barron	Virginia	Virginia
"	William F. Lynch	"	"
"	Isaac S. Sterett	Maryland	Maryland
"	S. S. Lee	Virginia	Virginia
"	William C. Whittle	"	"
"	Raphael Semmes	Maryland	Alabama
Captain in Pro. Navy	William W. Hunter	Pennsylvania	Louisiana
" "	E. Farrand	New York	Florida
"	John R. Tucker	D. C.	Virginia
Commander	S. S. Lee	Virginia	"
"	William C. Whittle	"	"
"	Robert D. Thorburn	"	"
"	Robert G. Robb	"	"
"	W. W. Hunter	Pennsylvania	Louisiana
"	Murray Mason	Virginia	Virginia
"	E. Farrand	New York	Florida
"	C. H. McBlair	Maryland	Maryland
"	A. B. Fairfax	Virginia	Virginia
"	Richard L. Page	"	"
"	Frederick Chatard	Maryland	Maryland
"	Arthur Sinclair	Virginia	Virginia
"	C. H. Kennedy	"	North Carolina
"	Thomas W. Brent	D. C.	Florida
"	John K. Mitchell	North Carolina	"
"	Matthew F. Maury	Virginia	Virginia
"	John R. Tucker	D. C.	"
"	Thomas Jeff. Page	Virginia	"
"	George Minor	"	"
"	R. F. Pinckney	Maryland	Maryland
"	Thomas R. Rootes	Virginia	Virginia
"	H. J. Hartstene	South Carolina	South Carolina
"	James L. Henderson	Virginia	Virginia
"	William T. Muse	North Carolina	North Carolina
"	Thomas T. Hunter	Virginia	Virginia
"	James W. Cooke	North Carolina	North Carolina
"	C. F. M. Spotswood	Virginia	Virginia
"	Isaac N. Brown	Kentucky	Mississippi
"	William L. Maury	Virginia	Virginia
"	John N. Maffit	Ireland	North Carolina
"	Joseph N. Barney	Maryland	Maryland
"	C. Ap. R. Jones	Virginia	Virginia
"	J. Taylor Wood	N. W. T.	Louisiana
Com'r for the War	James D. Bullock	Georgia	Georgia
" "	James H. North	South Carolina	South Carolina
" "	Robert B. Pegram	Virginia	Virginia
" "	John M. Brooke	Florida	Florida
" "	William A. Webb	Virginia	Virginia
Com'r in Pro. Navy	George T. Sinclair	"	"
" "	William T. Glassell	"	Alabama

First Lieutenants	77	Assistant Surgeons for the War	11
First Lieutenants Provisional Navy	2	Paymasters	12
Second Lieutenants	22	Assistant Paymasters	25
Lieutenants for the War	46	Masters in the line of promotion	16
Surgeons	22	Masters not in the line of promotion	46
Passed Assistant Surgeons	10	Passed Midshipmen	11
Assistant Surgeons	30	Midshipmen, Third Class, Senior	36

NAVY OF THE COFEDERATE STATES JANUARY 1, 1864.

ORIGINAL ENTRY INTO SERVICE OF C. S. N.	DATE OF PRESENT COMMISSION.	DATE OF PRESENT RANK.	PRESENT DUTY.
Sept. 5, 1861.	Aug. 21, 1862.	Aug. 21, 1862.	Commanding at Mobile.
Mch. 26, 1861.	Oct. 23, 1862.	Mch. 26, 1861.	Waiting orders.
June 10, 1861.	" "	" "	Commanding James River squadron.
Mch. 26, 1861.	" "	" "	Commanding naval station at Savannah.
" "	" "	" "	Waiting orders.
June 22, 1861.	" "	" "	
Mch. 26, 1861.	" "	" "	Commanding naval station at Charleston.
June 10, 1861.	" "	" "	Abroad.
" "	" "	" "	Commanding naval defences of North Carolina.
" "	" "	" "	Waiting orders.
" 11, 1861.	" "	Feb. 8, 1862.	Commanding at Drewry's Bluff.
" "	" "	" "	Waiting orders.
Mch. 26, 1861.	Aug. 25, 1862.	Aug. 21, 1862.	Commanding Confederate steamer Alabama.
June 6, 1861.	Jan. 7, 1864.	May 13, 1863.	Commanding naval squadron at Savannah.
Mch. 26, 1861.	" "	" "	Special service.
June 10. 1861.	" "	" "	Commanding naval squadron at Charleston.
" 11, 1861.	June 21, 1861.	Mch. 26, 1861.	Commanding at Drewry's Bluff.
" "	" "	" "	Waiting orders.
" 15, 1861.	Oct. 23, 1862.	" "	Naval station, Savannah.
" 10, 1861.	" "	" "	Commanding navy yard, Rocketts.
" 6, 1861.	June 6, 1861.	" "	Commanding squadron, Savannah.
" 10, 1861.	Oct. 23, 1862.	" "	Naval rendezvous, Richmond.
Mch. 26, 1861.	June 6, 1861.	" "	Special service.
Oct. 19, 1861.	Oct. 23, 1862.	" "	Commanding Confederate steamer Tuskaluza.
June 10, 1861.	" "	" "	Special service.
" "	" "	" "	Commanding naval station, Charlotte, N. C.
" 15, 1861.	" "	" "	Naval battery, Drewry's Bluff.
" 10, 1861.	" "	" "	Special service.
" 25, 1861.	" "	" "	Recruiting service, Macon, Georgia.
" 26, 1861.	" "	" "	Naval squadron, Mobile.
Nov. 11, 1861.	" "	" "	Office of Orders and Detail.
June 10, 1861.	" "	" "	Special service.
" "	June 6, 1861.	" "	Commanding squadron, Charleston.
" "	Oct. 23, 1862.	" "	Special service.
" "	" "	" "	Waiting orders.
" 24, 1861.	" "	" "	Commanding Confederate steamer Savannah.
" 10, 1861.	" "	" "	Special orders.
Mch. 26, 1861.	" "	" "	Waiting orders.
June 10, 1861.	" "	" "	Army duty.
" 24, 1861.	" "	" "	Commanding steamer North Carolina.
" 10, 1861.	" "	" "	Commanding steamer Chicora.
" 11, 1861.	July 15, 1862.	July 15, 1862.	Commanding steamer Albemarle.
" 10, 1861.	Feb. 13, 1863.	Aug. 25, 1862.	Recruiting service, Raleigh.
" 6, 1861.	Aug. 25, 1862.	" "	Commanding steamer Charleston.
" 10, 1861.	Feb 17, 1863.	Feb. 17, 1863.	Commanding steamer Georgia.
May 8, 1861.	Apl. 29, 1863.	Apl. 29, 1863.	Waiting orders.
July 2, 1861.	" "	" "	Commanding steamer Florida.
June 10, 1861.	" "	" "	Naval ordnance works, Selma, Ala.
Oct. 4, 1861.	Sept. 21, 1863.	Aug. 23, 1863.	Aid to the President.
Jan. 17, 1862.	Oct. 23, 1862.	Jan. 17, 1862.	Special service.
Mch. 26, 1861.	" "	May 6, 1862.	" "
June 10, 1861.	" "	Sept. 13, 1862.	Commanding steamer Richmond.
May 2, 1861.	" "	" "	Office Ordnance and Hydrography.
June 10, 1861.	Apl. 29, 1863.	Apl. 29, 1863.	Prisoner.
Apl. 20, 1861.	May 14, 1863.	May 14, 1863.	Special duty.
Aug. 5, 1862.	Jan. 7, 1864.	Oct. 5, 1863.	Prisoner.

Midshipmen, Third Class, Junior	22	Third Assistant Engineers	46
Midshipmen abroad	18	Boatswains	13
Engineer in Chief	1	Gunners	26
Chief Engineers	9	Carpenters	4
Engineer in Chief, Provisional Navy	1	Sail Makers	5
First Assistant Engineers	24	Naval Constructors	3
Second Assistant Engineers	27	Acting Master's Mates	15

LIST OF OFFICERS OF THE CONFEDERATE

RANK.	NAME.	STATE WHERE BORN.
Colonel Commandant	Lloyd J. Beall	U. S. Fort
Lieutenant-Colonel	Henry B. Tyler	Virginia
Major	George H. Ferrett	"
Paymaster, with the rank of Major	Richard T. Allison	Kentucky
Adjutant, with rank of Major	Israel Greene	New York
Quartermaster, with the rank of Major	A. S. Taylor	Virginia
Captain	John D. Simms	"
"	J. R. F. Tattnall	Connecticut
"	Andrew J. Hays	Alabama
"	George Holmes	Maine
"	R. T. Thom	Virginia
"	A. C. Van Benthuysen	Louisiana
"	J. E. Meiere	Connecticut
"	Thomas S. Wilson	Tennessee
First Lieutenant	C. L. Sayre	Alabama
"	B. K. Howell	Mississippi
"	K. H. Henderson	D. C.
"	David G. Raney	Florida
"	J. R. Y. Fendall	D. C.
"	T. P. Gwynn	Wisconsin
"	James Thurston	South Carolina
"	F. H. Cameron	North Carolina
"	Fergus MacRee	Florida
Second Lieutenant	David Bradford	Louisiana
"	N. E. Venable	Virginia
"	H. L. Graves	Georgia
"	Henry M. Doak	Tennessee
"	Albert S. Berry	Kentucky
"	E. F. Neufville	Georgia
"	Daniel G. Brent	D. C.
"	J. O. Murdoch	Maryland
"	S. M. Roberts	Pennsylvania
"	John L. Rapier	Louisiana

STATES MARINE CORPS, JANUARY 1, 1864.

State From Which Appointed.	Date of Entry into C. S. Marine Corps.	Date of Commission.	Present Duty.
Maryland..........	May 23, 1861.	May 23, 1861.	Headquarters.
Virginia...........	June 18, 1861.	June 18, 1861.	
"	" 20, 1861.	" 20, 1861.	Drewry's Bluff.
Maryland..........	May 10, 1861.	May 10, 1861.	Richmond, Virginia.
Virginia...........	June 19, 1861.	June 19, 1861.	Headquarters.
"	Dec. 3, 1861.	Dec. 4, 1861.	Richmond, Virginia.
"	July 15, 1861.	July 15, 1861.	Drewry's Bluff.
Georgia	Jan. 22, 1862.	Jan. 22, 1862.	Savannah, Georgia.
Alabama...........	Mch. 29, 1861.	Mch. 29, 1861.	With Army of Tennessee.
Florida	" 29, 1861.	" 29, 1861.	Drewry's Bluff.
Alabama......	" 25, 1861.	" 25, 1861.	With Army at Mobile.
Louisiana..........	" 30, 1861.	" 30, 1861.	
Maryland..........	May 8, 1861.	Dec. 5, 1861.	Mobile, Alabama.
Missouri	Jan. 24, 1862.	Oct. 10, 1862.	Drewry's Bluff.
Alabama...........	Mch. 29, 1861.	Mch. 29, 1861.	With Army at Mobile.
Louisiana..........	" "	" "	Steamer Alabama.
Virginia...........	Apl. 16, 1861.	Apl. 16, 1861.	Drewry's Bluff.
Florida	" 22, 1861.	Nov. 22, 1861.	Mobile, Alabama.
Mississippi........	June 15, 1861.	Dec. 5, 1861.	Mobile, Alabama.
Virginia...........	Sept. 20, 1861.	Feb. 15, 1862.	Drewry's Bluff.
South Carolina.....	" "	July 4, 1862.	Prisoner of War.
North Carolina.....	" "	Oct. 10, 1862.	Drewry's Bluff.
Missouri	Oct. 9, 1861.	" "	Drewry's Bluff.
Mississippi........	Nov. 22, 1861.	Nov. 22, 1861.	Navy Yard, Richmond.
Texas.............	Oct. 24, 1862.	Oct. 24, 1862.	Richmond, Virginia.
Georgia...........	" "	" "	Steamer Savannah.
Tennessee	Nov. 12, 1862.	Nov. 12, 1862.	Savannah, Georgia.
Kentucky..........	Mch. 6, 1863.	Mch. 6, 1863.	Steamer Charleston.
Georgia...........	" 6, 1863.	" 6, 1863.	Savannah, Georgia.
Florida	" 30, 1863.	" 30, 1863.	Savannah, Georgia.
Maryland..........	Apl. 8, 1863.	Apl. 8, 1863.	Steamer Richmond.
Louisiana..........	" "	" "	Schooner Gallego.
"	July 11, 1863.	July 11, 1863.	Drewry's Bluff.

ORGANIZATION OF THE CONFEDERATE STATES FORCES STATIONED NEAR TUPELO, MISS., JUNE 30, 1862.

COMMANDED BY GENERAL BRAXTON BRAGG.

ARMY OF THE MISSISSIPPI.

FIRST CORPS—MAJOR-GENERAL LEONIDAS POLK.

First Division—Brigadier-General C. Clark.

First Brigade—Colonel Russell—12th, 13th, 154th and 47th Tennessee regiments, and Bankhead's Light battery.

Second Brigade—Brigadier-General Stewart—4th, 5th, 31st and 33d Tennessee and 13th Arkansas regiments, and Stanford's Light battery.

Second Division—Major-General B. F. Cheatham.

First Brigade—Brigadier-General Donelson—8th, 15th, 16th and 51st Tennessee regiments, and Carnes' Light battery.

Second Brigade—Brigadier-General Manney—1st, 6th, 9th and 27th Tennessee regiments, and Smith's Light battery.

Detached Brigade—Brigadier-General Maxey—41st Georgia, 24th Mississippi and 9th Texas regiments, and Eldridge's Light battery.

SECOND CORPS—MAJOR-GENERAL SAMUEL JONES. ·

First Brigade—Brigadier-General Anderson—25th Louisiana and 30th, 37th and 41st Mississippi regiments, Florida and Confederate battalions and Slocumb's Light battery.

Second Brigade—Colonel Reichard—11th, 16th, 18th, 19th and 20th Louisiana and 45th Alabama regiments, and Burnett's Light battery.

Third Brigade—Brigadier-General Walker—21st, 13th and Cresent Louisiana, 1st Arkansas and Independent and 38th Tennessee regiments, and Lumsden's and Barrett's Light batteries.

THIRD CORPS—MAJOR-GENERAL WM. J. HARDEE.

First Brigade—Colonel J. R. Liddell—2d, 5th, 6th, 7th and 8th Arkansas regiments, Pioneer company and Roberts' Light battery.

Second Brigade—Brigadier-General Cleburne—2d, 5th, 24th and 48th Tennessee and 15th Arkansas regiments, and Calvert's Light battery.

Third Brigade—Brigadier-General Wood—44th Tennessee, 16th Alabama and 32d and 33d Mississippi regiments, and Baxter's Light battery.

Fourth Brigade—Brigadier-General Marmaduke—3d Confederate and 25th, 29th and 37th Tennessee regiments, and Sweet's Light battery.

Fifth Brigade—Colonel Hawthorne—17th, 21st and 23d Tennessee and 33d Alabama regiments, and Austin's Light battery.

RESERVE CORPS—BRIGADIER-GENERAL J. M. WITHERS.

First Brigade—Brigadier-General Gardner—19th, 22d, 25th, 26th and 39th Alabama regiments, Sharpshooters and Robertson's Light battery.

Second Brigade—Brigadier-General Chalmers—5th, 7th, 9th, 10th and 29th Mississippi regiments, Blythe's Mississippi regiment and Ketchum's Light battery.

Third Brigade—Brigadier-General Jackson—17th, 18th, 21st, 24th and 5th Alabama regiments, and Bortwell's Light battery.

Fourth Brigade—Colonel Manigault—10th and 19th South Carolina and 28th and 34th Alabama regiments, Waters' Light battery, and 1st Louisiana infantry, Lieutenant-Colonel Farrar, detached.

ARMY OF THE WEST.

MAJOR-GENERAL J. P. McCOWN.

First Division—Brigadier-General Little.

First Brigade—Colonel Gates—1st Missouri regiment dismounted cavalry, 2d and 3d Missouri and 16th Arkansas regiments infantry, battalion Missouri infantry and Wade's Light battery.

Second Brigade—Brigadier-General Hebert—3d Louisiana and 14th and 17th Arkansas regiments infantry, Whitfield's Texas legion and Greer's regiment dismounted cavalry, and McDonald's Light battery.

Third Brigade—Brigadier-General Green—4th Missouri regiment infantry, battalion Missouri infantry, battalion Missouri cavalry, dismounted, Confederate Rangers and King's Light battery.

Second Division—Major-General McCown.

First Brigade—Brigadier-General Cabell—McCray's Arkansas regiment infantry, 14th, 10th and 11th Texas dismounted cavalry, Andrews' Texas regiment infantry, and Goode's Light battery.

Second Brigade—Brigadier-General Churchill—4th Arkansas regiment infantry, 1st and 2d Arkansas regiments Riflemen, dismounted, 4th Arkansas battalion infantry, Turnbull's Arkansas battalion infantry, Humphrey's Light battery and Reves' Missouri Scouts.

THIRD DIVISION—BRIGADIER-GENERAL D. H. MAURY.

First Brigade—Colonel Dockery—18th, 19th and 20th Arkansas regiments, McCairn's and Jones' Arkansas battalions, Light battery.

Second Brigade—Brigadier-General Moore—2d Texas, 35th Mississippi and Hobbs' and Adam's Arkansas regiments infantry, and Bledsoe's Light battery.

Third Brigade—Brigadier-General Phifer—6th and 9th Texas and 3d Arkansas dismounted cavalry, Brooks battalion and McNally Light battery.

RESERVED LIGHT BATTERIES.

Hoxton's, Landis', Gaylor's and Brown's Light batteries.

CAVALRY.

Forrest's regiment, Webb's squadron, Savery's company, McCulloch's regiment and Price's Bodyguard.

ORGANIZATION OF THE ARMY OF TENNESSEE.

October 8th, 1863.

LIEUTENANT-GENERAL LONGSTREET'S CORPS.

MAJOR-GENERAL McLAW'S DIVISION.

First—Brigadier-General J. B. Kershaw's brigade—2d South Carolina regiment, Colonel John D. Kennedy; 3d South Carolina regiment, Colonel James D. Vance; 7th South Carolina regiment, Colonel D. Wyatt Aiken; 8th South Carolina regiment, Colonel John W. Hennegan; 15th South Carolina regiment, Lieutenant-Colonel James F. Gist; 3d South Carolina battalion, Lieutenant-Colonel W. G. Rice.

Second—Brigadier-General W. T. Wofford's brigade—18th Georgia regiment, Colonel S. Z. Ruff; 24th Georgia regiment, Colonel R. McMillan; 16th Georgia regiment, Lieutenant-Colonel H. P. Thomas; Cobb's Georgia legion, Lieutenant-Colonel L. J. Glenn; Phillips' Georgia legion, Lieutenant-Colonel E. S. Barclay; 3d battalion Georgia Sharpshooters, Lieutenant-Colonel N. H. Hutchins.

Third—Brigadier-General B. G. Humphries' brigade—13th Mississippi regiment, Colonel R. McLeroy; 17th Mississippi regiment, Colonel W. D. Hodge; 18th Mississippi regiment, Colonel F. M. Griffin; 21st Mississippi regiment, Colonel W. L. Brandon.

Fourth—Brigadier-General Goode Bryan's brigade—10th Georgia regiment, Colonel John B. Weems; 51st Georgia regiment, Colonel J. P. Simms; 50th Georgia regiment, Colonel P. McGlaskan; 53d Georgia regiment, Colonel E. N. Ball.

BRIGADIER-GENERAL M. JENKINS, COMMANDING HOOD'S DIVISION.

First—Brigadier-General J. B. Robertson's brigade—1st Texas regiment, Colonel A. T. Rainey; 4th Texas regiment, Colonel J. C. G. Key; 5th Texas regiment, Colonel R. M. Powell; 3d Arkansas regiment, Colonel V. H. Manning.

Second—Brigadier-General E. M. Law's brigade—4th Alabama regiment, Colonel P. D. Bowles; 15th Alabama regiment, Colonel W. C. Oats; 44th Alabama regiment, Colonel W. F. Perry; 47th Alabama regiment, Colonel M. J. Bulger; 48th Alabama regiment, Colonel J. T. Sheffield.

Third—Brigadier-General Henry L. Bennings' brigade—2d Georgia regiment, Colonel Butt; 17th Georgia regiment, Colonel Hodge; 20th Georgia regiment, Colonel Waddell; 15th Georgia, Colonel DuBose.

Fourth—Brigadier-General M. Jenkins' brigade—4th South Carolina regiment, Colonel John Bratton; 5th South Carolina regiment, Colonel A. Coward; 2d South Carolina regiment, Colonel Thomas Thomson; 1st South Carolina regiment, Colonel F. M. Kilpatrick; Palmetto Sharpshooters, Colonel James Walker; Hampton's Legion, Colonel M. W. Gary.

BRIGADIER-GENERAL W. PRESTON'S DIVISION.

First—Brigadier-General Gracie's brigade—43d Alabama regiment, Colonel Y. M. Moody; 63d Tennessee regiment, Colonel R. G. Fain; Alabama legion, Colonel Jack Thorington; 1st battalion, Lieutenant-Colonel J. H. Holt; 2d battalion, Lieutenant-Colonel B. Hall; 3d battalion, Lieutenant-Colonel J. W. A. Stanford; 4th battalion, Major McLemore.

Second—Colonel Twiggs' brigade—54th Virginia regiment, Colonel R. Twiggs; 1st Florida regiment, Colonel G. T. Maxwell; 6th Florida regiment, Colonel J. J. Finley; 7th Florida regiment, Colonel R. Bullock.

Third—Brigadier-General Kelly's brigade—58th North Carolina regiment, Colonel J. B. Palmer; 5th Kentucky regiment, Colonel H. Hawkins; 63d Virginia regiment, Major French; 65th Georgia regiment, Colonel R. H. Moore.

MAJOR-GENERAL W. H. T. WALKER'S DIVISION.

First—Brigadier-General Gregg's brigade—41st Tennessee regiment, Colonel R. Furguharson; 50th Tennessee regiment, Colonel C. H. Sugg; 7th Texas regiment, Colonel H. B. Granburn; 3d Tennessee regiment, Colonel C. H. Walker; 10th Tennessee regiment, Lieutenant-Colouel W. B. Grace; 30th Tennessee regiment, Lieutenant-Colonel Turner; 1st Tennessee battalion, Major S. H. Colms.

Second—Brigadier-General Gist's brigade—46th Georgia regiment, Lieutenant-Colonel W. A. Daniels; 24th South Carolina regiment, Colonel C. H. Stevens; 16th South Carolina regiment, Colonel J. M. McCullough; 8th Georgia battalion, Lieutenant-Colonel Leroy Napier.

Third—Colonel C. C. Wilson's brigade—25th Georgia regiment, Major W. J. Winn; 29th Georgia regiment, Colonel W. J. Young; 30th Georgia regiment, Colonel T. W. Mangham; 4th Louisiana battalion, Lieutenant-Colonel J. McEnery; 1st battalion Georgia Sharpshooters, Major A. Shaaff.

ARTILLERY OF LONGSTREET'S CORPS.

Major Robertson's battalion—Lumsden's battery, Captain Lumsden; Barret's battery, Captain Barrett; Havis' battery, Captain Havis; Messenburg's battery, Captain Messenburg; Orleans Guards, Captain LeGardeur.

Major Leydon's battalion—Wollham's battery, Captain Wollham; Peeples' battery, Captain Peeples; Everett's battery, Captain York; Jeffries' battery, Captain Jeffries.

Major Williams' battalion—Kolk's battery, Captain Kolk; Baxter's battery, Captain Baxter; McCants' battery, Captain McCants; Everett's battery, Lieutenant Everett.

Colonel Alexander's battalion—Jordan's battery, Captain Jordan; Woolfork's battery, Captain Woolfork; Parker's battery, Captain Parker; Taylor's battery, Captain Taylor; Fickling's battery, Captain Fickling; Moody's battery, Captain Moody.

LIEUTENANT-GENERAL POLK'S CORPS.

MAJOR-GENERAL B. F. CHEATHAM, COMMANDING.

Cheatham's Division—Brigadier-General Jackson commanding.

First—Jackson's brigade, Colonel J. C. Wilkinson—5th Georgia regiment, Colonel C. P. Daniel; 5th Mississippi regiment, Major J. B. Hening; 8th Mississippi regiment, Major Smith; 1st Confederate regiment; Major J. C. Gordon; 2d Georgia battalion Sharpshooters, Major R. H. Whitely.

Second brigade—Brigadier-General Maney—1st and 27th Tennessee regiments, Colonel H. R. Field; 4th Confederate regiment, Captain J. Bostick; 6th and 9th Confederate regiments, Colonel G. C. Porter; Maney's battalion Sharpshooters, Major F. Maney.

Third brigade—Brigadier-General Wright—8th Tennessee regiment, Colonel J. H. Anderson; 16th Tennessee regiment, Colonel D. M. Donnell; 28th Tennessee regiment, Colonel S. S. Stanton; 51st and 52d Tennessee regiments, Lieutenant-Colonel J. G. Hall; 38th Tennessee regiment, Colonel John C. Carter; Murray's battalion.

Fourth brigade—Brigadier-General Strahl—4th and 5th Tennessee regiments, Colonel J. J. Lamb; 31st Tennessee regiment, Colonel E. E. Tansill; 33d Tennessee regiment, Lieutenant-Colonel H. C. McNeil; 19th Tennessee regiment, Colonel F. M. Walker; 24th Tennessee regiment, Colonel John A. Wilson.

Fifth—Brigadier-General Smith's brigade, Colonel A. J. Vaughn—154th and 13th Tennessee regiments, Lieutenant-Colonel R. W. Pittman; 12th and 47th Tennessee regiments, Colonel W. M. Watkins; 29th Tennessee regiment, Colonel H. Rice; 11th Tennessee regiment, Colonel G. W. Gordon.

HINDMAN'S DIVISION—BRIGADIER-GENERAL PATTON ANDERSON.

First—Brigadier-General Anderson's brigade, Colonel J. H. Sharp—7th Mississippi regiment, Colonel W. H. Bishop; 9th Mississippi regiment, Major T. H. Lynam; 10th Mississippi regiment, Lieutenant-Colonel J. Barr; 41st Mississippi regiment, Colonel W. J. Tucker; 44th Mississippi regiment, Colonel J. H. Sharp; battalion Sharpshooters, Major W. C. Richards.

Second brigade—Brigadier-General Walthall—24th and 27th Mississippi regiments, Colonel J. A. Campbell; 29th and 30th Mississippi regiments, Colonel W. E. Brantley; 34th Mississippi regiment, Colonel Samuel Benton.

Third brigade—Brigadier-General Deas—19th Alabama regiment, Col. S. K. McSpadden; 22d Alabama regiment, Captain Toulmin; 25th Alabama regiment, Lieutenant-Colonel Johnson; 39th Alabama regiment, Colonel W. Clark; 50th Alabama regiment, Colonel J. G. Coltart; battalion Sharpshooters, Captain Nabers.

Fourth brigade—Brigadier-General Manigault—10th and 19th South Carolina regiments, Colonel J. F. Presly; 24th Alabama regiment, Colonel N. N. Davis; 28th Alabama regiment, Colonel John C. Reid; 34th Alabama regiment, Colonel J. C. B. Mitchell.

ARTILLERY OF POLK'S CORPS.

Scogin's battery, Captain John Scogin; Turner's battery, Lieutenant W. B. Turner; Carnes' battery, Captain W. W. Carnes; Stanford's battery, Captain J. H. Stanford; Scott's battery, Captain W. L. Scott; Garrity's battery, Captain J. Garrity; Fowler's battery, Captain W. H. Fowler; Dent's battery, Captain S. H. Dent; Hamilton's battery, Lieutenant W. P. Hamilton.

MAJOR-GENERAL D. H. HILL'S CORPS.

MAJOR-GENERAL P. R. CLEBURNE'S DIVISION.

First—Wood's brigade, Colonel M. P. Lowry—32d and 45th Mississippi regiments, Lieutenant-Colonel R. Charlton; 16th Alabama regiment, Captain T. A. Ashford; 33d Alabama regiment, Colonel Sam. Adams; 45th Alabama regiment, Colonel E. B. Breedlove; Sharpshooters, Captain Dave Coleman.

Second brigade—Brigadier-General Liddell—2d and 15th Arkansas regiments, Colonel D. C. Govan; 5th and 13th Arkansas regiments, Lieutenant-Colonel Murray; 6th and 7th Arkansas regiments, Lieutenant-Colonel P. Snyder; 8th Arkansas and 1st Louisiana regiments, Lieutenant-Colonel F. M. Kent.

Third brigade—Brigadier-General L. E. Polk—35th and 48th Tennessee regiments, Colonel B. J. Hill; 2d Tennessee regiment, Colonel W. D. Robeson; 1st Arkansas regiment, Colonel J. W. Colquitt; 3d and 5th Confederate regiment, Colonel J. A. Smith.

Fourth—Brigadier-General Deshler's brigade, Colonel R. Q. Mills—17th, 18th, 24th and 25th Texas regiments, Major W. A. Taylor; 6th, 10th and 15th Texas regiments, Lieutenant-Colonel T. S. Anderson; 19th and 24th Arkansas regiments, Lieutenant-Colonel A. S. Hutchinson.

MAJOR-GENERAL A. P. STEWART'S DIVISION.

First brigade—Brigadier-General Johnson—17th Tennessee regiment, Lieutenant-Colonel W. W. Floyd; 23d Tennessee regiment, Colonel R. H. Keeble; 25th Tennessee regiment, Lieutenant-Colonel R. B. Snowden; 44th Tennessee regiment, Colonel John S. Fulton.

Second brigade—Brigadier-General Brown—18th Tennessee regiment, Lieutenant-Colonel W. R. Butler; 26th Tennessee regiment, Major R. M. Saffell; 32d Tennessee regiment,

8

Colonel E. C. Cook; 45th Tennessee regiment, Colonel A. Searcy; Newman's battalion, Captain W. P. Simpson.

Third brigade—Brigadier-General Bates—20th Tennessee regiment, Captain J. T. Guthrie; 15th and 37th regiments, Colonel R. C. Tyler; 37th Georgia regiment, A. T. Rudler; 59th Alabama 'regiment, Colonel Bush. Jones; 4th Georgia battalion Sharpshooters, Lieutenant Joel Towers.

Fourth brigade—Brigadier-General Clayton—18th Alabama regiment, Major P. T. Hunley; 36th Alabama regiment, Colonel L. S. Woodruff; 38th Alabama regiment, Colonel C. T. Ketchum.

MAJOR-GENERAL JOHN C. BRECKINRIDGE'S DIVISION.

First brigade—Brigadier-General M. A. Stovall—1st and 3d Florida regiments, Colonel W. S. Dillworth; 4th Florida regiment, Lieutenant-Colonel E. Bader; 60th North Carolina regiment, Colonel W. M. Hardy; 47th Georgia regiment, Captain J. S. Cone.

Second—Brigadier-General Adams' brigade, Colonel R. L. Gibson—13th and 20th Louisiana regiments, Colonel Leon Von Zinken; 16th and 25th Louisiana regiments, Colonel D. Gober; 19th Louisiana regiment, Lieutenant-Colonel R. W. Turner; 32d Alabama regiment, Captain A. Kilpatrick; Austin's battalion, Major J. C. Austin.

Third—Brigadier-General Helm's brigade, Colonel James H. Lewis—2d Kentucky regiment, Lieutenant-Colonel J. W. Morse; 4th Kentucky regiment, Major T. W. Thompson; 6th Kentucky regiment, Major W. L. Clarke; 9th Kentucky regiment, Lieutenant-Colonel J. C. Wickliffe; 41st Alabama regiment, Colonel M. L. Stansel.

ARTILLERY OF HILL'S CORPS.

Semplis' battery, Lieutenant R. H. Goldthwait; Swett's battery, Captain Charles Swett; Calvert's battery, Lieutenant T. J. Key; Douglass' battery, Captain J. P. Douglass.

Major Eldridge's battalion—Darden's battery, Captain Pat. Darden; Dawson's battery, Lieutenant R. W. Anderson; Eufaula battery, Lieutenant W. J. McKenzie; Humphries' battery, Captain J. T. Humphries; Cobb's battery, Lieutenant T. P. Gracy; Slocomb's battery, Captain C. H. Slocomb; Mebane's battery, Captain J. W. Mebane.

ORGANIZATION OF ARMY OF NORTHERN VIRGINIA.

June 1st, 1863.

COMMANDED BY GENERAL R. E. LEE.

FIRST CORPS—LIEUTENANT-GENERAL JAMES LONGSTREET.

McLAWS' DIVISION—MAJOR-GENERAL L. McLAWS.

Kershaw's brigade—Brigadier-General J. B. Kershaw—15th South Carolina regiment, Colonel W. D. De Saussure; 8th South Carolina regiment, Colonel J. W. Memminger; 2d South Carolina regiment, Colonel John D. Kennedy; 3d South Carolina regiment, Colonel James D. Nance; 7th South Carolina regiment, Colonel D. Wyatt Aiken; 3d (James') battalion South Carolina infantry, Lieutenant-Colonel R. C. Rice.

Benning's brigade—Brigadier-General H. L. Benning—50th Georgia regiment, Colonel W. R. Manning; 51st Georgia regiment, Colonel W. M. Slaughter; 53d Georgia regiment, Colonel James P. Somms; 10th Georgia regiment, Lieutenant-Colonel John B. Weems.

Barksdale's brigade—Brigadier-General Wm. Barksdale—13th Mississippi regiment, Colonel J. W. Carter; 17th Mississippi regiment, Colonel W. D. Holder; 18th Mississippi regiment, Colonel Thomas M. Griffin; 21st Mississippi regiment, Colonel B. G. Humphreys.

Wofford's brigade—Brigadier-General W. T. Wofford—18th Georgia regiment, Major E. Griffis; Phillips' Georgia Legion, Colonel W. M. Phillips; 24th Georgia regiment, Colonel Robert McMillan; 16th Georgia regiment, Colonel Goode Bryan; Cobb's Georgia Legion, Lieutenant-Colonel L. D. Glenn.

PICKETT'S DIVISION—MAJOR-GENERAL GEORGE E. PICKETT.

Garnett's brigade—Brigadier-General R. B. Garnett—8th Virginia regiment, Colonel Eppa Hunton; 18th Virginia regiment, Colonel R. E. Withers; 19th Virginia regiment, Colonel Henry Gantt; 28th Virginia regiment, Colonel R. C. Allen; 56th Virginia regiment, Colonel W. D. Stuart.

Armistead's brigade—Brigadier-General L. A. Armistead—9th Virginia regiment, Lieutenant-Colonel J. S. Gilliam; 14th Virginia regiment, Colonel J. G. Hodges; 38th Virginia regiment, Colonel E. C. Edmonds; 53d Virginia regiment, Colonel John Grammer; 57th Virginia regiment, Colonel J. B. Magruder.

Kemper's brigade—Brigadier-General J. L. Kemper—1st Virginia regiment, Colonel Lewis B. Williams, Jr.; 3d Virginia regiment, Colonel Joseph Mayo, Jr.; 7th Virginia regiment, Colonel W. T. Patton; 11th Virginia regiment, Colonel David Funston; 24th Virginia regiment, Colonel W. R. Terry.

Toombs' brigade—Brigadier-General R. Toombs—2d Georgia regiment, Colonel E. M. Butt; 15th Georgia regiment, Colonel E. M. DuBose; 17th Georgia regiment, Colonel W. C. Hodges; 20th Georgia regiment, Colonel J. B. Cummings.

Corse's brigade—Brigadier-General M. D. Corse—15th Virginia regiment, Colonel T. P. August; 17th Virginia regiment, Colonel Morton Marye; 30th Virginia regiment, Colonel A. T. Harrison; 32d Virginia regiment, Colonel E. B. Montague.

HOOD'S DIVISION—MAJOR-GENERAL J. B. HOOD.

Robertson's brigade—Brigadier-General J. B. Robertson—1st Texas regiment, Colonel A. T. Rainey; 4th Texas regiment, Colonel J. C. G. Key; 5th Texas regiment, Colonel R. M. Powell; 3d Arkansas regiment, Colonel Van H. Manning.

Laws' brigade—Brigadier-General E. M. Laws—4th Alabama regiment, Colonel P. A. Bowles; 44th Alabama regiment, Colonel W. H. Perry; 15th Alabama regiment, Colonel Jas. Canty; 47th Alabama regiment, Colonel J. W. Jackson; 48th Alabama regiment, Colonel J. F. Shepherd.

Anderson's brigade—Brigadier-General G. T. Anderson—10th Georgia battalion, Major J. E. Rylander; 7th Georgia regiment, Colonel W. M. White; 8th Georgia regiment, Lieutenant-Colonel J. R. Towers; 9th Georgia regiment, Colonel B. F. Beck; 11th Georgia regiment, Colonel F. H. Little.

Jenkins' brigade—Brigadier-General M. Jenkins—2d South Carolina Rifles, Colonel Thomas Thompson; 1st South Carolina regiment, Lieutenant-Colonel David Livingston; 5th South Carolina regiment, Colonel A. Coward; 6th South Carolina regiment, Colonel John Bratton; Hampton's Legion, Colonel M. W. Gary.

SECOND CORPS—LIEUTENANT-GENERAL R. S. EWELL.

EARLY'S DIVISION—MAJOR-GENERAL J. A. EARLY.

Hays' brigade—Brigadier-General H. T. Hays—5th Louisiana regiment, Colonel Henry Forno; 6th Louisiana regiment, Colonel William Monaghan; 7th Louisiana regiment, Colonel D. B. Penn; 8th Louisiana regiment, Colonel Henry B. Kelley; 9th Louisiana regiment, Colonel A. L. Stafford.

Gordon's brigade—Brigadier-General J. B. Gordon—13th Georgia regiment, Colonel J. M. Smith; 26th Georgia regiment, Colonel E. N. Atkinson; 31st Georgia regiment, Colonel C. A. Evans; 38th Georgia regiment, Major J. D. Matthews; 60th Georgia regiment, Colonel W. H. Stiles; 61st Georgia regiment, Colonel J. H. Lamar.

Smith's brigade—Brigadier-General William Smith—13th Virginia regiment, Colonel J. E. B. Terrill; 31st Virginia regiment, Colonel John S. Hoffman; 49th Virginia regiment, Colonel Gibson; 52d Virginia regiment, Colonel Skinner; 58th Virginia regiment, Colonel F. H. Board.

Hoke's brigade—Colonel J. E. Avery commanding (General R. F. Hoke being absent; wounded)—6th North Carolina regiment, Colonel J. E. Avery; 21st North Carolina regiment, Colonel W. W. Kirkland; 54th North Carolina regiment, Colonel J. C. T. McDowell; 57th North Carolina regiment, Colonel A. C. Godwin; 1st North Carolina battalion, Major R. H. Wharton.

Rodes' Division—Major-General R. E. Rodes.

Daniel's brigade—Brigadier-General Junius Daniel—32d North Carolina regiment, Colonel E. C. Brabble; 43d North Carolina regiment, Colonel Thomas S. Keenan; 45th North Carolina regiment, Lieutenant-Colonel Samuel H. Boyd; 53d North Carolina regiment, Colonel W. A. Owens; Second North Carolina battalion, Lieutenant-Colonel H. S. Andrews.

Doles' brigade—Brigadier-General George Doles—4th Georgia regiment, Lieutenant-Colonel D. R. E. Winn; 12th Georgia regiment, Colonel Edward Willis; 21st Georgia regiment, Colonel John T. Mercer; 44th Georgia regiment, Colonel S. P. Lumpkin.

Iverson's brigade—Brigadier-General Alfred Iverson—Fifth North Carolina regiment, Captain S. B. West; 12th North Carolina regiment, Lieutenant-Colonel W. S. Davis; 20th North Carolina regiment, Lieutenant-Colonel N. Slough; 23d North Carolina regiment, Colonel D. H. Christie.

Ramseur's brigade—Brigadier-General S. D. Ramseur—2d North Carolina regiment, Major E. W. Hurt; 4th North Carolina regiment, Colonel Bryan Grimes; 14th North Carolina regiment, Colonel R. T. Bennett; 30th North Carolina regiment, Colonel F. M. Parker.

Rodes' brigade—Colonel E. A. O'Neal—3d Alabama regiment, Colonel C. A. Battle; 5th Alabama regiment, Colonel J. M. Hall; 6th Alabama regiment, Colonel J. N. Lightfoot; 12th Alabama regiment, Colonel S. B. Pickens; 26th Alabama regiment, Lieutenant-Colonel J. C. Goodgame.

THIRD CORPS—LIEUTENANT-GENERAL A. P. HILL.

R. H. Anderson's Division.

Wilcox's brigade—Brigadier-General C. M. Wilcox—8th Alabama regiment, Colonel T. L. Royster; 9th Alabama regiment, Colonel S. Henry; 10th Alabama regiment, Colonel W. H. Forney; 11th Alabama regiment, Colonel J. C. C. Saunders; 14th Alabama regiment, Colonel L. P. Pinkhard.

Mahone's brigade—Brigadier-General William Mahone—6th Virginia regiment, Colonel G. T. Rogers; 12th Virginia regiment, Colonel D. A. Weisiger; 16th Virginia regiment, Lieutenant-Colonel Joseph H. Ham; 41st Virginia regiment, Colonel W. A. Parham; 61st Virginia regiment, Colonel V. D. Groner.

Posey's brigade—Brigadier-General Canot Posey—46th Mississippi regiment, Colonel Jos. Jayne; 16th Mississippi regiment, Colonel Samuel E. Baker; 19th Mississippi regiment, Colonel John Mullins; 12th Mississippi regiment, Colonel W. H. Taylor.

Wright's brigade—Brigadier-General A. R. Wright—2d Georgia battalion, Major G. W. Ross; 3d Georgia regiment, Colonel E. J. Walker; 22d Georgia regiment, Colonel R. H. Jones; 48th Georgia regiment, Colonel William Gibson.

Perry's brigade—Brigadier-General E. A. Perry—2d Florida regiment, Lieutenant-Colonel S. G. Pyles; 5th Florida regiment, Colonel J. C. Hately; 8th Florida regiment, Colonel David Long.

Heth's Division.

First—Pettigrew's brigade—42d, 11th, 26th, 44th, 47th, 52d and 17th North Carolina regiments.

Second—Field's brigade—40th, 55th and 47th Virginia regiments.

Third—Archer's brigade—1st, 7th and 14th Tennessee and 13th Alabama regiments.

Fourth—Cooke's brigade—15th, 27th, 46th and 48th North Carolina regiments.

Pender's Division.

First—McGowan's brigade—1st, 12th, 13th and 14th South Carolina regiments and 1st South Carolina Rifles.

Second—Lane's brigade—7th, 18th, 28th, 33d and 37th North Carolina regiments.

Third—Thomas' brigade—14th, 35th, 45th and 49th Georgia regiments.

Fourth—Pender's Old brigade—13th, 16th, 22d, 34th and 38th North Carolina regiments.

NOTE—The foregoing organization of Lieutenant-General A. P. Hill's corps was perfected in obedience to the following order:

HEADQUARTERS ARMY NORTHERN VIRGINIA, 30th May, 1863.

Special Orders, } No. 146. }

* * * , *

VIII. The following changes are made in the organization of corps and divisions of this army:

1. The brigades of Heth and Archer, of A. P. Hill's division, with Pettigrew's and Cooke's, will constitute a division, and be under the command of Major-General Henry Heth.

2. The brigades of Pender, Lane, Thomas and McGowan will constitute a division, and be under the command of Major-General W. D. Pender.

3. The divisions of Major-Generals Early, Johnson and Rodes will constitute the Second corps, and be under the command of Lieutenant-General R. S. Ewell.

4. The division of Major-General R. H. Anderson is detached from the First corps, and, together with the divisions of Major-Generals Heth and Pender, will constitute the Third corps, and be under the command of Lieutenant-General A. P. Hill.

5. The chief of artillery will designate the battalions of artillery to serve with the three corps, and the chief quartermaster make the necessary division of the transportation. * *

By command of General R. E. Lee. W. H. TAYLOR, A. A. General.

ARTILLERY OF ARMY OF NORTHERN VIRGINIA.

[NOTE.—The following roster of the artillery is kindly furnished by Rev. George W. Peterkin, of Baltimore, who served on the staff of Brigadier-General W. N. Pendleton, chief of artillery Army of Northern Virginia. It is copied from a roster made out by him, from reports on hand, for General Pendleton's use, and he vouches for its completeness and accuracy. The date is not given, but is was evidently soon after the organization of the artillery into three corps, and before Colonels E. P. Alexander, A. L. Long and R. L. Walker were made brigadier-generals and assigned respectively to the First, Second and Third corps].

FIRST CORPS—COLONEL J. B. WALTON.

		20-lb. Parrotts.	10-lb. Parrotts.	3-inch Rifles.	Napoleons.	12-lb. Howitzers.	24-lb. Howitzers.	Other Guns.
Col. H. C. Cabell...... } Major Hamilton........}	McCarty............				2	2		
	Manly.............				2	2		
	Carlton...........			2		1	1	
	Fraser............			1	1		1	*1
9 rifles ; 5 Naps.; 2 Hows.								
Major Dearing........} Major Reed...........}	Macon.............		2		4			
	Blount............	2	1	1				
	Stribling.........				4			
	Caskie............				4			
6 rifles ; 12 Napoleons.								
Major Henry.............	Bachman...........				4			
	Rielly............		2	2	2			
	Latham............				2	1		*1
	Gordon............				3	1		
6 rifles ; 11 Naps.; 2 Hows.								

* Blakely.

FIRST CORPS—*Continued.*

		20-lb. Parrotts.	10-lb. Parrotts.	3-inch Rifles.	Napoleons.	12-lb. Howitzers.	24-lb. Howitzers.	Other Guns.
Col. E. P. Alexander... } Major Huger............ }	Jordan................	....	......	4	......	......	......	......
	Rhett................	3	......	......	......	......	......	......
	Moody	......	......	......	2	......	4	......
	Parker	......	1	3	......	......	......	......
	Taylor...............	......	......	......	4	......	......	......
11 rifles; 6 Naps.; 4 Hows.								
Major Eshleman.........	Squiers...............	......	......	......	......	......	......	......
	Miller................	......	......	......	2	1	......	......
	Richardson...........	......	......	......	3	1	......	......
	Norcom...............	......	......	......	3	......	......	......
8 Napoleons; 2 Hows.		5	9	15	42	6	4	2

Total number of rifles.. 31
Total number of Napoleons... 42
Total number of Howitzers... 10
———
Total number of pieces.. 83
Total number of battalions.. 5
Total number of companies.. 21

SECOND CORPS—COLONEL S. CRUTCHFIELD.

		20-lb. Parrotts.	10-lb. Parrotts.	3-inch Rifles.	Napoleons.	12-lb. Howitzers.	24-lb. Howitzers.	Other Guns.
Lt. Col. Thos. H. Carter } Maj. Carter M. Braxton }	Page	......	......	......	4	......	......	......
	Fry...................	......	2	......	......	......	1	......
	Carter................	......	2	......	1	......	1	......
	Reese.................	......	......	3	1	......	......	......
7 rifles; 6 Naps.; 2 Hows.								
Lt. Col. H. P. Jones.... } Major Brockenborough }	Carrington............	......	......	......	4	......	......	......
	Garber................	......	......	......	4	......	......	......
	Thompson	......	2	......	......	1	......	......
	Tanner................	......	......	2	......	1	......	......
4 rifles; 8 Naps.; 2 Hows.								
Lt. Col. S. Andrews.... } Major Latimer......... }	Brown.................	......	4	......	......	......	......	......
	Dermot................	......	......	......	4	......	......	......
	Carpenter.............	......	......	2	2	......	......	......
	Raine	......	2	2	......	......	......	......
10 rifles; 6 Napoleons.								
Lt. Col. Nelson......... } Major Page............. }	Kirkpatrick	......	......	......	4	2	......	......
	Massie................	......	......	......	4	2	......	......
	Millege...............	......	1	3	......	......	......	*2
6 rifles; 8 Naps.; 4 Hows.								
Col. J. T. Brown....... } Major Hardaway ...... }	Dance.................	......	......	......	2	......	2	......
	Watson	......	2	......	2	......	......	......
	Smith.................	......	2	1	......	......	......	......
	Huff..................	......	......	......	......	2	2	......
	Graham................	2	2	......	......	......	......	......
11 rifles; 4 Naps.; 4 Hows.		2	19	15	32	10	2	2

Total number of rifles... 38
Total number of Napoleons... 32
Total number of Howitzers... 12
———
Total number of pieces.. 82
Total number of battalions.. 5
Total number of companies 20

* Kind not known.

THIRD CORPS—COLONEL R. LINDSAY WALKER.

		20-lb. Parrotts.	10-lb. Parrotts.	3-Inch Rifles.	Napoleons.	12-lb. Howitzers.	24-lb. Howitzers.	Other Guns.
Maj. D. G. McIntosh...⎱ Maj. W. F. Poague....⎰	Hurt	......	......	2	......	......	......	*2
	Rice..............	......	......	......	4	......	......	......
	Luck.............	......	......	4	......	......	......	......
10 rifles; 6 Napoleons.	Johnson..........	......	......	2	2	......	......	......
Lt. Col. Garnett........⎱ Major Richardson......⎰	Lewis............	......	1	3	......	......	......	......
	Maurin...........	......	1	2	2	......	......	......
	Moore............	......	1	1	2	......	......	......
11 rifles; 4 Naps.; 2 Hows.	Grandy...........	......	......	2	......	2	......	......
Major Cutshaw..........	Wyatt............	......	1	1	2	2	......	......
	Woolfolk..........	......	......	......	......	4	......	......
2 rifles; 5 Naps.; 7 Hows.	Brookes..........	......	......	......	3	1	......	......
Maj. Willie J. Pegram...	Brunson..........	......	......	3	......	1	......	......
	Davidson.........	......	......	......	3	1	......	......
	Crenshaw	......	2	1	......	......	......	......
	McGraw..........	......	......	......	4	......	......	......
8 rifles; 9 Naps.; 2 Hows.	Marye............	......	2	......	2	......	......	......
Lt. Col. Cutts...........⎱ Major Lane.............⎰	Wingfield..........	2	3	......	......	......	......	*1
	Ross	......	3	1	1	......	......	......
10 rifles; 3 Naps.; 4 Hows.	Patterson.........	......	......	......	2	......	4	......
		2	14	22	27	15	......	3

```
Total number of rifles..... ...........................................  41
Total number of Napoleons...........................................  27
Total number of Howitzers,..........................................  15
                                                                      ——
Total number of pieces,.........................................  83
Total number of battalions..........................................  5
Total number of companies........... ..............................  19
```

SUMMARY OF ARTILLERY OF ARMY OF NORTHERN VIRGINIA (EXCLUSIVE OF HORSE ARTILLERY).

	Battalions.	Companies.	Rifles.	Napoleons.	Howitzers.	Total.
Artillery of First corps.....	5	21	31	42	10	83
Artillery of Second corps..................	5	20	38	32	12	82
Artillery of Third corps............................	5	19	41	27	15	63
Total...................................	15	60	110	101	37	249

NOTE.—It is to be regretted that we have been thus far unable to secure a roster of the cavalry of the Army of Northern Virginia sufficiently complete to publish.

* Whitworth.

ORGANIZATION OF THE CONFEDERATE STATES ARMY.

May 21st, 1864.

COMMANDED BY GENERAL G. T. BEAUREGARD.

HOKE'S DIVISION.

First—Brigadier-General Hagood's brigade—7th South Carolina battalion, and 11th, 21st, 25th and 27th South Carolina Volunteers.

Second—Brigadier-General Colquitt's brigade—6th, 19th, 23d, 27th and 28th Georgia Volunteers.

Third—Brigadier-General Clingman's brigade—8th, 31st, 51st and 61st North Carolina Volunteers.

Fourth—Brigadier-General Martin's brigade—17th, 42d and 66th North Carolina Volunteers.

JOHNSON'S DIVISION.

First—Brigadier-General Walker's brigade—17th, 18th, 22d and 26th South Carolina Volunteers.

Second—Brigadier-General Ransom's brigade—24th, 25th, 35th, 49th and 56th North Carolina Volunteers.

Third—Brigadier-General Johnson's brigade—63d, 17th, 23d, 25th and 44th Tennessee Volunteers.

Fourth—Brigadier-General Wise's brigade—26th, 34th, 46th and 59th Virginia Volunteers.

ARTILLERY.

Read's battalion (38th Virginia) of artillery—Blount's battery, Caskie's battery, Macon battery and Marshall battery.

Washington battalion of artillery—1st and 3d companies.

Owen's battalion of artillery—Martin's battery and Slaton's battery.

Caskie's battalion of artillery—1st section of Graham's battery, 1st section of Wright's battery and Miller's battery.

Field Return of Troops commanded by General G. T. Beauregard, May 21st, 1864.

	For Duty																	Sick		Ex. Duty		In ar		Total		Aggregate	Total Absent		Aggregate present and absent
	General	Brigadier-Generals	A. A. Generals	Ordnance Officers	Aides de Camp	Colonels	Lieutenant-Colonels	Majors	Quartermasters	Commissaries	Adjutants	Surgeons	Captains	Lieutenants	Chaplains	Non-Commissioned Officers	Enlisted Men	Officers	Enlisted Men	Officers	Enlisted Men	Officers	Enlisted Men	Officers	Enlisted Men	Aggregate	Officers	Enlisted Men	
General and staff	1	1	5	1	2	2	2	2	1	1	2	2	1											13		13			
Hoke's division		1	1	1	1	2	2	2	4	1	2	2	21	90	1	210	1,612	2	68	6	156	1	1	100	1,709	1,955	94	1,831	3,734
Martin's brigade		1	2	1	1	2	2	2	1	2	2	1	18	51	1	191	1,253	2	1	1	37			125	1,471	1,596	80	1,224	2,900
Ragoon's brigade			2	1		2	2	2	5	2	2	5	25	66		211	1,222	2	7	4	31			141	1,428	1,869	71	1,032	2,971
Chapman's brigade																													
Colquitt's brigade		1	2	1	1	3	2	4	3	2	2	5	26	32	4	285	1,584	2	70	4	86								
Johnson's division																							3	145	2,134	2,279	45	801	3,125
Wise's brigade		1	1			3	2	3	3	1	3	6	30	51	3	281	1,683	2	117	2	62	1	1	140	1,702	1,842	92	979	1,971
Walker's brigade		1	2	1	1	3	3	3	2	1	1	7	25	90	4	241	1,461	2	62	12	169	3		93	814	907			
Johnson's brigade		1	1			3	4	4	2	1	1	6	14	46	2	107	474	6	48		131		3	153	2,331	2,484	42	1,203	3,729
Ransom's brigade												9	32	89	1	281	1,892												
Total Infantry	1	5	16	5	8	20	20	24	22	14	21	22	191	594	15	1,807	10,581	15	366	25	671	5	7	44	14,744				
Two companies																													
Washington battalion artillery			1	1		1	1	1	1	1	1	3	1	3	3	9	152		4		10				162	167	3	75	241
Owen's battalion artillery						1		1				2	2	6	4	25	127	1			10		2	5	166	173		56	229
Caskie's battalion artillery				1				1					3	5	2		212				14			7	133	241		361	376
Read's battalion artillery						1			1				2	11	1	62	293		9	1	35			17	401	418	3	104	629
Portion of Third																													
Alabama cavalry			1			1	1	1	1	1	1		9	28		84	440	1		1	52		9	55	576	620	3	339	956
Grand total	1	5	16	6	8	20	24	24	21	14	22	54	203	647	15	1,987	12,105	16	381	26	792	5	9	79		16,363			

*Reports not complete.

Statement of the Confederate Forces in the Field, November 27th, 1863.

COMMAND.	DATE OF RETURN.	Effective total.	Total present.	Aggregate present.	Total present and absent.	Aggregate present and absent.	REMARKS.
Army of Northern Virginia..........	Nov. 20, 1863.	48,269	51,980	56,068	40,498	96,576	Gen. Imboden's command not included.
Army of Tennessee................	Nov. 1, 1863.	46,496	60,353	65,603	95,376	102,990	
Department of S. C., Georgia and Florida.	Nov. 15, 1863.	29,393	33,126	35,004	46,191	49,588	
Department of Cape Fear...........	Nov. 20, 1863.	6,363	7,038	7,380	8,799	9,231	
District of the Gulf...............	Oct. 20, 1863.	6,997	8,251	6,837	12,053	12,890	Returns incomplete.
Department of Southwest Virginia....	Oct. 31, 1863.	7,975	8,794	2,471	16,010	17,067	Returns incomplete.
Department of Richmond...........	Nov. 20, 1863.	6,392	7,417	7,891	11,151	11,783	
Department of Mississippi..........	Nov. 7, 1863.	17,209	19,260	20,325	35,569	36,623	
		169,099	196,219	211,099	266,236	336,723	

NOTE.—The above statement does not include returns from the Trans-Mississippi Department. Returns from the Department of North Carolina are also wanting.

Light Artillery of the Army of Tennessee, General Joseph E. Johnston, June 10th, 1864.

ARMY CORPS.	BATTALION.	BATTALION COMMANDER.	BATTERY.	COMMANDER OF BATTERY.	
Lieut. Gen. W. J. Hardee......	Hoxton's........	Major Hoxton..........	Turner's.........	Capt. W. B. Turner.......	
			Phelan's.........	2d Lieut. N. Venable...	
			Perry's..........	Capt. T. J. Perry.......	
			Swett's..........	1st Lieut. H. Shannon...	
			Key's............	1st Lieut. J. G. Marshall.	
	Hotchkiss'......	Major Hotchkiss.........	Goldthwaite's....	Capt. R. W. Goldthwaite.	Commanded by Colonel M. Smith.
			Bledsoe's........	Capt. H. M. Bledsoe.....	
			Ferguson's.......	Capt. R. T. Beauregard..	
			Howell's.........	1st Lieut. W. G. Robson..	
	Martin's........	Major Martin..........	Slocum's.........	Capt. C. H. Slocum......	
			Mebane's.........	Capt. J. W. Mebane......	
	Cobb's..........	Major Cobb..........	Gracey's.........	Capt. F. P. Gracey......	
			Douglass'........	Capt. J. P. Douglass....	
			Garrett's........	Lieut. Phillip Bond.....	
Lieut. Gen. Jno. B. Hood......	Courtney's......	Major Courtney..........	Dent's...........	Capt. J. H. Dent........	
			Fenner's.........	Capt. C. E. Fenner......	
			Oliver's.........	Capt. McD. Oliver.......	
	Eldridge's......	Major Eldridge..........	Stanford's.......	Lieut. J. S. Kaye.......	
			Corput's.........	Lieut. W. S. Kaye.......	
			Marshall's.......	Capt. L. G. Marshall....	
	Johnston's......	Major Johnston..........	Rowan's..........	Capt. Jno. B. Rowan.....	
			White's..........	1st Lieut. A. Pugh, Jr...	
Major-Gen. Jos. Wheeler......	Robertson's.....	Lt. Col. F. H. Robertson..	Huggins's........	Capt. A. L. Huggins.....	
			Ramsay's.........	1st Lieut. B. B. Ramsay..	One section.
			Wiggins's........	1st Lieut. J. P. Bryant..	
Reserve Artillery...............	Williams'.......	Major Williams..........	Terrell's........	2d Lieut. Davis.........	
			Jeffrey's........	Capt. W. C. Jeffrey.....	
			Kolb's...........	Capt. R. F. Kolb........	
			Darden's.........	Capt. P. Darden........	
	Palmer's........	Major Palmer..........	Lumsden's........	Capt. C. L. Lumsden.....	Commanded by Lieut. Col. J. H. Hollonquist.
			Havis'...........	Capt. M. W. Havis.......	
			Anderson's.......	Capt. K. W. Anderson....	
	Waddell's.......	Major Waddell..........	Barret's.........	Capt. O. W. Barret......	
			Emery's..........	Capt. W. D. Emery.......	
			Bellamy's........	Capt. R. H. Bellamy.....	

Light Batteries in the Department of South Carolina, Georgia and Florida, December, 1864.

Col. A. Gonzales, Chief of Artillery Departm't of S. C., Ga. and Fla. Lt. Col. Chas. C. Jones, Jr., Chief of Artillery Military Dis. of Georgia and Third Military Dis. of South Carolina.

	NAME.	STATE.	COMMANDING OFFICER.	12-lb. Napoleons.	12-lb. Howitzers.	6-lb. Guns.	10-lb. Parrotts.	3-inch Rifles.	3½-inch Blakely.
1	Waccamaw Light Artillery	South Carolina	Capt. Nehan Ward	2	2	2			
2	German Light Artillery	"	Capt. F. W. Wagener	2	1	1			
3	Orleans Guard Battery	"	Capt. G. LeGardeur, Jr.	2	2				
4	Marion Artillery	South Carolina	Capt. E. L. Parker	4	2				
5	Wagner Artillery	"	Capt. C. E. Kanapaux	2					
6	Chestnut Artillery	"	Capt. F. C. Shultz	2	2				
7	Washington Artillery	"	Capt. G. H. Walter	1	2		2		
8	Furman Artillery	"	Capt. W. E. Earle	3			1		
9	Beaufort Volunteer Artillery	"	Capt. H. M. Stuart	4	2				
10	German Artillery	"	Capt. W. K. Backman	4	2				
11	Lafayette Artillery	"	Capt. J. F. Kanapaux		4				
12	Santee Light Artillery	"	Capt. C. Gaillard						
13	Inglis Light Artillery	"	Capt. Wm. E. Charles	2					
14	DePass' Light Artillery	"	Capt. W. L. DePass						
15	Colcock's Light Artillery (section)	"	Lieut. Johnson	2		2	2	2	
16	Chatham Artillery	Georgia	Capt. J. F. Wheaton	4	2				
17	Regular Light Battery	"	Capt. J. A. Maxwell	4		2			
18	Guerard's Light Battery	"	Capt. Jno. M. Guerard	4		4			
19	Daniell's Light Battery	"	Capt. Chas. Daniell	4					
20	Terrell Light Battery	"	Capt. Jno. W. Brooks	4					
21	Barnwell's Light Battery	"	Capt. A. S. Barnwell	4					
22	Anderson's Light Battery	"	Capt. Anderson	4					
23	Jo. Thompson Artillery	"	Capt. C. K. Hanleiter						
24	Hamilton's Batt'n Light Artillery		Major Hamilton		2	2	2	4	4
25	Girardey's Batt'y Light Artillery	Florida	Capt. C. E. Girardey		4				
26	Gamble's Battery Light Artillery	"	Capt. C. E. Dyke	4	2			2	
27	Dunham's Battery Light Artillery	"	Capt. J. L. Dunham	4	2				
28	Abell's Battery Light Artillery	"	Capt. H. F. Abell	2	2				
29	Kilcrease Battery Light Artillery	Georgia	Capt. F. L. Villipigue		2				
30	Clinch's Battery Light Battery	"	Capt. N. E. Clinch	2	2	2			
				57	37	13	7	8	4

Total, 126 guns.

DEPUTIES TO THE PROVISIONAL CONGRESS OF THE CONFEDERATE STATES.

Assembled at Montgomery, Alabama, February, 1861.

Hon. Howell Cobb............	Georgia..........	President of the Provisional Congress; afterwards Brigadier-General and Major-General in the Confederate army.
Hon. J. J. Hooper............	Alabama..........	Secretary of the Provisional Congress.
Hon. Wm. P. Chilton.......	"	Afterwards member of Congress.
Hon. Jabez L. M. Curry.....	"	Afterwards member of Congress and Lieutenant-Colonel of cavalry.
Hon. Thomas Fearn.........	"	
Hon. Stephen F. Hale.......	"	
Hon. David P. Lewis........	"	
Hon. Colin J. McRae.........	"	Afterwards special agent to London and Paris.
Hon. John Gill Shorter......	"	Afterwards Governor of Alabama.
Hon. Robert H. Smith.......	"	Afterwards Colonel in Confederate Army.
Hon. Richard W. Walker....	"	Afterwards Confederate Senator from Alabama.
Hon. J. Patton Anderson....	Florida..........	Afterwards Brigadier-General and Major-General in the Confederate army.
Hon. Jackson Morton........	"	
Hon. James B. Owens.......	"	
Hon. Frank S. Bartow.......	Georgia..........	Afterwards Brigadier-General in the Confederate army.
Hon. Howell Cobb...........	"	Afterwards Brigadier-General and Major-General in the Confederate army.
Hon. Thomas R. R. Cobb....	"	Afterwards Brigadier-General in the Confederate army.
Hon. Martin J. Crawford....	"	Afterwards delegate to the United States.
Hon. Benjamin H. Hill......	"	Afterwards Confederate Senator from Georgia.
Hon. Augustus H. Kenan....	"	Afterwards member of Confederate Congress.
Hon. Eugenius A. Nisbet....	"	
Hon. Alexander H. Stephens	"	Elected Vice-President of the Confederate States.
Hon. Robert Toombs........	"	Secretary of State; Brigadier-General in the Confederate army, &c.
Hon. Augustus R. Wright....	"	Afterwards member of Confederate Congress.
Hon. Alexander de Clouet...	Louisiana.........	
Hon. Charles M. Conrad.....	"	Afterwards member of Confederate Congress.
Hon. Duncan F. Kenner.....	"	Afterwards member of Confederate Congress.
Hon. Henry Marshall.......	"	Afterwards member of Confederate Congress.
Hon. John Perkins, Jr.......	"	Afterwards member of Confederate Congress.
Hon. Edward Sparrow.......	"	Afterwards Confederate Senator from Louisiana.
Hon. William S. Barry.......	Mississippi........	Afterwards Brigadier-General in Confederate service.
Hon. Walker Brooke........	"	
Hon. J. A. P. Campbell......	"	
Hon. Alexander M. Clayton..	"	
Hon. W. P. Harris..........	"	
Hon. James T. Harrison.....	"	
Hon. W. S. Wilson...........	"	
Hon. Robert W. Barnwell....	South Carolina....	Afterwards Confederate Senator from South Carolina.
Hon. William W. Boyce......	"	Afterwards member of Confederate Congress.
Hon. James Chestnut, Jr...	"	Afterwards A. D. C. to the President, with rank of Colonel, and subsequently Brigadier-General C. S. A.
Hon. Lawrence M. Keitt.....	"	Afterwards Colonel in the Confederate army.
Hon. Charles G. Memminger	"	Afterwards Secretary of the Treasury.
Hon. Wm. Porcher Miles....	"	Afterwards member of Confederate Congress.
Hon. R. Barnwell Rhett......	"	
Hon. Thomas J. Withers....	"	
Hon. John Gregg...........	Texas.............	Afterwards Brigadier-General in the Confederate army.
Hon. John Hemphill........	"	
Hon. W. B. Ochiltree........	"	

Deputies to the Provisional Congress.—Continued.

Hon. Williamson S. Oldham..	Texas............	Afterwards Confederate Senator from Texas.
Hon. John H. Reagan........	"	Afterwards Postmaster-General.
Hon. Thomas N. Waul.......	"	Afterwards Brigadier-General in the Confederate army.
Hon. Louis T. Wigfall.......	"	Afterwards Brigadier-General in the Confederate army, and Confederate Senator from Texas.

ADDITIONAL DELEGATES TO THE PROVISIONAL CONGRESS,

Upon its Assembling in Richmond, Virginia, in July, 1861.

Hon William W. Avery......	North Carolina....	
Hon. Burton Craige....	"	
Hon. Andrew T. Davidson...	"	Afterwards member of Confederate Congress.
Hon. George Davis..........	"	Afterwards Confederate Senator from North Carolina, and Attorney General of the Confederacy.
Hon. Thomas D. McDowell..	"	Afterwards member of Confederate Congress.
Hon. John M. Morehead.....	"	
Hon. Robert C. Puryear......	"	
Hon. Thomas Ruffin...... .	"	
Hon. Wm. N. H. Smith......	"	Afterwards member of Confederate Congress.
Hon. Ab'm W. Venable.....	"	
Hon. John D. C. Atkins......	Tennessee	Afterwards member of Confederate Congress.
Hon. Robt. L. Caruthers.....	"	Elected Governor of Tennessee in 1863, but never inaugurated.
Hon. David M. Currin........	"	Afterwards member of Confederate Congress.
Hon. W. H. DeWitt........	"	
Hon. John F. House........	"	
Hon. George W. Jones......	"	Afterwards member of Confederate Congress.
Hon. James H. Thomas......	"	
Hon. Thomas S. Bocock.....	Virginia	Afterwards member of Congress and speaker of the house.
Hon. J. W. Brockenborough..	"	Afterwards Confederate Senator from Virginia; Secretary of State, &c.
Hon. R. M. T. Hunter........	"	
Hon. Robert Johnson........	"	Afterwards member of Congress.
Hon. Wm. H. McFarland....	"	
Hon. James M. Mason.......	"	Afterwards commissioner to Europe.
Hon. Walter Preston.........	"	Afterwards member of Congress.
Hon. Wm. Ballard Preston..	"	Afterwards Confederate Senator from Virginia.
Hon. Roger A. Pryor........	"	Afterwards member of Congress; Brigadier-General in the Confederate army, &c.
Hon. William C. Rives.......	"	Afterwards member of Congress.
Hon. Charles W. Russell.....	"	Afterwards member of Congress.
Hon. Robert E. Scott........	"	
Hon. James A. Seddon.......	"	Afterwards Secretary of War.
Hon. Waller R. Staples......	"	Afterwards member of Congress.
Hon. John Tyler	"	Afterwards member of Congress.

CONFEDERATE SENATORS.

Hon. Alexander H. Stephens	Georgia	Vice-President of the Confederate States, and president of the senate.
R. M. T. Hunter	Virginia	President pro tempore; at one time Secretary of State.
James H. Nash	South Carolina	Secretary.
Clement C. Clay, Jr.	Alabama	First Congress.
William L. Yancey	"	First Congress; afterwards commissioner Europe.
Robert Jemison, Jr.	"	Second Congress.
Richard W. Walker	"	Second Congress.
Robert W. Johnson	Arkansas	First and Second Congress.
Charles B. Mitchel	"	First Congress.
Augustus H. Garland	"	Second Congress.
James M. Baker	Florida	First and Second Congress.
Augustus E. Maxwell	"	First and Second Congress.
Benjamin H. Hill	Georgia	First and Second Congress.
John W. Lewis	"	First Congress.
Herschel V. Johnson	"	Second Congress.
Henry C. Burnett	Kentucky	First and Second Congress.
William E. Simms	"	First and Second Congress.
Thomas J. Semmes	Louisiana	First and Second Congress.
Edward Sparrow	"	First and Second Congress.
Albert G. Brown	Mississippi	First and Second Congress.
James Phelan	"	First Congress.
J. W. C. Watson	"	Second Congress.
John B. Clark	Missouri	First Congress.
R. L. Y. Peyton	"	First Congress.
Waldo P. Johnson	"	Second Congress.
L. M. Louis	"	Second Congress.
William T. Dortch	North Carolina	First and Second Congress.
George Davis	"	First Congress; afterwards Attorney Gen.
William A. Graham	"	Second Congress.
E. G. Reade	"	Second Congress.
Robert W. Barnwell	South Carolina	First and Second Congress.
James L. Orr	"	First and Second Congress.
Gustavus A. Henry	Tennessee	First and Second Congress.
Landon C. Haynes	"	First and Second Congress.
Louis T. Wigfall	Texas	First and Second Congress; had been Brigadier-General in Confederate army.
Williamson S. Oldham	"	First and Second Congress.
Robert M. T. Hunter	Virginia	First and Second Congress; president pro tempore of the senate; had been Secretary of State.
Wm. Ballard Preston	"	First Congress.
Allen T. Caperton	"	Second Congress.

MEMBERS OF THE FIRST AND SECOND CONGRESSES OF THE CONFEDERATE STATES.

First Congress from February 22d, 1862, to February 22d, 1864.
Second Congress from February 22d, 1864, to the overthrow of the Confederacy.

Hon. Thomas S. Bocock	Virginia	Speaker of both Congresses.
Albert R. Lamar	Georgia	Clerk of both Congresses; assistant clerk of the First Congress.
Robert E. Dixon	"	Clerk of First Congress.
William P. Chilton	Alabama	Member of First and Second Congress.
David Clopton	"	" " "
Williamson R. W. Cobb	"	Member of Second Congress.
M. H. Cruikshank	"	"
Jabez L. M. Curry	"	Member of First Congress.
Edward S. Dargan	"	"
J. S. Dickinson	"	Member of Second Congress.
Thomas J. Foster	"	Member of First and Second Congress.
Francis S. Lyon	"	" " "
James L. Pugh	"	" " "
John P. Ralls	"	Member of First Congress.

Members of First and Second Congresses.—Continued.

Hon. William R. Smith......	Alabama..........	Member of First and Second Congress.
Felix J. Batson........	Arkansas	" "
Augustus H. Garland..	"	Member of First Congress.
Rufus K. Garland......	"	Member of First and Second Congress.
Thomas B. Hanly......	"	" "
Grandison D. Royston.	"	Member of First Congress.
James B. Dawkins.....	Florida	" "
Robert B. Hilton......	"	Member of First and Second Congress.
John M. Martin.......	"	" "
St. George Rogers.....	"	" "
J. P. Sanderson,.......	"	" "
George T. Ward........	"	Member of Second Congress; had been Colonel in Confederate service.
Warren Akin.......	Georgia..........	Member of Second Congress.
Clifford Anderson.....	"	Member of First and Second Congress.
H. P. Bell.............	"	" "
Mark H. Blanford.....	"	" "
William W. Clark......	"	Member of First Congress.
Joseph H. Echols,.....	"	Member of Second Congress.
Lucius J. Gartrell.....	"	Member of First Congress; afterwards Brigadier-General in Confederate service.
Julian Hartridge.....	"	Member of First and Second Congress.
Hines Holt...........	"	Member of First Congress.
Augustus H. Kenan...	"	" "
George N. Lester.....	"	Member of Second Congress.
David W. Lewis.......	"	Member of First Congress.
Charles J. Munnerlyn..	"	" "
John T. Shewmake....	"	Member of Second Congress.
James M. Smith........	"	Member of Second Congress; had been Colonel in Confederate service.
William E. Smith.....	"	Member of Second Congress.
Hardy Strickland.....	"	Member of First Congress.
Robert P. Trippe.....	"	" "
Augustus R. Wright...	"	
Benj. F. Bradley......	Kentucky........	Member of Second Congress.
R. J. Breckinridge, Jr..	"	Member of First and Second Congress.
Eli M. Bruce..........	"	" "
H. W. Bruce..........	"	" "
Theodore L. Burnett...	"	" "
James S. Chrisman....	"	" "
John W. Crockett....	"	" "
John M. Elliott.......	"	" "
George W. Ewing.....	"	" "
George B. Hodge.....	"	Member of First Congress; afterwards Brigadier-Gen'l in Confederate service.
Willie B. Machen.....	"	Member of First and Second Congress.
Humphrey Marshall...	"	Member of Second Congress; had been Brigadier-General in Confederate service.
James W. Moore.......	"	Member of First and Second Congress.
Henry E. Reed.......	"	" "
George W. Triplett....	"	Member of Second Congress.
Charles M. Conrad...	Louisiana........	Member of First and Second Congress.
Lucius J. Dupre......	"	" "
Duncan F. Kenner.....	"	" "
Henry Marshall......	"	Member of First Congress.
John Perkins, Jr......	"	Member of First and Second Congress.
Charles J. Villiere..	"	" "
Ethel Barksdale.......	Mississippi.......	" "
Henry C. Chambers....	"	" "
J. W. Clapp........	"	Member of First Congress.
Reuben Davis.........	"	" "
W. D. Holder........	"	Member of Second Congress.
J. T. Lampkin........	"	" "
John J. McRae.......	"	Member of First Congress.
John A. Orr........	"	Member of Second Congress.
Otho R. Singleton....	"	Member of First and Second Congress.
Israel Welch........	"	" "
Casper W. Bell........	Missouri.........	Member of First Congress.
John B. Clark........	"	Member of Second Congress; Brigadier-General in Confederate service.
A. H. Conrow........	"	Member of First and Second Congress.
Wm. M. Cooke,........	"	Member of First Congress.

Members of *First* and *Second* Congresses.—Continued.

Hon. Thomas W. Freeman..	Missouri	Member of First Congress.
Thomas A. Harris......	"	Member of First Congress; Brigadier-Gen. in Confederate service.
R. A. Hatcher.........	"	Member of Second Congress.
N. L. Norton......... ..	"	"
Thomas L. Snead......	"	
George G. Vest	"	Member of First and Second Congress.
Peter D. Wilkes........	"	Member of Second Congress.
Archibald H. Arrington	North Carolina....	Member of First Congress.
Thomas S. Ashe.......	"	"
Robert R. Bridgers....	"	"
A. T. Davidson........	"	"
Thomas C. Fuller......	"	Member of Second Congress.
B. S. Gaither.........	"	Member of First and Second Congress.
John A. Gilmer.......	"	Member of Second Congress.
Owen R. Kenan......	"	Member of First Congress.
William Lander........	"	"
James M. Leach.......	"	Member of Second Congress.
J. T. Leach...........	"	"
George W. Logan......	"	"
T. D. McDowell.......	" ...	Member of First Congress.
J. R. McLean........	" ...	"
James G. Ramsay.....	" ...	Member of Second Congress.
W. H.-N. Smith......	" ...	Member of First Congress.
Josiah Turner, Jr......	" ...	Member of Second Congress.
Lewis M. Ayer........	South Carolina....	Member of First and Second Congress.
M. L. Bonham........	"	Member of First Congress; Brigadier-Gen. in Confederate service; Governor of South Carolina, &c.
William W. Boyce.....	" ...	Member of First and Second Congress.
James Farrow........	" ...	"
John McQueen.......	" ...	Member of First Congress.
Wm. Porcher Miles....	" ...	Member of First and Second Congress.
Wm. D. Simpson......	" ...	"
James M. Witherspoon	"	Member of Second Congress.
John D. C. Atkins.....	Tennessee	Member of First and Second Congress.
Mich'l W. Cluskey....	"	Member of Second Congress.
A. S. Colyar........	"	"
David M. Currin.......	"	Member of First Congress.
Henry S. Foote.......	"	Member of First and Second Congress.
E. L. Gardenhier.......	"	Member of First Congress.
Meredith P. Gentry....	"	"
James B. Heiskell.... .	"	Member of First and Second Congress.
George W. Jones......	"	Member of First Congress.
E. A. Keeble.........	"	Member of Second Congress.
James McCallum.....	"	"
Thomas Menees.......	"	Member of First and Second Congress.
John P. Murray........	"	Member of Second Congress.
W. G. Swan..........	"	Member of First and Second Congress.
Wm. H. Tibbs...... ..	"	Member of First Congress.
John V. Wright........	"	Member of First and Second Congress.
T. R. Baylor...........	Texas..	Member of Second Congress.
A. M. Branch.........	"	"
Stephen H. Darden....	"	"
B. H. Epperson......	"	Member of First Congress.
M. D. Graham........	"	"
P. W. Gray.........	"	"
C. C. Herbert.........	"	Member of First and Second Congress.
S. H. Morgan.........	"	Member of Second Congress.
Frank B. Sexton......	"	Member of First and Second Congress.
John R. Wilcox......	"	Member of First Congress.
William B. Wright.....	"	"
John B. Baldwin.......	Virginia..........	Member of First and Second Congress.
Thomas S. Bocock.....	"	Member of First and Second Congress; speaker.
Alexander R. Boteler..	"	Member of First Congress.
John R. Chambliss....	"	Member of First Congress; afterwards Brigadier-General.
D. C. DeJarnette.......	"	Member of First and Second Congress.
David Funsten........	"	Member of Second Congress.
M. R. H. Garnett......	"	Member of First Congress.
Thomas S. Gholson....	"	Member of Second Congress.
John Goode, Jr........	"	Member of First and Second Congress.

9

Members of First and Second Congresses.—Continued.

James P. Holcombe....	Virginia...........	Member of First Congress; afterwards special agent to Canada.
Hon. F. W. M. Holliday......	"	Member of Second Congress.
Albert G. Jenkins......	"	Member of First Congress; afterwards Brigadier-General in Confederate service.
Robert Johnson........	"	Member of First and Second Congress.
Fayette McMullen.....	"	Member of Second Congress.
Sam'l A. Miller........		"
Rob't L. Montague.....		
Walter Preston........	"	Member of First Congress.
Roger A. Pryor........	"	Member of First Congress; afterwards Brigadier-General in Confederate service.
William C. Rives......	"	Member of Second Congress.
Charles W. Russell....	"	Member of First and Second Congress.
William Smith.........	"	Member of First Congress; afterwards Brigadier-General and Major-General in Confederate service, and Governor of Virginia.
Waller R. Staples......	"	Member of First and Second Congress.
John Tyler............	"	Member of First Congress.
Rob't H. Whitfield.....	"	Member of Second Congress.
Wm. C. Wickham......	"	Member of Second Congress; Brigadier-General in Confederate service.

Territorial Delegates to First and Second Congress.

Hon. M. H. McWillie, Arizona.
Hon. E. C. Boudinot, Cherokee Nation.
Hon. R. M. Jones, Choctaw Nation.
Hon. S. B. Callahan, Creek and Seminole Nations.